THE PSYCHEDELIC DJ

A Practical Guide to
Therapeutic Music Curation
and Psilocybin-Assisted Therapy

MATT XAVIER

Copyright & Trademark Notice
© 2025 Matt Xavier. All rights reserved.

No part of this publication may be reproduced, stored in a retrieval system, or transmitted in any form or by any means—electronic, mechanical, photocopying, recording, or otherwise—without the prior written permission of the author, except in the case of brief quotations embodied in critical articles or reviews.

This book is intended for educational and informational purposes only and does not constitute medical advice, diagnosis, or treatment. Always consult with a qualified health professional before undertaking any therapeutic or psychedelic practices described herein.

Creative Commons License & Attribution Request
License & Use
The following original terms and frameworks—*The Psychedelic DJ*, *Therapeutic DJing*, *Psychedelic Soundtracking*, *Therapeutic Music Curation*, and *Certified Psychedelic DJ (CPDJ)*—are offered under a Creative Commons Attribution-NonCommercial-ShareAlike 4.0 International License.

You are welcome to reference or adapt these specific terms for non-commercial purposes, provided proper credit is given to the author, Matt Xavier, including the title of the book and a link to www.integratedpsychedelics.com. Any adaptations must be shared under the same license.

Ethical Use & Community Respect
These terms emerged from decades of clinical, musical, and personal work. If you plan to use them in professional settings, trainings, or published materials, please:

- Attribute Matt Xavier and *The Psychedelic DJ*
- Reference the original source where appropriate
- Avoid presenting these terms or frameworks as your own
- Contact the author for licensing, collaboration, or commercial use

A formal trademark process is under consideration. This Creative Commons license reflects a balance between open sharing and protecting creative integrity.

For media requests or collaboration inquiries, please visit: www.integratedpsychedelics.com

ISBNs
Ebook: 979-8-9986806-0-1
Paperback: 979-8-9986806-1-8
Hardcover: 979-8-9986806-2-5

Project consultant: Doug Reil
Developmental editing: Danielle Polgar, Noelle Armstrong, Doug Reil
Copyeditor: Allison Felus
Creative consultant: Trevor Wyse
Cover design and image: Myck Stewart
Interior design: Chris Williams
Project manager: Donnel McLohon

To Captain Dickie in heaven—ya don't stop

To my wife Destiny—we don't stop

To my mom and family—ya don't stop

To my friends that I love—ya don't stop

To my clients on their journeys—ya don't stop

To all composers and musicians—ya don't stop

To the DJs and the ravers—ya don't stop

To the sounds of music—ya don't stop

To all the psychedelics—ya don't stop

To the Universe and God—ya don't stop

To the Spirit that's within me—ya don't stop

To all parts of my being—ya don't stop

To all the readers of this book—ya don't stop

To A Tribe Called Quest—ya don't stop

With love and gratitude—I don't stop.

M. Magic

RIP RJB 5:22 / 12:44

CONTENTS

Important Note/Disclaimer	*xi*
Ethics and Training in Psychedelic Therapy	*xiii*
Introduction	*1*
My Journey with Music, Psychedelics, and Therapy	*5*
Chapter 1: Pairing Psychedelic Therapy with Music	*11*
What Is Psychedelic Therapy?	*11*
Music as Universal Language	*13*
Musical Sense Memories	*15*
Music as Medicine: Harnessing Sound for Set, Setting, and Healing	*18*
Chapter 2: Psilocybin Mushrooms—Past, Present, and Future	*27*
History and Traditions	*27*
Music and Ritual: Sound in Psychedelic Traditions	*30*
Chapter 3: Therapeutic DJing—Curation and Soundtracking for Psychedelic Therapy	*37*
Therapeutic DJing	*38*
Therapeutic Music Curation: Laying the Foundation	*40*

Psychedelic Soundtracking: Scoring the Hero's Journey	42
Tempo and Energy in Music Curation	46
Volume as Setting	50
The Sound of Silence: The Space Between the Notes	52
Modern Soundscapes: Integrating Ambient, Electronic, and Neoclassical Music in Psychedelic Therapy	53
Advanced Techniques	55
Beatmatching: Synchronizing Rhythm and Flow	56
Harmonic Mixing: Enhancing Therapeutic DJing	58
Chapter 4: The Psilocybin Experience	**67**
Physical Effects	67
Psychological and Sensory Effects with Music	68
Therapeutic Benefits and Challenges	71
Broad Dosage Guidelines	73
Dosing Delivery Methods	77
Chapter 5: Psilocybin Mushroom Journey Protocol	**79**
Screening and Journey Preparation	80
Prejourney Writing	85
Preparation Counseling Sessions	86
Dietary and Activity Suggestions	89
Prejourney Considerations for Practitioners	91
Journey Day Supply List	93
Chapter 6: Journey Day—Creating a Safe Setting	**95**
Welcome	95
Orientation	96
Timekeeping	98
Eyeshade Use	99

Bathroom Use	*100*
Ceremony	*101*
Crisis Prevention: Proper Dosing, Music Adjustments, and Preparation	*104*
Ego Death	*106*
Crisis Intervention Plan	*108*
Crisis Support: Nonphysical Guiding Intervention	*110*
Crisis Intervention: Training and Resources	*112*
Postcrisis Integration	*113*

Chapter 7: Stages of a Mushroom Journey	***115***
Timeline of Psychedelic Effects and Journey Stages	*115*
Trailhead: The Imbibing Ceremony	*116*
Stage One: Hike to Basecamp (Onset)	*117*
Basecamp: Bathroom and Booster Break	*121*
Stage Two: Climbing the Mountain (Ascent)	*122*
Stage Three: The Summit (Peak)	*126*
Stage Four: Return to Basecamp (Descent)	*128*
Stage Five: Basecamp (Landing and Processing)	*130*
Stage Six: Closing Ceremony (Baseline Sobriety)	*133*
Table of Stages: Timeline and Recommended Music	*136*

Chapter 8: Psychedelic Audio Presentation—A Technical Guide to Journey Space Setup	***137***
DJ Software	*138*
Speaker Recommendations: Creating the Foundation for Immersion	*138*
My Journey Space Setup	*139*
Basic Setup: Simplicity and Affordability	*141*
Intermediate Setup: Balancing Performance and Control	*141*

Advanced Setup: Immersive and Professional	142
Headphones Versus Speakers: Preparing the Sound System	143
Using Headphones: Ensuring Redundancy	144
Bluetooth and Wi-Fi Audio	144
Your Personalized Audio Environment	145
Testing Your Setup: Audio Mixing	145

Chapter 9: Therapeutic Music Collecting — *147*

Building Your Record Box and Digging Deep	147
Sustainability: Purchasing Music Versus Streaming	151

Chapter 10: Assembling the Parts—Gestalt Therapy and Music in Postjourney Integration — *155*

Psychedelic Integration	155
Guiding Integration: Methods and Best Practices	156
Gestalt Experiential Integration	159
Music for Psychedelic Integration	162
Clinical Vignettes: Music, Gestalt, and Somatic Therapies in Action	164
Follow-up and Future Journeys	173

Chapter 11: Practitioner Self-Care in Psychedelic Therapy — *175*

Checking In Before Sessions	175
Grounding Practices and Setting Boundaries	176
Burnout and Compassion Fatigue: Building Resilience	177
Vicarious Traumatization and Somatic Countertransference	180
Emotional Detox	181
Journey Planning: How Many Are Enough?	182
Sustaining the Sacred Work	183

Chapter 12: Life Beyond the Journey—What's Next?	*185*
To the Guides, Witnesses, and DJs	*188*
Looking Ahead	*189*
Acknowledgments	*191*
Appendix: Audio Protocols, QR Code, Resources, and Instructions	*197*
Notes	*203*
Index of Artists and Remixers	*213*
About the Author	*221*

IMPORTANT NOTE/ DISCLAIMER

This book is intended for informational and educational purposes only, to share the author's personal experiences, insights, and opinions on music curation and psychedelic integration counseling in jurisdictions where such practices are legally permitted. It is not a manual for illegal activity or a substitute for professional training, supervision, or legal counsel.

The author strictly adheres to a harm reduction model designed to minimize risks associated with psychedelic use by creating a safe and supportive environment for clients (also known as journeyers). The author never provides, sells, distributes, or facilitates access to any psychedelic substances under any circumstances. Any substances used in therapeutic sessions are independently sourced by the client, in full compliance with applicable laws. This approach ensures that therapeutic work remains focused solely on safety, support, and intentionality, while protecting practitioners from legal accusations related to the distribution or provision of illicit substances.

All guided sessions described in this book were conducted in a controlled, intentional, and therapeutic capacity with harm reduction principles in place. The author acted exclusively as a guide, providing emotional, spiritual, and psychological counseling support within jurisdictions where such practices are legally permitted—whether through legal frameworks, decriminalization, or exemptions for religious, therapeutic, or personal use. In every instance, the author's role was strictly limited to providing harm reduction support and facilitating safe psychedelic experiences aligned with each client's personal, spiritual, or therapeutic goals.

This book is not a substitute for professional advice or training. Readers are strongly advised not to attempt to use the material contained in this book without proper education, licensure, and legal counsel. **Any actions taken based on the information in this book are done entirely at the reader's own risk and responsibility.**

The author, publisher, and any associated parties involved in the creation, release, or promotion of this material expressly disclaim any liability for outcomes, damages, or adverse effects resulting from the use or misuse of this material. By using this book, readers agree to

- acknowledge both that the author never provides substances under any circumstances and that any mention of substances in this book pertains solely to contexts where clients have independently sourced them in compliance with applicable laws;
- recognize that the author's role is limited to sharing personal experiences, insights, and general guidance; and
- assume full responsibility for their own decisions and actions, including any legal, medical, or psychological consequences.

The information presented in this book is intended to encourage thoughtful, informed, and responsible exploration of therapeutic practices in jurisdictions where they are legally permitted. Readers are solely responsible for ensuring that any actions they take are lawful, ethical, and safe. The author, publisher, and associated parties do not condone any illegal activity and will not be held liable for the misuse or misinterpretation of this material. This disclaimer serves as a clear boundary to protect all parties involved, reinforcing the principle that ultimate responsibility lies with the reader.

ETHICS AND TRAINING IN PSYCHEDELIC THERAPY

Let's take a moment to talk about the differences between counseling, psychotherapy, and psychedelic therapy and why it's so important to approach this work with care. Psychedelic therapy is unique because it opens the door to deeper layers of the subconscious in ways traditional talk therapy often can't. This is fascinating and powerful, but it's also why the stakes are higher and why ethical guidelines and proper training are nonnegotiable.

In counseling, the focus is often on practical support and helping clients navigate specific challenges in their lives. Psychotherapy goes a step deeper, exploring patterns, unresolved issues, and emotional wounds that might be driving behavior. Psychedelic therapy and guiding, on the other hand, take all of this to another level by working with powerful substances that provide clients with direct access to their subconscious.

This isn't just about talking—it's about creating a safe space where clients can navigate the buried emotions, vivid memories, and profound insights that often arise during the journey. As practitioners, we're not here to fix, direct, or impose our beliefs on their process. This isn't a time for indoctrination; it's a time for listening and supporting the client's unique journey of self-discovery. The medicine is the key, and we're simply the container that holds space for the unfolding experience.

Because psychedelic therapy and guiding invite people into such vulnerable, emotional spaces, ethics are imperative at every stage of the process. At its core, ethical practice means ensuring that the client's well-being is always the priority. That might sound obvious, but when we're working with tools as powerful as psychedelics, it becomes even more important to pause, reflect, and double-check how we're showing up in this space.

What Ethical Practice Looks Like

Here are some hallmarks of what ethical practice looks like in action.

- Informed consent. Clients need to know what they're signing up for; they need you to tell them about the potential risks, benefits, and unique nature of psychedelic therapy. Transparency builds trust.
- Confidentiality. Clients may share deeply personal and even transformative experiences with you. Protecting their privacy is a baseline requirement.
- Nondirective support. The magic of this work happens when clients feel free to follow their inner process without interference or the imposition of an agenda from the guide. We're the lighthouse, not the ship's captain.
- Cultural awareness. Clients come from all walks of life, and it's crucial that we honor their diverse perspectives and experiences. This isn't about our worldview—it's about creating space for theirs.
- Encouraging ethical sourcing. While we don't source the medicines ourselves, we do encourage clients to research and select their medicines responsibly. This includes being mindful of sustainability, respecting cultural origins, and understanding the impact of their choices.

It's also OK to acknowledge when you're not ready for a certain situation. If you ever feel unsure about your ability to safely guide someone, take a step back. Trust your intuition and seek out additional training or refer the client to someone with more experience. There's no shame in being honest about your limits—in fact, it's the most ethical thing you can do.

That same ethical awareness applies when deciding whether to work with a particular client. If something doesn't feel right, it's better to decline than to move forward with uncertainty. Saying no doesn't protect just you—it also protects the client by ensuring they're matched with someone

ETHICS AND TRAINING IN PSYCHEDELIC THERAPY

who is better suited to their needs. Knowing who *not* to work with is just as important as knowing who you do want to work with, if not more so.

And remember, as with all things psychedelic: go slow, dose low. You can always take more, but you can't take less.

For additional information about ethical guidelines in psychedelic therapy, I encourage you to consult the Council on Spiritual Practices' Code of Ethics for Spiritual Guides, the Multidisciplinary Association for Psychedelic Studies (MAPS) MDMA-Assisted Therapy Code of Ethics, and The Conclave's Recommended Model for Best Practices.[1] These resources will provide further insight into best practices and help deepen your understanding of the responsibility we carry as psychedelic practitioners.

Let's be honest—this work isn't always easy. The emotional intensity of counseling, guiding, and psychedelic therapy can be taxing, even for experienced practitioners. Burnout, compassion fatigue, and vicarious trauma are real risks, so we need to prioritize our own self-care, which is discussed later in this book. That means checking in with ourselves before and after sessions, seeking support when we need it, and making sure we're not overextending our boundaries.

INTRODUCTION

In the world of psychedelic therapy, music has often been overlooked for its potent role as cotherapist, capable of guiding and amplifying emotional and spiritual experiences. While many acknowledge the transformative power of psychedelics themselves, few understand how deeply music can shape the journey, offering both structure and support to the unfolding process. My hope is that this book will illuminate the underappreciated synergy between music and psychedelics and offer helpful insights for those new to the practice of creating a soundtrack for a client's mind-altering journey as well as for those seeking to deepen their understanding of this powerful combination.

At the heart of this synergy lies an intuitive practice that many of us already engage in, often without realizing its full potential: DJing. At its core, DJing is more than a technical skill or a profession—it's an ancient, intuitive practice of fostering connection through music. While the word *DJ* might first evoke images of turntables and nightclubs, the essence of DJing has always been about reading the energy of a space, understanding the emotional state of an audience, and creating a musical flow that brings people together. The act of curating soundscapes is something we all engage in, whether we realize it or not. It's fascinating how often people, even those unfamiliar with DJ culture, instinctively describe the act of playing music for others as "DJing." Whether it's a carefully crafted playlist or live selections during a session, this shorthand captures the transformative power of music to shape an experience.

THE PSYCHEDELIC DJ

It's also a perfect metaphor for the work of a guide in psilocybin therapy. Much like a DJ, a psychedelic guide senses the emotional and spiritual state of the journeyer and uses music to support, uplift, or ground them as needed.

So in the context of psilocybin therapy, this combined role of DJ and guide takes on even greater importance as music becomes a profound tool for healing, a bridge to deeper states of consciousness, and a path through the peaks and valleys of a journey. Whether it's through an ambient soundscape, a cathartic swell, or a moment of silence, the right soundtrack holds space for transformation, supporting the journeyer as they navigate their inner world.

This book invites you to embrace DJing in its most universal and therapeutic sense: as an intuitive practice of connection and healing. You don't need to be a professional DJ or know how to beatmatch to engage in this work. If you've ever put together a playlist to set a mood, evoke an emotion, or create a meaningful experience, you've already practiced a form of DJing. By expanding your understanding of what it means to DJ, this book will empower you to harness the transformative potential of music, no matter your background. Whether you're a clinician, a guide, or someone seeking to deepen your connection with music in therapeutic spaces, you'll find practical tools and inspiration for creating soundscapes that heal, guide, and transform.

My own journey into this work reflects this very concept of DJing—an intuitive and organic unfolding that led me from collecting music to curating therapeutic experiences. Similarly, this book didn't actually begin as a book; it started as a DJ mix, a curated compilation of tracks I've used in sessions, drawing from my vast collection of psychedelic ambient, chill-out, and downtempo electronic music. What began as a simple instructional guide to accompany the mix quickly evolved into something much larger as a narrative unfolded about my journey as a DJ, my experiences as a psychedelic guide, and my work as a mental health counselor. The music that fills these sessions is the product of over 30 years of collecting, testing, and refining. Each track mentioned here has been carefully chosen to enhance the therapeutic potential of a journey.

INTRODUCTION

My intention with this book is to highlight the transformative capacity of weaving together psychedelic medicine, music curation, and both clinical and shamanic counseling practices. However, this book does not dive heavily into the scientific evidence; it instead focuses on how the use of music for the purpose of psychedelic counseling informs the healing potential of our psychology. The product of many years of clinical and experiential practice, this book explores how integrating music with psychedelics has impacted the biological, psychological, social, and spiritual lives of the clients I've worked with.

I cover the importance of mind-set and the need for careful screening before a psychedelic journey, inviting the client to explore their intentions, goals, and beliefs. This preparation creates a foundation for the journey, helping clients understand what they are seeking and how to approach their experience with mindfulness. In addition, the book includes practical protocols for administering psychedelics in an intentional and therapeutic capacity, ensuring that facilitators are equipped to provide a secure container for clients. It also offers experiential counseling techniques for guiding clients through their journeys and assisting them in processing and integrating the insights and realizations that emerge during the experience.

There is also detailed information on setting that provides suggestions on how to curate an environment that ensures a safe and supportive container. Though for our purposes here the most important element will be the curation of a nonverbal musical soundtrack that elicits thoughts, memories, visions, and emotions, it is just as important to remember to properly address the other four senses. This includes providing comfortable bedding, soft lighting and artwork, and pleasant scents.

However, in my practice, I've found that music is not just an element of the setting—it is often the most vital component. Each track should be carefully selected to support the unfolding journey, whether that means guiding a client through moments of emotional intensity or helping them settle into a place of introspection. The music I use in sessions spans various electronic subgenres such as ambient, chill-out, neoclassical, downtempo, and, on rare occasions, house, techno, trance, or drum and bass. I've curated these selections from tens of thousands of compositions, continuously testing them in both altered and nonaltered states of consciousness. You'll find some of these specific track recommendations sprinkled throughout the pages that follow; think of them like small musical acorns waiting to be discovered. I hope that coming across these while you read feels much like those moments when you're digging through record bins in search of that one perfect vinyl to add to your collection, a true rite of passage for any DJ. Over time, I've learned to map out which tracks work best for the different stages of a journey, blending them into a continuous set that evolves with each client's needs. Musical curation thus becomes a powerful tool for guiding clients through their inner landscapes, amplifying the therapeutic potential of each session.

Music, in its own right, is a powerful medicine that can dramatically shape the course of a journey. Understanding how and when to present music with the least amount of disruption is crucial to creating a safe and transformative environment for healing. It is this understanding that I hope to share with you, drawing on the knowledge I've gained through many years of curating music, DJing events, guiding clients, and integrating ancient traditions with modern therapeutic practices.

The practices in this book welcome beginners as well as those seeking to incorporate more advanced techniques. However, the insights shared here are not prescriptive—they reflect my personal journey and experiences with music, counseling, and psychedelics for healing. There's no expectation for anyone to mirror my methods, as many of these are advanced skill sets developed over extensive practice, long before I became a mental health counselor and psychedelic guide. That said, I hope this book can serve as a guideline for those who wish to expand their practice as they gain more comfort and confidence. I encourage readers to remain mindful before attempting any of the exercises or techniques, particularly those related to psychedelic therapy, as it involves counseling skills that require significant training and supervision. Attempting these without proper preparation could result in unintended harm.

At the time of publishing, this book references a series of recorded DJ mix protocols, designed as examples of the practices discussed throughout

INTRODUCTION

these pages. These mixes, developed over hundreds of psychedelic-assisted counseling sessions, serve as reference tools for readers, offering practical illustrations of the approaches described in the book. They highlight my over 30 years of experience as a DJ, collecting and blending psychedelic compositions in ways that respond to the emerging needs of each client. The sequence of tracks is crafted to support the first four stages of a psilocybin journey, providing soundscapes that can unlock memories, amplify emotional processing, and evoke a sense of safety and surrender. These DJ mixes, along with specific track previews and links to purchase, can be accessed via the QR code found in the appendix. The information available via the link offers an additional way to engage with the material presented throughout the text, inviting you to explore the mixes I've put together or preview individual tracks for yourself while also offering a way to directly support the artists whenever possible.

Whether you're exploring the mix as part of your own journey or using it to support a client, family member, or friend, I wish you a beautiful, enriching experience. Remember, the power of music—much like psychedelics—should never be underestimated. Use it with care, stay mindful, and allow the sounds to guide you on a safe and transformative journey!

My Journey with Music, Psychedelics, and Therapy

This book and my work in the field of psychedelic therapy are the result of a winding, decades-long journey filled with music, transformation, and a deep desire to help others find healing. While music and psychedelics are the heart of my current practice, it's important to understand how I arrived at this intersection, where my passions converged with my purpose.

The foundation of my path began in childhood, where music was a sanctuary—a constant companion and one of my life's greatest loves. My attempts at learning how to play instruments were hindered by anxiety and frustration, but my love for listening never wavered. My earliest influences included classic rock staples like the Beatles, the Doors, and Fleetwood Mac. It wasn't until my tween years at our family's basketball camp in upstate New York that my world expanded to the sounds of early rap and hip-hop. Artists like Run-DMC, Beastie Boys, Eric B. &

THE PSYCHEDELIC DJ

Rakim, Special Ed, EPMD, and Gang Starr provided the backdrop for those formative years.

At age 16, I had my first encounters with cannabis and LSD, and those experiences transformed my life and relationship with music. My doors of perception swung open, revealing the vast potential of sound. Pink Floyd, Jimi Hendrix, Cream, and Led Zeppelin became the new soundtrack to my psychedelic explorations. A year later, my journey took a major turn when I walked into NASA, a pioneering rave club in downtown Manhattan, where I encountered the vibrant world of early '90s house, techno, jungle, and electronic ambient music. I was captivated by the sights, sounds, energy, and openness of the rave scene, which inspired my friends and me to organize underground raves in clandestine locations across Long Island and Brooklyn.

In those early years, I stumbled into DJing and learned the craft by watching legends like Frankie Bones, Adam X, and Jimmy Crash. I was drawn to their artistry, confidence, and raw Brooklyn style. But my DJing journey truly took off after a tense episode with my mother. I persuaded her to sell my car after she'd confiscated it following an argument, and with the proceeds, I purchased my first set of turntables. While studying audio engineering in college, I spent countless hours mixing records at home, acquiring my first vinyl treasures like Cari Lekebusch's *Hybrid EP - 1 and 2* (under his Braincell moniker) and Richie Hawtin's alias Plastikman's *Sheet One* from Groove Records in Brooklyn.

My brother, born with perfect pitch, couldn't stand my novice, off-key mixes and devised a system for harmonic mixing—a technique that was pioneering at the time. This became my secret weapon, allowing me to refine my auditory and technical skills and deliver polished performances in the North American rave, nightclub, and psychedelic trance scenes. My exploration of music expanded into Goa trance, inspiring me to create my first DJ alias, Matthew Magic. Soon after, I cofounded two pioneering production companies, Project Beyond and Tsunami Productions, which became well known for their cutting-edge psychedelic trance events.

Despite my public DJ sets being dominated by techno, house, and trance, my private love for ambient and chill-out music never waned.

INTRODUCTION

Artists like Mixmaster Morris, the Future Sound of London, the Orb, Moby, and Aphex Twin soundtracked my drives home from raves and subsequent moments decompressing in my childhood basement. As rave culture shifted toward harder beats and the chill-out rooms began to disappear, I held onto these soothing sounds, wondering if I'd ever have the opportunity to share this type of music with others.

By 2000, the shadows of the psychedelic party scene had become too obvious to ignore. Many friends slid into problematic drug use, and I decided to step back from psychedelics to focus on self-care and spiritual pursuits. My creativity flourished during those three years of burgeoning sobriety. I began performing regularly as Matt Xavier and producing house and techno records under the moniker grüvhaus as well. After this period, I moved to Los Angeles, where I cofounded international techno and house music label Railyard Recordings with my high school friend Sean as a tribute to our roots in New York's electronic underground. In 2007, I moved our operations to Berlin, Germany, immersing myself in that city's rich electronic music scene. Shortly after, I felt a call to change directions once again, returning to Los Angeles to pursue addiction counselor training in Gestalt therapy.

For the next several years, I worked as a full-time addiction counselor, helping people navigate the challenges of addiction and co-occurring mental health disorders. In 2015, after a 15-year hiatus from psychedelics, a close friend gifted me some psilocybin mushroom chocolates. The experience of consuming these was unlike any of my earlier recreational trips—it was deeply healing and life changing. This led me to explore other plant medicines like ayahuasca, which further opened my eyes to the power of blending music with psychedelics. In 2017, I even revisited cannabis with a more mature and intentional approach, understanding it as a tool for healing rather than recreation. These experiences helped me realize that my work could bridge ancient ceremonial practices with modern therapeutic techniques.

By 2018, I experienced significant burnout, compassion fatigue, and vicarious trauma. The devastating OxyContin, heroin, and fentanyl addiction epidemic had swept through the nation, taking a heavy toll on both clients and counselors. Feeling the weight of this crisis, I reached out to a peer in the Los Angeles harm reduction community who was also a psychedelic therapist and MDMA researcher. We discussed the possibility of blending my background in DJing, psychedelics, and mental health counseling as a means of self-preservation.

Around this time, I connected with the emerging world of psychedelic integration circles—distinctive gathering spaces where individuals could share and process their psychedelic experiences. As someone with a background in group therapy, these circles felt like a homecoming. Soon, I enrolled in training programs that further shaped my approach, including training in Integrative Harm Reduction Psychotherapy in New York City, which offered a compassionate approach aligned with my counseling work. I also completed an extensive, experiential psychedelic therapy program where I learned a modified version of the MAPS MDMA therapy protocol. Upon completion, I adapted that training for use with psilocybin mushrooms, which became a cornerstone of my practice.

As I delved deeper into combining music with psychedelic therapy, I found that the music I'd been collecting and curating for decades was uniquely suited to this work. I began to experiment with different soundscapes, testing each track in both altered and nonaltered states. This allowed me to observe how each piece influenced the emotional and psychological experiences of clients, helping me to refine my approach and create more effective music sets for each stage of a psychedelic journey.

Those preliminary sessions revealed the profound impact that music could have on the therapeutic process, whether by unlocking long-held memories, facilitating emotional breakthroughs, or providing a sense of safety and surrender. I began to see my DJing skills in a new light—not just as a way to entertain but also as a means to guide and support clients on their healing journeys. This realization marked the beginning of a new chapter in my life, where my love for music, my passion for counseling, and my desire to help others came together to form a dynamic whole. These elements were no longer just individual passions—they fused into something greater, a true gestalt that brought

INTRODUCTION

depth and direction to my path. Through this synthesis, I found a way to channel my skills into a unified, transformative practice, offering clients the space to pull up roots, process old patterns, and plant seeds for change.

1
PAIRING PSYCHEDELIC THERAPY WITH MUSIC

What Is Psychedelic Therapy?
Psychedelic therapy is an expressive, experiential treatment that integrates psychedelic substances with traditional and nontraditional psychotherapeutic and psychosomatic counseling techniques to explore the subconscious mind and emotional landscape. The substances used can provide profound insights, cathartic emotional releases, new neural pathways, and healing for trauma and mental health conditions such as anxiety, depression, PTSD, OCD, and addiction.

Due to their chemical properties, psychedelics activate various regions of the brain that facilitate access to otherworldly spiritual experiences and visions, leading to greater self-awareness, peace, and clarity. This activation bypasses coping mechanisms and ingrained responses, allowing individuals to challenge habitual beliefs and behaviors, fostering new insights.

Psychedelic therapy deepens vulnerability (often suppressed by trauma), revealing the knowns and unknowns, as well as the unknown unknowns, within us. It's a courageous process that allows suppressed material to surface for healing. As Brené Brown notes in her TED Talk "Listening to Shame," "Vulnerability is the birthplace of innovation, creativity, and change." This courage can lead to creative visions and innovative solutions, facilitating psychological, emotional, and spiritual transformation.

Psychedelic therapy also reveals that the human experience is more expansive than day-to-day awareness allows. When combined with experiential counseling, psychedelics guide individuals beyond the conscious mind into subconscious realms where vast, often unknown landscapes exist.

Carl Jung, the father of analytical psychology, described this subconscious territory as "the shadow"—those primal, emotional parts of the psyche that remain concealed in an attempt to protect the ego. The conscious mind, encompassing our thoughts, beliefs, and narratives, guides our behavior and reactions, while the default mode network (DMN), the interconnected brain regions active during introspection and self-referential thinking, represents how we see ourselves and react to stimuli. Although the conscious mind is undeniably powerful, unconscious influences often have a greater impact on behavior.

The subconscious serves as a lifetime memory bank, recording our entire existence. It operates in the background, driven by nonrational influences that shape emotions and automatic behaviors. Ignoring or avoiding subconscious content can trap unprocessed emotions and traumas, causing psychological strain that hinders value-aligned decision-making.

I often explain this with a simple metaphor: When a person's need to go to the bathroom is acknowledged, the urge prompts action, leading to relief and allowing attention to shift to other needs. When the need is ignored, discomfort grows, siphoning energy and creating distraction. Similarly, unresolved psychological or emotional needs left unattended can lead to significant distress.

Psychedelics, especially psilocybin, can heighten awareness of subconscious patterns and neurotic behaviors by releasing long-suppressed emotions and memories. This release can manifest cognitively, visually, emotionally, physically, or spiritually, breaking down the ego's control and easing decades of accumulated psychological strain. The result is often a profound sense of relief and harmony in mind, body, and spirit.

Psychedelics function as amplifiers, root pullers, and transformational agents that break through defenses and support the fulfillment of unmet needs. They help us to see how coping strategies can actually block access to emotional and psychospiritual discomfort.

In combination with other therapies like Gestalt therapy, Reichian therapy, Somatic Experiencing, Internal Family Systems, breathwork, mindfulness meditation, and EMDR, psychedelics can offer catharsis and enhanced awareness. These therapeutic modalities act as portals to the unconscious as well as nonordinary states of consciousness, opening what William Blake described as "the doors of perception," revealing the infinite nature of existence.

Historically, nonordinary states of consciousness were accessed through music, rituals, chanting, meditation, dreaming, and ceremonial psychedelic use. Meditation and dreams remain effective ways to observe and process subconscious content without interference from the conscious ego. For instance, meditation quiets mental chatter through observation, while dreams allow automatic release of collected subconscious content.

But psychedelics can help us go further by creating an awakened dream state that frees the subconscious from avoidance patterns, enabling the resolution of unfinished issues. This release redirects energy toward healing and regeneration. The brain forms new connections and insights, repairing ruptures caused by trauma. As fragmented parts become integrated, clarity, psychological resilience, and a calmer nervous system response emerge, producing life-changing shifts.

For thousands of years, psychedelics have been used by medicine practitioners for various purposes. Today, their integration with intentional, experiential therapies transcends traditional talk therapy, allowing individuals to face both the light and dark aspects of their being and access new depths of their innate healing potential.

This book will explore the world of psychedelic mushrooms specifically and how to incorporate music into psychedelic therapy sessions. Often called "magic mushrooms," these natural substances contain psilocybin, a compound that has been studied extensively for its therapeutic benefits, and have a rich history in spiritual and medicinal practices.

Music as Universal Language

In the grand soundscape of existence, there is a medium that permeates the universe, a rhythm that beats in every heart, and a harmony that binds us all. This is music—the universal language of the soul and the divine vibration that resonates within and around us. Music, like the fleeting arc of a rainbow or the gentle fade of a sunset, belongs to no one and yet is a gift to all. A rainbow splits light into colors we can see but not touch; likewise, music takes us beyond the limits of what words can express. The colors of a sunset remind us of the day's end, but in that fading light, there's a sense of something bigger—a connection that runs deeper than we can fully understand. In a psychedelic therapy session, music works in much the same way. It is a psychedelic journey that takes us beyond the confines of our personal identities, allowing us to experience the interconnectedness of all things. It is a shared celebration, a communal trance-dance, a collective ecstasy trip that reminds us of our common humanity.

As the 1990s Swedish ambient-techno music pioneer Robert Leiner says on his album *Visions of the Past*, "It has always been there; you just have to discover it." This profound statement sums up the essence of music. It is not something that is created, but rather discovered, uprooted from the depths of the cosmos and the soul.

In a world where everything is energy, this collection and composition of rhythmic sounds, frequencies, notes, chords, and vibrations has the capacity to change us as beings. We don't just listen to music—we are music, resonating with its rhythms and harmonies on a fundamental level. Our first experience of rhythm and frequency is hearing our mother's heartbeat in utero. This rhythm is echoed in the sequence and timing of our breath, our own heartbeat, and the energetic pulse of life.

Music serves as a soundtrack to the unfolding movie of our lives. It elevates the heart and mind, triggers our imagination and memories, activates our emotions, and resonates on the deepest levels of the human experience. There is a quote I've always loved—its origins unknown—that beautifully captures this: "Music gives a soul to the universe, wings to the mind, flight to the imagination, and life to everything."

Music is a powerful and creative method of self-expression that transcends both the spoken word and nonverbal communication. It acts as a channel to the divine and gives form to the formless, or as Aldous Huxley once eloquently said, "After silence, that which comes nearest to expressing the inexpressible is music." Beyond its role as a sonic sculpture and a pathway to the heavens, music is a storyteller that weaves together narratives transcending culture and time.

PAIRING PSYCHEDELIC THERAPY WITH MUSIC

Each sound, note, and chord possesses the ability to convey even the most subtle of human emotions. Throughout our existence, music remains our companion, resonating with the emotions we feel as we navigate life's challenges. Whether it's the pounding rhythms of a drum or the expansive, otherworldly sounds of modern synthesizers, music grants us the ability to touch the untouchable. As we listen, feel, and become entranced by its power, music reminds us that we exist within a vast, colorful universe of sound. It is a potent psychedelic in and of itself, a healing medicine for the soul, capable of manifesting visions, triggering pleasure, soothing pain, lifting spirits, and igniting hope.

The power of music can bridge the divides that separate us, smoothing out the rough edges of misunderstanding and fostering a sense of unity and togetherness. Though we may come from different backgrounds and experiences, we are all part of the same journey—and music, in its infinite wisdom, reminds us of this interconnectedness. It has the power to bring us into the same boat, carrying us beyond the illusion of separation and toward a deeper understanding of our shared humanity. As Martin Luther King Jr. envisioned, a world where people come together in brotherhood and mutual respect is possible—and music, in its unifying embrace, helps us take steps toward that dream, reminding us that we can all dance together as one, free from judgment and separation.

Musical Sense Memories

Our senses serve as triggers for recollection. To feel is to remember. To see is to remember. To smell is to remember. Every scent can become a portal to the past, evoking memories of our initial encounters with it. For instance, a musty, moldy aroma instantly brings me back to my grandparents' country home in Yaphank, New York. The smell vividly brings back memories of running around in the thick, leaf-covered woods behind the house, as my mind attempts to reconstruct the scenes I experienced in very specific detail. I remember running through the woods with my siblings and favorite cousins, playing tag or hide-and-seek. The air was warm and humid, filled with the scent of wet soil and leaves. I can still feel the excitement of being there, the joy of playing among the trees, and the contrast to the more crowded, organized spaces of our suburban home.

And just as scent evokes memory, sounds can do so as well. Each musical note and frequency can carry a person back in time and allow them to access the moment-to-moment emotions unfolding as that memory was created.

For example, I was recently eating in a restaurant when one of Billy Joel's most popular songs came on the sound system. It immediately transported me back to my childhood in New York during the '80s and '90s. I had visions of the Italian restaurant I went to with my mother, where she gave us coins to make selections from the jukebox. I recalled the smells and tastes of the food—the delicious bread, the sweet dipping sauce, and the syrupy flavor of fountain Coca-Cola.

When I tuned in more deeply, I heard the kitchen door swinging open and closed as servers dressed in red-and-white aprons hurried around. I remembered sitting at the table as a young boy with my family, feeling small and innocent but also excited to eat my favorite ravioli and garlic bread. My mother drank red wine, which I hated the taste of when she let me try it. I was eager to play video games but only after finishing my dinner. Details came flooding back to me as visual memories while bodily feelings of comfort, joy, agitation, and conflict rose to the surface—all of it triggered decades later by the sound of this one song.

Perhaps you too can hear theme songs from your favorite childhood shows or commercials in your head right now. What characters or scenes do you remember? What emotions do you feel? What memories or visions pop into your head as you feel those emotions? Do you remember your age or the time, place, or circumstances in your life when you first watched those films or heard those songs?

Just as hearing a song can transport you to a moment in time, the music in a film shapes how we experience and remember it. The emotional impact of a movie often depends on its soundtrack—try rewatching a powerful scene without music, and you'll notice how much depth is lost. Search YouTube, and you'll find some fascinating examples of popular movie scenes edited to play without the supporting music. Stripped of the soundtrack, these scenes lose much of the director's vision, as well as the overall energy and emotionality of the story. What remains is only a shell of the powerful experience represented on the screen. Without his ominous theme song, Darth Vader becomes a much less scary character, just someone in a black robot suit bossing others around.

Similar to how music supervisors for a movie select songs to facilitate emotional reactions in viewers as part of the wider journey of the film, psychedelic facilitators work with music to bring forth deeply held subconscious thoughts, feelings, visions, body sensations, and otherworldly imaginations during a session. Each sound played during a journey acts as a brushstroke on the canvas of the mind, highlighting subconscious material. As memories resurface, psychedelic medicine dismantles our defenses, creating an open space where music and medicine collaborate. Together, they unearth thoughts and memories so they can be cleared and resolved in the present moment.

In my client sessions, I have discovered that certain movie soundtracks naturally align with the emotional landscapes of psychedelic journeys, evoking powerful visions and feelings that guide clients through transformative moments.

Jonny Greenwood's "Tree Strings" from *You Were Never Really Here* is intense and evocative, with strings that create a sense of urgency, perfectly suited for moments of deep reflection or emotional release. "Some Other Place" and "Dimensions" from Arcade Fire and Owen Pallett's soundtrack to the movie *Her* are ethereal and melancholic, blending ambient textures with emotional depth, ideal for encouraging introspection and relatedness. Hans Zimmer's "Where We're Going" and "I'm Going Home" from *Interstellar* are mysterious, expansive, and otherworldly, instilling a sense of awe and exploration that opens pathways to profound states of being. Thomas Newman's "Road to Perdition" from *Road to Perdition* is deeply sentimental and contemplative, with rich orchestration that evokes powerful feelings of reflection and melancholy. Jóhann Jóhannsson's "Kangaru" from *Arrival* carries a mystical and transcendent quality, offering a playful yet powerful soundscape that fosters an uplifting sense of otherworldly presence. Finally, Lisa Gerrard's "Biking Home" and "Go Forward" from *Whale Rider* are both hopeful and grounding, blending traditional Māoriinspired elements with modern instrumentation to help clients integrate their journey and carry its insights and optimism into the future.

Contemporary and neoclassical soundtracks such as these combine classic instrumentation with modern synthesizers, serving as portals to expansive emotional terrains. Their ability to evoke vivid emotions and memories mirrors the way our senses connect us to the past, reminding us that music is more than just background noise. It is a bridge to deeper self-awareness. In psychedelic therapy, these soundtracks become tools not just for catharsis and connection but also for helping clients access long-buried memories and emotional states, bringing them into the present for reflection and healing.

Music as Medicine: Harnessing Sound for Set, Setting, and Healing

Music and psychedelics are both powerful medicines on their own, but pairing them creates an incredibly potent synergy, where one magnifies the effects of the other. When combined, music enhances the qualities, traits, power, and emotional depth of the psychedelic journey, while psychedelics amplify the thoughts, feelings, and emotions that music evokes.

In ancient shamanic practices, chants and repetitive drumming were used to help override the ego and enhance all five senses by triggering a hypnotic, transcendent, nonordinary state of consciousness. These traditional methods are still used today by shamans, ceremony leaders, therapists, and psychedelic guides who often blend them with modern instruments like acoustic or electric guitars, electronic drums, synthesizers, microphones, turntables, and effects such as reverb and delay. Played through high quality sound systems, these enhanced sonic experiences can add more power, intensity, and vibrational energy to a session than through traditional methods alone.

However, many psychedelic therapists see incorporating music as a daunting task, one that brings up fear or trepidation. This hesitation severs the essential connection between sound and its power to support psychedelic therapy. Yet within this challenge lies an incredible opportunity—to be intentional and well informed about how music can be paired with healing. When approached with care, music becomes a transformative tool, uniquely amplifying the emotional, psychological, and spiritual dimensions of the journey.

Music curation for psychedelic therapy is a creative process where the client, practitioner, medicine, music, and setting work together to enhance the benefits of nonordinary states of consciousness induced by psychedelics. Incorporating DJing into psychedelic therapy provides clients and guides alike with a refined, responsive, and customized approach to any given journey. Selections can be made in the present moment or preselected in a playlist. Creating a playlist or DJ mix serves as an accompaniment to the emotional flow and energetic shifts that may unfold for the client in their altered state.

The twin goals of music in psychedelic therapy are to utilize frequencies and vibrations that elicit powerful responses in the journeyer while simultaneously providing support for engaging and exploring the subconscious material that arises. In psychedelic therapy and guiding, music provides a nonverbal support system whose presence transcends the need for speech. The selections, arrangements, and intentional transitions between tracks can create a seamless, responsive soundscape, amplifying the journeyer's stated intentions and emerging needs.

An essential part of my approach is incorporating what I call music for remembering—tracks that evoke nostalgia, familiarity, and a deep sense of reconnection. This type of music gently opens the door to moments of reflection and helps clients tap into memories and feelings that are meaningful for their healing. By weaving these pieces throughout the journey, I provide a grounding and emotionally resonant anchor that can support insight, integration, and a sense of homecoming.

Building on this, the emotional potency of music deepens when we consider the unique power of sad yet beautiful compositions. Tracks with this quality often evoke bittersweet emotions that tap into deeply rooted memories, creating a paradoxical sense of both sorrow and solace. The sadness this music evokes invites empathy and introspection, while their aesthetic beauty provides relief, offering a cathartic experience that feels comforting and safe—much like the soothing presence of a caregiver. This response, rooted in the brain's reward system, enhances our ability to process and make sense of complex emotions, creating a space for reflection and healing.[1]

Neurobiological research has shown that listening to sad music releases dopamine, a neurotransmitter associated with pleasure and reward, particularly at emotional peaks. This explains why sadness, paradoxically, can feel comforting or even euphoric in a musical context. Prolactin—a hormone linked to consolation and comfort—is released as well, fostering a soothing and caregiving response in listeners. Together, these neurochemical reactions create a bittersweet emotional experience, where the sorrow evoked by the music invites introspection and empathy, while the associated biochemical rewards provide relief and a sense of safety. This process mirrors the emotional bonding and solace experienced through social connectedness, offering listeners a cathartic and healing interaction with the music.[2]

During a psychedelic journey, this effect becomes even more profound. The heightened emotional and sensory states amplify the listener's connection to the music, allowing them to safely explore and release pent-up grief, sorrow, or unresolved memories. These compositions act as emotional caretakers, holding space for vulnerability while gently guiding the journeyer through waves of sadness and sublimation. By curating tracks with both emotional depth and aesthetic beauty, guides can foster an unparalleled sense of reconnection and transformation, helping journeyers navigate the full spectrum of their inner world.

I've discovered and utilized the power of sublimation extensively in my own client journey sessions. This approach is a cornerstone of the reference DJ mix protocols included in this book, which lean heavily on sublimative elements to support the emotional arc of a session. These mixes offer readers a practical lens through which to understand how sublimation shapes track selection, helping clients process and integrate challenging emotions while enhancing the therapeutic potential of music in psychedelic therapy.

Expanding on this approach, my concept of careful musical adaptation takes these elements further by uniquely curating musical compositions that provide an essential layer of energetic and emotional structure. This intentional curation enhances the wide range of mental, emotional, and spiritual experiences that it is possible to have during psychedelic journeys. The musical soundtrack becomes a rich and evocative tool that stirs emotions and brings up specific visions, memories, and thoughts in the journeyer.

When compositions are aligned with each moment of the journey, they can trigger powerful reactions while also being supportive, blissful, and making the reactions more easy to digest. To achieve this goal, it's helpful to understand the qualities, themes, chord structures, and root notes of each composition and how those frequencies will likely affect the journeyer during stages of a mushroom journey.

While thoughtfully curated playlists provide a strong foundation, the ability to adjust and respond to the journeyer's evolving emotional and energetic states is essential. These adjustments, informed by careful observation and intuitive attunement, ensure the music remains a supportive partner throughout the experience.

As the potency of the psychedelic substance increases, so does the sensitivity of the journeyer. This heightened sensitivity can lead to abrupt physiological, emotional, or energetic reactions: A journeyer may suddenly sit up and attempt to remove their eyeshades; their body may shake or tremble; they may begin to cry, yell, laugh, or cough; they may even report uncomfortable changes in body temperature, feelings of nausea, or, in rare cases with psilocybin mushrooms, the need to physically purge.

Clients often seek additional support during these challenging moments. While vocal coaching or simple hand-holding may suffice, there are instances when the music itself might be triggering the current reaction. In such cases, the guide can provide powerful nonverbal support by thoughtfully adjusting the next musical selection to either soften or enhance the emerging reaction, significantly impacting the client's journey.

While music holds incredible potential to transform and deepen psychedelic experiences, it also has the power to unintentionally amplify unproductive emotional states if used carelessly. For example, melancholic or repetitive music can trap a journeyer in cycles of rumination, reinforcing sadness or despair rather than guiding them toward resolution. Similarly, overly cheerful or otherwise incongruent tracks may suppress the journeyer's deeper emotional truths, creating a disconnect that hinders their ability to process and transform. These pitfalls highlight the importance of selecting music that aligns with the emotional flow of the journeyer, fostering coherence rather than inadvertently amplifying resistance or avoidance.

This approach to music curation in psychedelic therapy is much like a game of musical chess. Every track selection becomes a calculated move, as the therapist anticipates how it might resonate with the journeyer while simultaneously responding to their current state. Through practice, guides expand their capacity for attention—listening not only to the client's verbal and nonverbal cues but also to the subtle shifts in energy and emotion brought on by each track. The guide must stay several moves ahead, predicting where the journey might go and preparing the music to meet the evolving needs of the moment. This strategic, moment-to-moment awareness mirrors the dynamic interplay of Therapeutic DJing, where preparation (curation) and real-time responsiveness (soundtracking) come together to create an emotionally attuned and transformative experience.

A psychedelic guide does more than merely hit play and hold space; they are an active participant in the journey, moving and manipulating the soundscape to alter the setting. When music selections elicit emotional responses, repressed memories, traumas, or unexpressed or unmet needs, they can help journeyers lean into the discomfort of their past. The guide follows those experiences, making various adjustments based upon the client's reactions to selected sounds.

The personal needs and experiences of each client often change from session to session. One journey may focus on trauma, grief, or depression, and then, once addressed or resolved, the next journey might call for exploring other layers of repressed shadow material, such as anxiety, anger, fear, love, joy, or happiness, that have been lying dormant underneath the first layer of unexpressed or unresolved material. As the cup is emptied, greater space is made for other subconscious material to seek resolution through awareness.

With the lens of the mind's eye cleansed and cleared, greater attention can be given to the emerging material as the journeyer travels into deeper subconscious layers. Pairing the best possible music with a psychedelic experience is essential and, like most aspects of a therapeutic alliance, each person and moment calls for a different intervention. The music must resonate with the unfolding process, offering a dynamic response that supports the client's evolving emotional and energetic needs.

A psilocybin mushroom journey is similar to a book or novel in that it contains themes, chapters, and acts. Rather than dictating the story, the music acts as a partner, reflecting the journeyer's inner narrative and providing emotional resonance for each stage. Music provides the energy behind the overall storyline of the journey and mirrors the unique characteristics of the medicine, music, and journeyer alike. To understand the role that music will play, it's important to understand the specific traits of the medicine being used and the commonly reported qualities and characteristics of the substance or strain, as well as its effects across a timeline from activation to sobriety.

With psilocybin mushrooms, in particular, there is often a sense of gradual unfolding, as the experience oscillates from moments of emotional depth to spiritual connection and profound introspection. These qualities inform how I pair music with the mushroom journey. Early on, I may use subtle, grounding soundscapes or rhythms that ease the journeyer into the unfolding experience. As the trip deepens, more expansive, transcendent, and emotionally evocative music can reflect the complexity and richness of what's emerging internally, while lighter, softer tones can help guide the journeyer back toward integration and calm near the end.

Specific mushroom strains can sometimes influence the type of music I choose as well. For example, when using Albino Penis Envy, Ghost, Shakti, Enigma, or Toque, the effects are noticeably stronger due to the higher amount of psilocybin in the material, while strains like Golden Teacher, B+, or Mazatapec are less strong. Knowing this helps guide my selections to prevent an over- or underwhelming experience by matching the music's energy to the strain's intensity. In my experience, and according to reports from some clients and colleagues, Albino Penis Envy often induces open-eye visuals that are playful, surreal, and pastel—reminiscent of a van Gogh painting. These journeys tend to focus more on dreamy, transpersonal, and external spiritual content. In such cases, I find that larger, spacier, and more "colorful" musical pieces with a rising, expansive feeling pair with this mushroom beautifully, giving a sense of out-of-body, otherworldly travel—much like the elements of air and ether.

In contrast, traditional strains like Mazatapec provide a more grounded, internal feeling, with visuals that are static and tightly woven, featuring darker shades. These journeys often dive deep into the content of one's psyche and involve confronting or releasing repressed emotions or trauma. For these experiences, I might choose tracks that evoke self-reflection, with more subdued and perhaps darker, moodier tones that align with shadow work and introspection, offering a soundtrack that matches the internal, grounded nature of the trip—much like the element of earth.

Just as storytelling searches for the perfect word or phrase to best describe a scene and its depth, selecting music in psychedelic therapy becomes a search for sounds that can hold space for the journeyer's emotions, offering guidance and safety without controlling the narrative. Musical notes and sounds become the guide's tools for catalyzing a physical, mental, or emotional release of the nonverbal storyline held within the journeyer. This musical word search requires a dedication to listening to, examining, and understanding the powers, traits, and behaviors of each piece of music and how it works with the song before it, after it, and within the overall body of the entire journey.

If you think of a psychedelic journey as a literal journey up to and back down from the top of a mountain, the process of selecting music entails finding the best fit for the hike to basecamp (onset), climb (ascent), summit (peak), return (descent), landing, and processing stages of the journey. Sometimes certain pieces of music can be useful in multiple stages. Compositions during the onset may be softer, have less complexity, and less movement, which can also be useful during the expansive summit, softening activation as the strength of the medicine reaches its peak.

Sublimative compositions often shine during moments of catharsis, such as the dynamic and emotionally charged ascent stage or the reflective descent stage, when clients are integrating the intensity of their experience. These tracks guide journeyers through waves of emotional release, transforming challenging emotions into a sense of peace and closure.

PAIRING PSYCHEDELIC THERAPY WITH MUSIC

This approach allows the journeyer's imagination to soar through their own inner or outer heavens without feeling overwhelmed. On the other hand, certain energetic, rhythmic, and emotionally moving pieces can be brought in during either the ascent or descent stages. These pieces can provide a sense of momentum and motivation, offering a boost of energy that aids in the uphill climb of the ascent. Similarly, the rhythm and flow of these tracks can lend a sense of ease and support during the descent, helping the journeyer maintain a smooth and steady pace as they navigate their way back down. While the ascent requires more effort and dynamic energy, and the descent leans toward a more reserved and gentle energy, both stages benefit from a rhythmic foundation to support the process. By balancing sublimative tracks with rhythmic and energetic pieces, the guide ensures that the emotional arc of the journey is both expansive and grounded.

In some instances, certain pieces of music may not fit any of the four primary stages. They may instead be better suited to later stages, such as the landing and processing stage, or to more recreational situations where the criteria for music selection often differ from those chosen for intimate, intentional, focused, therapeutic journeys.

Therapeutic Music Curation for the primary stages of psychedelic mushroom therapy requires actively listening to each piece before incorporating it into sessions. During the evaluation process, it's crucial to ask: "Does this specific piece of music evoke feelings of a pleasant hike, a climb, flying, or a return or homecoming?" Proper evaluation ensures that each track is thoughtfully chosen to resonate with the journeyer's experience at each stage, enhancing the therapeutic potential and overall coherence of the session.

In my exploration, I've identified several qualities and traits that can be relevant across each stage of the psychedelic journey, though the emphasis may shift depending on the needs of any given stage. These musical qualities help facilitate nonordinary states of consciousness, whether in conjunction with psychedelic substances or without.

For instance, more uplifting and expansive music might support the ascent, while deeper, more introspective tracks may resonate during the descent. However, many of these qualities can be adaptable and beneficial throughout the entire process.

I recommend music selections that align with desired qualities such as mind-manifesting psychedelic sounds, trippy and hypnotic rhythms, and expansive or spacious compositions. Music can also be spacey, elastic, deep, and stretchy, creating a colorful or cerebral atmosphere.

Emotional tracks can range from heady, laid-back, cuddly, and gentle to those that are loving, supportive, happy, and playful. Mellow pieces offer a soothing presence, while more challenging, intense, dark, or even sinister tracks can invite deeper introspection.

Musical selections may include sublime or reflective compositions that resonate with a journeyer's inner landscape, inviting deeper self-awareness or closure. Self-reflective compositions help bring a sense of resolution to the experience.

When I test musical selections, I consider factors like emotional impact, color, timbral complexity (sound quality), tone, synesthetic effects (what songs might evoke hearing colors and seeing sounds), and spatial depth. When combined, these factors create compositions that sound exceptional under the influence of psychedelic substances, creating unique, transformative, and emotional experiences.

These elements correlate with the music's effectiveness in psychedelic therapy by enhancing feelings, triggering cathartic responses, releasing blockages, unlocking repressed memories, and activating visual or transpersonal imagery during altered states of consciousness.

By thoughtfully selecting and adapting music to match each phase of the journey, guides can amplify the therapeutic potential of psychedelic experiences while fostering emotional integration and resolution. This process of intentional curation is further expanded upon in chapter 3, where we delve into the nuances of therapeutic music selection, exploring its profound connection to memory, medicine, and healing, while offering practical tools to deepen your practice.

2
PSILOCYBIN MUSHROOMS—PAST, PRESENT, AND FUTURE

History and Traditions

As psilocybin mushrooms and other natural psychedelics continue to gain recognition for their therapeutic and spiritual applications, it is important to acknowledge the deep cultural and ecological roots of these substances. Historically used by a wide array of cultures around the world in healing and ceremonial contexts, these traditions remind us of the need for thoughtful and respectful practices when engaging with these powerful natural resources. Ethical considerations in sourcing and using psilocybin include ensuring that cultivation respects both the environment and the communities that have long safeguarded these traditions. Additionally, it is vital to be mindful, respectful, and informed about the history of psychedelic medicines as well as about any ceremonial practices that you wish to or already have integrated into your therapeutic sessions, honoring their origins and significance whenever possible.

Psilocybin-containing mushrooms, commonly known as magic mushrooms in the West, have been used throughout history for healing and a variety of rituals, thanks to their psychoactive properties. Archaeological evidence suggests that early psychedelic mushroom use may have been depicted in murals found in the Tassili n'Ajjer region of the Sahara Desert, dating back between 9000 and 7000 BCE. Additional murals from the Upper and Middle Paleolithic periods (6000–4000 BCE) also appear to illustrate the use of mushrooms, potentially in ritualistic or shamanic contexts.[1] Psychedelic mushroom use was documented in 9th-century Japan, where the *Konjaku Monogatari Shū* describes nuns consuming mushrooms that caused dancing and laughter, suggesting psychoactive effects.[2] Some scholars also speculate that rock art in South Africa and Australia from the same period depicts ritualistic mushroom use, though this remains unproven.[3] The Aztecs referred to psychedelic mushrooms as *teonanácatl*, a Nahuatl term that translates to "flesh of the gods." Various Mesoamerican cultures, including the Mazatec, Nahua, and Mixtec, have long used these mushrooms in ritualistic and spiritual ceremonies to communicate with the spirit world, seeking wisdom from deceased ancestors.[4] In the Amazon basin, certain Indigenous tribes have also been reported to use psychoactive mushrooms for spiritual and shamanic purposes, although documentation is less extensive than for Mesoamerican traditions.[5]

Among the numerous species of psychedelic mushrooms, some of the most recognized include *Psilocybe cubensis*, *Psilocybe azurescens*, *Psilocybe cyanescens*, and *Psilocybe semilanceata*.[6] These species encompass a wide range of varieties such as Mazatapec, Golden Teacher, Penis Envy, Liberty Cap, Melmak, Flying Saucer, Pink Buffalo, and Enigma.[7] There are hundreds of known species that contain the psychoactive alkaloids psilocybin and psilocin, with new types continually being discovered as mycological research advances.[8]

More than 180 mushroom species contain psychoactive compounds like psilocybin and psilocin. The most common belong to the *Psilocybe* genus, which thrives in humid subtropical forests.[9] While Mexico has the greatest variety, these mushrooms grow all over the world, including in Japan, Siberia, Europe, Hawaii, Australia, New Zealand, and South America.[10] Other genera, like *Gymnopilus*, *Panaeolus*, and *Copelandia*, also contain psychoactive species, though they are less common.[11]

Foraging for wild mushrooms carries significant risks, as toxic varieties such as *Pholiota* and *Galerina* can closely resemble psilocybin-containing species.[12] A safer approach is to cultivate mushrooms at home or obtain them from reputable sources. Cultivation allows for controlled conditions, reducing the risk of consuming misidentified or contaminated mushrooms.

The effects of psilocybin mushrooms were documented as early as 1598 by Indigenous historian Hernando Alvarado Tezozómoc in *Crónica Mexicana*, describing their use during the coronation of Moctezuma II in 1502.[13]

PSILOCYBIN MUSHROOMS—PAST, PRESENT, AND FUTURE

Spanish chroniclers, including Fray Bernardino de Sahagún, also recorded the religious and ceremonial significance of these mushrooms among the Aztecs and other Mesoamerican cultures.[14] However, these practices were condemned as heretical, leading to the persecution of shamans and healers who used them. Despite colonial suppression, indigenous communities preserved their sacred mushroom traditions in secrecy for centuries.[15]

Western interest in psychedelic mushrooms began in the 20th century. In 1938, researchers Blas Pablo Reko, Richard Evans Schultes, Roberto J. Weitlaner, and Jean Bassett Johnson documented the use of psilocybin mushrooms in Oaxaca, Mexico.[16] This research later inspired R. Gordon Wasson and his wife, Valentina Pavlovna Wasson, who began studying Mazatec mushroom rituals in 1952. In 1955, the Wassons and photographer Allan Richardson attended a psilocybin ceremony led by Mazatec shaman María Sabina. Wasson's reports, published in *Life* magazine, introduced these traditions to the Western world but also brought unwanted attention and the exploitation of Sabina's practices.[17]

However, this research and firsthand experience contributed significantly to the understanding of these powerful natural substances in the West, and the "flesh of the gods" continues to be a source of spiritual, medicinal, and scientific interest today for recreational, therapeutic, and spiritual purposes. Recreational use often occurs in social settings such as concerts and nightclubs, while spiritual journeyers may gravitate to quieter settings in nature. Therapeutically, psilocybin shows promise in helping to treat or manage conditions including addiction, depression, end-stage cancer, and mood disorders.[18] However, it's important to note that research into psilocybin's potential uses as a medicine remains ongoing.

The Johns Hopkins Center for Psychedelic and Consciousness Research is leading the way in exploring innovative treatments using psilocybin. Backed by significant funding, researchers are expanding their studies on psychedelics for illness and wellness. The aim is to develop new treatments for a wider variety of psychiatric and behavioral disorders, tailored to the specific needs of individual patients.

Research to date demonstrates the safety of psilocybin when consumed over a series of guided sessions in regulated spaces facilitated by a medical team.[19] As part of cognitive behavioral therapy, psilocybin has been found to help reduce anxiety in some cancer patients and encourage smoking cessation for others.[20]

The National Institute on Drug Abuse (NIDA) is supporting research into psilocybin as a potential clinical treatment for substance use disorders and other mental illnesses.[21] In addition, NIDA is conducting preclinical studies to further explore psilocybin's effects on the brain and body, aiming to better understand its therapeutic potential and risks.[22]

Psilocybin mushrooms are part of a continuously unfolding history, with much still to be understood about their potential therapeutic applications, along with an evolving role in the spiritual practices of journeyers today.

Music and Ritual: Sound in Psychedelic Traditions

For as long as people have explored the effects of psilocybin mushrooms, music has been a natural companion, helping to guide the experience. Whether it's the steady beat of a drum, used in traditions around the world to support altered states, or the flowing soundscapes of modern electronic music, sound has a way of grounding us in these vast and sometimes overwhelming journeys. From ancient rituals to contemporary therapy sessions, music and mushrooms have long been intertwined, each amplifying the other's transformative power. In this section, I want to explore the profound relationship between psilocybin and music—two universal forces that, when combined, create a psychedelic gestalt, something greater than the sum of their parts.

While cultural traditions develop independently, they often share common threads, including rhythms, chants, and melodies that guide and ground the psychedelic experience. For example, we see this relationship in the sacred mushroom ceremonies of Indigenous cultures, like the Mazatec people of Mexico. Their *veladas*—mushroom ceremonies—are not just about consuming psilocybin; they are deeply intertwined with music. The chants, drumming, and rhythmic patterns are there to guide participants, not just provide background accompaniment. The shamans, or *curanderos*, sing *cantitos*, or healing songs, that mirror the natural rhythms of the body and mind. These songs allow participants to feel held and supported as they move through the journey. The music is selected with intention, often to call on protective spirits or to help release negative energy.[23]

The Mazatec *veladas* are deeply rooted in the power of spoken and sung word, with the *curandero's* voice acting as a guide throughout the experience. María Sabina, one of the most well-known Mazatec shamans, described her chants as coming directly from the mushrooms themselves—a sacred language meant to bring healing and insight.[24] While there isn't much documentation on specific instruments used in *veladas*, Mesoamerican cultures, including those in Oaxaca, have long incorporated instruments like the *teponaztli* (wooden slit drum) and the *tlapitzalli* (ceremonial flute) in their spiritual traditions. The *teponaztli*, used in religious and royal ceremonies, produces distinct percussive tones, while the *tlapitzalli*—often crafted from clay or bone—was decorated with images of deities and played in sacred rites.[25] Whether through the steady rhythm of a drum, the airy tones of a flute, or the raw beauty of the human voice, sound has long been a way to anchor and shape the psilocybin experience, offering both structure and a sense of deeper connection.[26]

Across Central and South America, Indigenous traditions have long embraced psychedelics as part of ritual and healing practices. Among the Mixtec, Zapotec, and Maya, psilocybin-containing mushrooms are believed to have played a role in ceremonies designed to deepen spiritual connection and provide insight.[27] While the details of these traditions vary, many Indigenous groups across the region have been known to integrate sound, rhythm, and song into their ceremonial practices.

Beyond psilocybin, the relationship between music and altered states of consciousness is deeply embedded in other traditions as well. In South America, ayahuasca ceremonies are often guided by shamans who sing *icaros*—medicine songs—believed to help participants navigate their visions and emotions. Similarly, Native American peyote ceremonies rely on group singing and drumming, which create a sacred space for introspection, connection, and shared experience.

In Siberian shamanism, the *Amanita muscaria* mushroom has long been associated with ritual practices, believed to facilitate altered states of consciousness and spiritual journeys.[28] These ceremonies reflect a deep connection to the natural and spiritual worlds, with shamans using rhythmic drumming, chanting, and singing to enter trance states. The steady beat of the drum is thought to create a sonic landscape that helps guide the shaman and participants between realms. This use of sound establishes a sacred space where healing, divination, and communication with the spirit world can take place. The frame drum, often considered the shaman's most essential tool, plays a key role in these rituals—its resonant tones are said to mirror the heartbeat of the earth, grounding the experience and deepening the connection to unseen forces.[29]

The ancient Celts held music in high regard, with bards and druids using chants, harp drones, and pipes in their rituals to foster a sense of connection with the natural and spiritual worlds. While some speculate that hallucinogenic mushrooms like *Amanita muscaria* may have played a role in pre-Christian Celtic traditions, concrete historical evidence remains limited, with much of the discussion based on folklore rather than direct documentation. Sacred groves were central to Celtic spiritual practices, and their natural acoustics may have enhanced the impact of music, creating an immersive sonic space for ritual and introspection. Instruments such as the bodhrán, a handheld drum, and the Celtic harp, known for its ethereal resonance, were integral to musical traditions, likely playing a role in ceremonial and spiritual settings where sound was used to invoke altered states of awareness.[30]

The Sámi people of Northern Europe have traditionally used rhythmic drumming and chanting, known as *joik*, to enter transcendent states, aligning their inner rhythms with the natural world. Sámi shamans, or *noaidi*, utilized drums adorned with various symbols to facilitate their spiritual journeys. The sound of the drum in these ceremonies was believed to bridge the physical and spiritual realms, guiding the shaman on their journey.

Bringing their understanding of the potency of music in ceremony into the mid 20th century, psychedelic therapists adapted classical music to support emotional awareness and spiritual exploration during their guided sessions. Psychedelic therapy practitioners such as Walter Pahnke and Bill Richards incorporated compositions by Bach, Beethoven, and Mozart into their therapy trials. These compositions, with their intricate harmonies and emotional depth, were deliberately chosen to reflect the inner landscapes explored during psychedelic sessions, allowing participants to engage with their emotions more fully. The therapeutic setting emphasized a structured, carefully curated musical experience, with classical pieces guiding the journey in distinct movements, contrasting with the more fluid, immersive soundscapes commonly used in contemporary psychedelic therapy.[31]

Other pioneering figures like Hermina E. Browne and Helen Bonny helped shape the foundations of Therapeutic Music Curation in psychedelic therapy as we would recognize it today. Browne developed an early approach to sequencing music in LSD-assisted treatment for alcoholism that involved mapping selections to reflect the natural arc of a psychedelic journey—from relaxation and tension to spiritual ascent, then resolution. Bonny's promising early work on psychedelic therapy was unfortunately halted, though she later developed the Guided Imagery and Music (GIM) modality, showing that evocative music in and of itself could open doorways to deep inner exploration. Their contributions have reinforced what many have come to recognize both experientially and theoretically in the years since—that music, when chosen with intention, has the power to guide and shape the psychedelic experience in profound ways.[32]

By the 1960s and '70s, the notion of pairing of music with psychedelics began to reach a wider, and often less formal, audience. Festivals and concerts featuring bands like Pink Floyd and the Grateful Dead demonstrated how live, improvisational music could become an integral part of the psychedelic experience. These performances were not just concerts—they were musical journeys, blending rock, jazz, and other genres to create shared, immersive soundscapes for the audience's unfolding trips.

By the 1990s, the rave scene and the psychedelic trance movement took this connection between music and altered states to new levels. Electronic music, with its repetitive beats and hypnotic rhythms, became the soundtrack for communal experiences of expanded consciousness.

THE PSYCHEDELIC DJ

This evolution laid the groundwork for modern festivals like Boom, Electric Daisy Carnival, and Coachella, where electronic music continues to be a powerful medium for collective exploration and spiritual growth, crystallizing the enduring bond between music and psychedelics.

Fast-forward to the present, and we see a shift toward modern ambient and electronic chill-out music for psychedelic journeys in a world where technology has also transformed how we combine music with psychedelics. While classical music focuses attention on the complexity of intricate orchestral arrangements, ambient and chill-out music instead encourages emotional expression by evoking feelings of calm, introspection, and aliveness. Unlike classical pieces, which can be densely structured, the spaciousness of ambient and chill-out music allows room for the imagination to fill in the empty spaces with memories and emotions. The spaciousness of ambient-electronic soundscapes hold the potential to more effectively induce the visual and synesthetic effects (e.g., hearing colors or seeing sounds) frequently encountered during psychedelic experiences. The depth and sonic textures in these soundscapes, ranging from ethereal drones to pulsating rhythms, make for powerfully textured, futuristic sounds that resonate with the various sensations often intensified by psychedelic substances.

As journeyers close their eyes and surrender to the music, they begin to experience vivid visual imagery and hallucinations that dance in sync with the deeper rhythms and surreal textures of electronic music. After the peak psychedelic experience subsides, electronic ambient music serves as a powerful tool for soothing or grounding the postjourney experience, as well as for activating reflections or memories.

In the last six years, we have seen a shift toward the use of personalized soundscapes that are now possible via the adaptive music technology available on platforms such as Wavepaths (https://wavepaths.com/). These platforms align music with the participant's evolving emotional and psychological state, creating an auditory framework that is both intentional and responsive. This approach echoes the structured methods of earlier therapeutic practices while incorporating new technology meant to deepen the experience. And while this technology is an incredible tool, it does have its limitations. The available music remains proprietary to the platform, a restriction at odds with the open-ended possibilities of DJing or other spontaneous curation methods. Additionally, the magic of prerecorded music often lies in the organic, unrepeatable moments captured during its creation—moments that are difficult to recreate within a proprietary framework.

Despite these constraints, Wavepaths continues to evolve, offering multiple protocols specifically designed for psilocybin-assisted therapy that allow users to upload personalized sounds such as voice prompts or field recordings. While the use of copyrighted music is still discouraged, creative users might find ways to work around these limitations.

Meanwhile, research at institutions like Johns Hopkins University and Imperial College London continues to reveal the profound impact of music in psychedelic therapy. At Johns Hopkins, researchers developed a carefully curated playlist, primarily featuring classical music, to accompany psilocybin therapy sessions. This playlist is designed to align with the trajectory of a medium- to high-dose psilocybin experience, facilitating elevated states of consciousness and introspection.[33] Similarly, research from the Centre for Psychedelic Research at Imperial College London has demonstrated that psilocybin, when combined with a structured music playlist and psychological support, can be at least as effective as traditional antidepressants for treating depression.[34] The music plays a critical role in enhancing the mystical and transcendent qualities of the psilocybin experience, which have been strongly linked to long-term improvements in mental health, including reductions in anxiety, depression, and feelings of isolation.[35] Studies confirm that well-crafted playlists can amplify feelings of connection, emotional insight, and transformation during psilocybin sessions, reinforcing music's role as an essential therapeutic tool.[36]

No matter where or when it happens, music has always been there in the psilocybin experience. From ancient Mazatec and Celtic rituals to modern therapy rooms, sound has the power to bring clarity when things get confusing, comfort when fear arises, and insight when deep revelations unfold. While technology and research have given us new tools to understand this relationship, at its core, the pairing of music and psilocybin is timeless. As we continue to explore the synergy between music and psychedelics, we honor the legacy of the past while embracing the boundless possibilities of today's electronic music technology.

This book is a reflection on what's possible with a modern perspective on psilocybin journeys, blending traditional wisdom with contemporary approaches to sound and healing. Drawing from my experiences as an experiential counselor, DJ, and music curator, it serves as a guide for using music as a powerful tool in therapeutic settings. My goal is to bridge the established techniques of psychedelic therapy with the possibilities of modern sound healing technologies, offering you fresh, experiential recommendations for best practices in how music can guide, deepen, and transform the psychedelic journey.

3
THERAPEUTIC DJING—CURATION AND SOUNDTRACKING FOR PSYCHEDELIC THERAPY

The essence of DJing—the intuitive ability to connect people through music—takes on a profound dimension in the context of psilocybin therapy. Here, music becomes more than a medium for connection; it transforms into a vehicle for greater emotional resonance, enhanced spiritual insight, and profound inner healing. But how does all this unfold in practice, especially within such a sensitive and transformative setting?

Therapeutic DJing is a dynamic practice that encompasses two complementary approaches: Therapeutic Music Curation and Psychedelic Soundtracking. Together, these techniques allow for the creation of an immersive and responsive soundtrack, meeting the journeyer where they are in each moment and then guiding them toward healing.

To begin with, we'll explore and define the interrelated facets of this art form. We'll consider Therapeutic DJing as the broad, overarching practice that combines advance preparation with real-time responsiveness and technical skills to facilitate meaningful psychedelic experiences. We'll then segue into a look at Therapeutic Music Curation and examine how the creation of playlists will form the backbone of your session, as you tailor them both to your clients' therapeutic goals and to the phases of the psilocybin journey. And we'll round things out with an exploration of Psychedelic Soundtracking, learning how to dynamically adapt music midsession to best align with the client's energy and unfolding process, creating a living, evolving musical experience.

We'll then delve into advanced techniques like harmonic mixing, tempo control, and seamless transitions that will serve to amplify the therapeutic impact of your sessions. These tools and techniques are more than just technical skills—they are a means of deepening your attunement to the client's needs, enabling you to create a more profound and intentional healing experience.

For those new to Therapeutic DJing, it's important to begin with foundational skills. Start by focusing on how different tracks align with the emotional and energetic flow of a psilocybin journey. As you gain confidence, you'll develop the ability to adapt in the moment, identifying and adjusting the music to better suit your client's evolving process.

With these core ideas in mind, this chapter offers a comprehensive introduction to the art and science of Therapeutic DJing. From understanding tempo and energy flow to mastering harmonic blending and advanced mixing strategies, Therapeutic DJing is about much more than just selecting songs—it's about shaping an adaptive, meaningful soundtrack that supports the journeyer's unique process.

Through music, you can create a transformative container that amplifies the healing potential of the psychedelic journey. By attuning to the peaks and valleys of the experience and responding to subtle cues, therapeutic DJs become conavigators of the client's inner world. Whether you're curating playlists, using DJ software, or crafting live sessions, the practices outlined in this chapter will empower you to offer profound musical experiences that support your clients' emotional and psychological healing.

Therapeutic DJing

For those drawn to exploring the art of music curation within a therapeutic context, Therapeutic DJing offers a profound and transformative approach to healing. It's not simply about playing music; it's about weaving soundscapes that hold space, evoke memories, and guide emotional or spiritual processes. Therapeutic DJing elevates the traditional art of DJing into a creative and spiritual practice, inviting both journeyers and curators alike to explore the deeper layers of sound and self.

As hip-hop legend DJ Craze remarked, "DJing is not just about matching two beats together; DJing is an art form that has many levels to it—selection, technical skills, showmanship, crowd control, and knowledge of music." In a therapeutic setting, this art transforms into an act of sonic stewardship, achieved through careful selection, experimentation, and a deep sense of empathy. The therapeutic DJ becomes a guide, creating an environment where music is truly a partner in the client's healing process.

At its core, Therapeutic DJing is also a form of detective work. It involves extensive research, hunting, collecting, and curating to build a library of tracks that stimulate psychological, emotional, and behavioral responses. Music curators and DJs must intentionally tune into the thoughts, memories, emotions, physical sensations, and otherworldly experiences that each song has the potential to evoke. This process requires a blend of intuition and technical skill, supported by an ongoing commitment to understanding how music affects the mind, body, and spirit.

A key part of this practice is recognizing the unique qualities of each track—its rhythm, energy, tempo, key, melody, harmony, pitch, tone, timbre, color, dynamics, and texture. Therapeutic DJs use their technical skills to blend these elements into a seamless, continuous presentation that aligns with the stages of the client's journey. Though, for beginners, it may be helpful to first focus on broad themes or on tracks that evoke specific emotions, gradually building a more nuanced approach as your confidence grows.

As Richie Hawtin once put it, "Records are like words. The way that you put them together creates a story: the sentences, the paragraphs. That's the beauty of electronic music. . . . You're fusing those two things. It's a magical new emotion that didn't exist before, and may never exist again."[1]

In this setting, much like the way music and psilocybin combine to create a psychedelic gestalt, DJing transforms into a harmonious synergy, where the music seamlessly intertwines to create an experience that transcends its individual elements. Each song brings its own flavor, yet when woven together, they create something cohesive and alive—a dynamic soundscape that unfolds with each transition. It's not just a playlist; it's a living, breathing experience during which every track supports the journeyer's process, carrying them deeper into their healing.

This is where Therapeutic DJing naturally evolves into Psychedelic Soundtracking, where music is adapted moment to moment to reflect the client's unfolding experience. Each piece of music is chosen not to impose a narrative but to harmonize with the client's inner process. As you refine your skills, the ability to adjust and adapt in the moment becomes an exciting development, allowing you to meet the client's energy and guide the journey with greater precision and care.

For those new to this practice, the focus should be on experimenting with how different tracks resonate with the client's state and then adjusting for flow. Over time, you'll develop the ability to craft cohesive soundscapes, blending them into an integrated experience that deeply resonates with the journeyer's unique needs.

Ultimately, Therapeutic DJing is not about perfection—it's about presence. By tuning into the client's energy and responding with intention, you create a unique and supportive container where healing can unfold organically. This practice invites you to blend technical knowledge with empathy and intuition, crafting soundscapes that amplify the transformative power of music in psychedelic therapy.

Therapeutic Music Curation: Laying the Foundation

Curating music for a client during a psychedelic therapy session is less about adhering to their musical preferences and more about attuning to their psychological, emotional, and spiritual needs as they journey through the medicine. Therapeutic Music Curation is the foundational stage of this process, where playlists are thoughtfully prepared to align with the anticipated phases of the psilocybin journey and the client's therapeutic goals. This preparatory work establishes a framework for the session, providing a reliable backbone upon which spontaneous adjustments can be made during the journey.

While I consider the client's presenting issues—such as unresolved emotions or memories—that were identified during the screening, writing, and preparation sessions, the actual music selection is something I've honed over time through deep listening and experimentation. Clients trust my ability to select tracks that resonate with their evolving emotional and energetic states, knowing that each song is chosen for its unique capacity to support specific moments in the process.

Much as the ayahuasca shamans I've sat with over the years don't ask participants about their musical preferences beforehand, instead drawing on their knowledge of songs to guide and support the energy of the ceremony, intuitively responding to what's happening in the room with them, I similarly avoid involving clients too much in the music selection process. While it might seem collaborative, overinvolvement can actually introduce too much complexity into the process and disrupt the client's ability to surrender. If a track doesn't match the client's expectations, it can lead to unnecessary distractions—for example, identifiable vocals in a session can pull someone out of their experience and into their head.

That said, I always provide transparency during the screening process. I inform clients about the general type of music I use so they can make an informed decision about whether my approach aligns with their expectations and needs. In rare cases, particularly with professional musicians or DJs, clients may request the inclusion of specific tracks. I carefully review these requests, ensuring they align with the client's therapeutic goals, lack identifiable vocals, and won't disrupt the flow. If a moment calls for it, I may incorporate these tracks, but in most cases, clients ultimately prefer to surrender fully to my curated selections. After the session, many report that letting go and trusting the process significantly enhanced their experience.

Each session is thus a blend of expertise and intuition, and I often start with a playlist of options that leaves room for flexibility. No two journeys are the same. Each session provides unique insights that refine my understanding and inform my future work. This ongoing process of reflection and adjustment deepens my ability to attune to clients and create more personalized journeys over time.

For beginners, though, it's helpful to focus on broad themes or moods for playlists rather than becoming overly concerned with granular details. Starting with foundational tracks that align with specific stages of the psilocybin journey provides an accessible entry point. Over time, you'll develop a deeper understanding of how to fine-tune your selections and create nuanced soundtracks that resonate with the unique needs of each journeyer.

It's important to remember that each practitioner operates differently, and that's OK. Some take personal preferences, cultural backgrounds, and spiritual contexts into account, while others do not. Both approaches can be valid. However, it's always best to check with clients to see if these elements are particularly significant to them. If a practitioner doesn't feel confident in their musical knowledge or lacks a robust enough library to customize a session to meet specific needs, referring the client to another guide may be the most ethical choice. Music profoundly shapes the therapeutic experience, and having the right soundtrack can greatly enhance the quality and benefits of a journey.

Therapeutic Music Curation is not about perfection—it's about presence, preparation, and creating a flexible foundation. By crafting playlists with care and intention, you establish a strong framework for the session while leaving room for the spontaneous, adaptive process of Psychedelic Soundtracking to unfold.

Psychedelic Soundtracking: Scoring the Hero's Journey

Psychedelic Soundtracking is the art of using music to create a responsive and supportive soundtrack that mirrors the client's unfolding journey. It is both a mind-set and a technique within Therapeutic DJing, distinct yet complementary to Therapeutic Music Curation. While Therapeutic Music Curation establishes a carefully prepared framework tailored to the client's therapeutic goals, Psychedelic Soundtracking aligns music fluidly and in direct connection with the client's evolving emotional and energetic states, creating a cinematic experience that adapts to their inner journey.

A well-executed soundtrack amplifies transformation as the client navigates inner landscapes, offering emotional resonance and energetic guidance without imposing a narrative. The goal is to meet the client where they are in each phase of the psilocybin journey—onset, ascent, peak, descent, and landing—enhancing each stage with depth, immersion, and attunement.

The DJ mix protocols emphasized in this book prioritize emotional flow over traditional beatmatching. Rather than syncing tracks by beats per minute (bpm) for seamless transitions, my approach weaves a journey through diverse styles, tempos, genres, and subgenres, using intentional track selection, timing, and dynamic flow. This variety enriches the session's emotional depth and minimizes disruption, fostering an experience where the client remains fully engaged with their unfolding process. Each track serves as a chapter in the client's experience, supporting them through moments of tension, release, and revelation, mirroring the natural rhythms of a psilocybin journey.

Real-Time Adaptation

Psychedelic Soundtracking requires keen attunement to the client's emotional and energetic cues, allowing music to adapt fluidly in real time. For example, if a track feels too intense or otherwise mismatched with the client's current state, I might transition to a gentler composition to provide grounding. Conversely, if the client appears stuck or blocked, increasing the tempo or introducing a more activating track can encourage movement and breakthrough.

This process requires nonverbal dialogue. Observing subtle signals such as body language, breathing patterns, and emotional expressions allows the psychedelic DJ to respond with the appropriate sound (or silence). This attunement creates a dynamic, living soundtrack that evolves as a partner to the client's journey, offering a supportive presence without imposing direction.

A Cinematic Approach

In many ways, soundtracking is akin to scoring a film. Music evokes emotions, deepens the experience of the moment, and guides the listener through a structured progression. The stages of a psilocybin journey—launch, hike, climb, summit, descent—mirror the structure of a film, where music builds moods, introduces tension, and provides closure. However, unlike a film's static soundtrack, Psychedelic Soundtracking is fluid, adapting responsively to the client's shifts in energy and emotion.

I can think of one particular session that exemplifies this art. A return client—a seasoned psychonaut—began sobbing while listening to the sublime "Forever in a Moment" by Endless Melancholy and Black Swan.

THE PSYCHEDELIC DJ

As his sadness transformed into an eruption of intense joy, I sensed that that track no longer matched his rising energy. Confident in the client's mind-set, I shifted to "The Art of Luxurious Intergalactic Time Travel (MX Custom Edit)" by Junkie XL, a higher energy, more psychedelic track with a playful quality that mirrored his celebratory release. The track's crescendo aligned with his emotional evolution, allowing his experience to shift from yells to joyful laughter, creating a harmonious climax. Once he reached this peak, I transitioned into the more mellow "Lunar Landscape" by Sacred Seeds, now gently guiding him inward for reflection and rest after the emotional release.

As the session continued and the client's affect stabilized, I matched the apparent calm that had followed his big release while subtly increasing the energy from the previous beatless track. I transitioned to the more rhythmic yet whimsical, hopeful track "Collaborative Survival" by Lav. With its heart-opening sense of sublimation and beautifully delicate breakbeat, this piece evoked the feeling of soaring through the innerverse—mirroring the way his arms spread wide. The energetic yet gentle rhythm felt like the perfect companion for this powerful phase of the ascent, resonating with the heart-opening sensation I was picking up on after his profound emotional release. I could see the client experiencing this as well—his hands now resting over his heart, tears still streaming, a gentle smile on his face as he whispered unintelligibly to himself. The music supported the moment, reinforcing the depth of emotion I, too, felt in the room.

As the track gently faded, I followed with James Bernard's lovely "Out into Light," an equally expansive composition, again beatless, offering the same spacious, floating quality as the previous piece but with a touch less energy. The continuity between the two selections preserved the soaring expansiveness while providing a supportive space for the client to continue processing whatever emerging material he might be encountering. In this moment, I felt yet another shift—not just in his emotional state but in my own as well. As I remained attuned to his experience, I found myself moved by the profound beauty of the unfolding journey, witnessing how sound itself, once again, became an invisible guide—shaping the space and deepening the shared moment of transformation.

THERAPEUTIC DJING

The Practice of Deep Listening

The ability to adjust music in the moment is at the heart of Psychedelic Soundtracking. Though I often draw on my personal experiences with both the chosen medicine and the available tracks, applying my knowledge of how I've seen or felt their effects work in the past to guide my choices in the present moment, I mainly rely on a deep, empathetic connection with the client. One particularly effective technique is synchronizing my breathing with theirs, creating a shared rhythm that helps me connect with their present state. Taking things a step beyond traditional beatmatching—where one ear attunes to the track playing and the other to the track coming in—this process requires splitting my attention between the rhythm of the music currently playing, the rhythm of the next composition, and the rhythm of the journeyer's breath. This intricate balancing act blends technical skill with intuitive responsiveness, ensuring that the flow remains seamless and adaptive.

Mindfulness and Adaptability

As with reading the energy of a dance floor, Psychedelic Soundtracking involves constant responsiveness. Staying mindful and present allows me to observe how the music resonates with the client and make subtle adjustments as needed. If a piece feels too powerful—such as "Decay Waves" by Rafael Anton Irisarri, "Redacted" by Spinger, "Interstellar Superstructure" by Peter Benisch, "Midnight" by Charlie May, "I Eat Air (Marcel Dettmann Space Version)" by Mathilde Nobel, or "Said and Done" by Nils Frahm—I may ease into something gentler, like "Requiem" by Sasha, "Peace for Earth" by Four Tet, "Bloom" by Robert Babicz, "Dream as a Memory" by Tycho, "33,000 Feet Over" by Vibrasphere, "Golden Tunic" by Saphileaum, "Lotus Vajra (feat. Light Hawk)" by Liquid Bloom, or the first half of "K1" by Donato Dozzy.

If the client seems stuck or blocked, I might increase the tempo or shift to a more activating track, such as "Kothluwalawa" by Eat Static, "Plane" by Doctrina Natura, "The Call for Total Surrender" by Byron Metcalf and Steve Roach, "Manekin" by Amandra x Mattheis, or "Sun in Your Eyes" by Above & Beyond. For a more expansive lift, I might introduce an epic piece like "Madagascar (Michael Woods Chill Out Mix)" by Art of Trance. If the client has demonstrated significant psychonaut experience, I may even select the extended single version of "RITUAL (evocation) feat. Ishq, feat. Cherif Hashizume (Original Mix)" by Jon Hopkins, though this track is highly activating and should be introduced with care. Each choice is a response to the client's evolving experience, fostering a nonverbal conversation through sound.

Audience of One

Unlike playing to a crowd, soundtracking in psychedelic therapy is entirely attuned to one individual's needs and energy. The client becomes the sole audience member, and the music reflects this dynamic. The result is an experience shared by the DJ and the client that feels deeply personal, profoundly moving, and ultimately unique to each session.

For beginners, the idea of soundtracking a full session may feel daunting, but starting with foundational principles can make the process more approachable. Begin by observing how tracks align with specific stages of a psilocybin journey and experimenting with different moods or tempos. Focus on alignment rather than perfection, and don't be afraid to adjust tracks as you gain confidence. Over time, the ability to swap a track while you're in the flow will become a natural and exciting part of your practice, allowing for deeper engagement and responsiveness.

The intimate connection created through soundtracking is enhanced by technical elements like tempo and energy. Understanding how these qualities interact with emotional states allows you to tailor the music's pace to the client's unfolding journey, creating moments of grounding, activation, or release as needed. These subtle yet powerful tools allow guides to craft soundtracks that feel attuned to the journeyer's inner world, supporting them through every phase of the experience.

Tempo and Energy in Music Curation

Tempo, measured in bpm, is the pace or speed of a song, forming the technical backbone of a composition. It plays a significant role in setting the tone and pace of a psychedelic journey, even influencing physiological responses such as heart rate and breathing.

While tempo provides an objective measurement of speed, the perceived energy of a song is shaped by subjective qualities like instrumentation, rhythm, and dynamics. For example, a slow-tempo track with driving percussion and dynamic crescendos can feel energizing, while a fast-tempo piece with minimal instrumentation and soft tones may feel calm and soothing. This interaction highlights that tempo sets the foundation, but energy sets the emotional tone, making it an equally important consideration in Therapeutic Music Curation. Together, tempo and energy interact to shape a track's emotional and physical resonance, creating a sonic setting that guides clients through moments of release, introspection, or breakthrough.

In classical music, tempos are denoted by descriptive terms such as *grave, lento, adagio,* and *allegro,* offering a spectrum of emotional and technical possibilities. These terms reflect not only the speed but also the character of a piece, from the measured solemnity of *largo* to the vibrant urgency of *presto*. In contrast, modern genres like electronic music primarily use precise bpm to indicate tempo. Despite this difference, the interplay of tempo and energy remains a timeless tool for shaping musical experiences across genres.[2]

Tempo also affects how well a song pairs with others played before or after it. Here are some common tempos for various modern electronic music genres:

Ambient: 50 to 80 bpm
Dub: 60 to 90 bpm
Downtempo/chill-out: 80 to 110 bpm
Hip-hop: 85 to 110 bpm
Dubstep/chillstep: 140 bpm (or half time of 70 bpm)
Glitch-hop: 105 to 115 bpm
Breakbeat: 110 to 130 bpm
House: 115 to 130 bpm
Trance: 120 to 140 bpm
Psytrance: 130 to 150 bpm
Techno: 120 to 140 bpm
Tech House: 120 to 130 bpm

THE PSYCHEDELIC DJ

> Hardstyle: 140 bpm to 160 bpm
> Drum and bass: 165 to 180 bpm

Selecting tempo and energy levels for psychedelic journeywork is essential in creating a comfortable, relaxing, and inviting setting for clients to lie down, trust the process, surrender to the experience, and open themselves up to receiving what they need. Curating the best tempo greatly impacts the session's overall vibe and energy level.

Because tempo can impact heart rate and relaxation levels, choosing an appropriate speed is particularly important for creating the right setting in psychedelic therapy. Studies have shown that the heart and respiratory rate of listeners can naturally increase based on the tempo of the music they are listening to. One study suggested that tempo is a crucial factor in determining whether music has an exciting or relaxing effect.[3] Energy levels, however, are not tied as directly to physiological responses as tempo. Instead, they reflect the emotional and contextual impact of a track. A client's perception of energy is influenced by their internal state, the journey stage, and the music's arrangement. For instance, soft ambient tones may feel deeply calming during the climbing stage but could evoke euphoria when paired with a client's heightened emotional state at the summit.

Assessing and choosing the appropriate tempo for the journey can be done during journey preparation sessions and in the moments before or after launch as new needs emerge. In my experience, slower tempos support a more comfortable and palatable setting for the vast majority of journeywork, especially since clients are often lying down with eyeshades. Thus slower tempos are more conducive to resting and relaxing. Faster tempo musical styles, such as house, techno, trance, or drum and bass, run the risk of creating unnecessary intensity and can lead to feelings of overwhelm, particularly for clients who lack experience navigating psychedelic experiences.

Tempo and energy also shift in importance depending on the stage of the journey. During the onset hiking stage, slower tempos with low-energy instrumentation will help ease anxiety and encourage relaxation. As the journey deepens, higher energy dynamics—conveyed by the swell of a synthesizer or the driving rhythm of a drum—can complement moments of catharsis or breakthrough, even if the tempo remains moderate. This balance ensures that the music aligns with the client's emotional and physical needs at every stage.

Many clients often arrive to the journey with strong feelings of excitement or anxiety, and certain types of music can further exacerbate their already fragile prejourney state. So starting off with music at a slower or more moderate tempo creates a calmer, less distracting, and more supportive setting that supports deep exploration for a wider range of listeners. However, the use of higher tempos should not be completely avoided, as there are specific states of being where these tempos can be beneficial.

For instance, when clients exhibit signs of being in a more ecstatic or euphoric state—characterized by energetic body language, laughter, or spontaneous movement—a higher tempo song or playlist can amplify these feelings and help them fully embrace the moment. Or, if clients feel stuck in their heads or weighed down in their bodies, which creates a block to a more desired aspect of the experience, faster tempos may help them break through. If clients express sentiments like, "I'm still here. I'm having trouble letting go. I need something more to override this blockage," while manifesting physical responses like turning in bed or sighing audibly with frustration, it might be time to bring in a piece with a faster tempo.

Additionally, if you notice a client becoming more engaged and expressive during a session, this may indicate a readiness to leave behind their egoic defenses. In such cases, faster tempos can match their heightened energy and encourage them to surrender to the experience more deeply. Certain moments in the medicine timeline, such as during the climbing/ascent stage, may also call for increased tempos. The amplified energy of the music during these moments can help clients navigate intense emotions, facilitate catharsis, and release pent-up energy. Being able to recognize these shifts in energy and emotional state allows you to adapt the musical selection to best support their journey.

In practice, tempo often guides the physiological aspects of a journey, such as calming a racing heart or encouraging steady breathing. Energy, on the other hand, is more relevant when aiming to evoke or heighten specific emotional states. For example, when a client feels stuck or blocked, introducing a high-energy track—regardless of tempo—can create the momentum needed to move forward. Conversely, when grounding or soothing is required, a low-energy piece can be more effective, even at a similar tempo.

When modern recorded music feels too intricate or stimulating, I turn to recorded drumming patterns to bring on powerful altered states of consciousness. The natural sound of a single drum, especially when played in simple and repetitive rhythm, has a hypnotic, trance-inducing effect that is both calming and grounding. This calming effect allows clients to feel greater comfort and confidence in turning inward, enabling them to more fully engage with and explore emerging emotional or spiritual material.

When in doubt, I have discovered it's best practice to match the music to the administered protocol. If the client is asked to lie down, wear eyeshades, and focus for many hours, it may be best to select music that matches a slower and more relaxed setting rather than using active tempos. If the protocol creates space for greater movement—such as with certain psycholytic protocols or recreational psychedelic experiences—then perhaps a higher tempo will be a more appropriate choice. Ultimately, the aim is to create the most supportive and inviting environment possible, one without distractions that enhances the transformative potential of the session.

Volume as Setting

Back in 1993, I purchased a T-shirt at the pioneering rave club NASA in New York City that was emblazoned with the unforgettable motto "Volume Is Job #1." This simple yet profound statement captures the essential role of volume in music presentation, particularly in psychedelic therapy.

As important as tempo and energy are for guiding the rhythm of a journey, volume—or the lack thereof—plays an equally crucial role in shaping the sonic environment. Volume determines how the music is experienced, influencing its emotional impact, the depth of connection with the journeyer, and how it supports moments of stillness, movement, or catharsis. Understanding and fine-tuning volume becomes a vital part of crafting the journey space.

Music curators are experts at achieving continuity in a sonic space by gluing together multiple pieces of music without lapsing into overly long periods of silence, introducing abrupt changes, or causing unexpected endings. Engineering, blending, and mixing all contribute to the magic that makes this happen seamlessly. These particular skills emphasize the importance of adjusting the volume to create a more cinematic quality in the transitions between tracks. Since volume significantly influences the psychedelic setting, it is an essential tool for facilitating or expanding altered states of consciousness.

Understanding the traits of each composition can help prevent large jumps in volume or energy between songs, which can be disruptive to the amplified sensitivity of the client's psychedelic experience. Intense volume can feel overwhelming and create unnecessary discomfort, distracting the client from the primary goal of connecting with their inner voice and healer, while too little volume can be underwhelming, causing the dynamics and emotional impact of a song to fall flat.

One way to think about volume during a psychedelic journey is to consider it in terms of foreground, background, or middle ground. Foreground represents the sound closest to the journeyer, background reflects sound further away, and middle ground sits in the space between. Similarly, volume can be conceptualized as being above, below, or at "eye level" with the client's experience.

Sometimes the moment or musical selection calls for the volume to be set in the background (below eye level), offering the client the ability to hear and interact with their own inner experience without interference. Other times, the moment or music selection calls for the volume to be placed in the foreground (above eye level) to facilitate greater impact and enhance emotional or bodily sensations. For the majority of the experience, however, it is best to set volume levels in the middle ground (at eye level) for the perfect balance between allowing the music to actively provide a supportive backdrop and leaving space for the client's ability to hear, feel, and experience any emerging material.

Since volume is subjective and preferences differ from person to person, it's always important to check in with the client to ensure the volume is comfortable. During the orientation, assess the client's sensitivity to sound and their volume preferences while encouraging them to collaborate with you on volume adjustments throughout the experience in a way that will maintain their comfort without disruption. Of course, it's important for you to continue to observe their reactions to determine whether adjustments are needed. When in doubt, a less-is-more approach is best.

Something fascinating about volume is that it can change the effect of a song. For example, higher energy music played at low volumes can be experienced as relaxing and uplifting, whereas a low-energy piece of music played at a high volume can be experienced as intense. If using a left/right stereo speaker configuration instead of headphones, the best overall volume for a journey sits somewhere between 50 and 70 decibels, though this range can be exceeded if the client requests an increase in volume. (You can measure the overall volume with a free smartphone app, such as "Decibel: dB Sound Level Meter.") This volume range provides just enough impact without overwhelming the client's ability to hear or experience themselves. This also helps with client/guide communication and ensures conversation can be picked up if a recording device is being used to capture the session. If the client has approved the use of a recording device, be sure to place the microphone near the client instead of near the speaker, as the music will overwhelm the microphone and may prevent their statements from being recorded.

Volume—or its deliberate absence—is a powerful tool for shaping the session's dynamics. The intentional use of silence, much like the use of sound, creates space for reflection, integration, and connection with the journeyer's inner experience.

The Sound of Silence: The Space Between the Notes

In music, silence is the canvas upon which music is painted, a space where emotions take root and meaning unfolds. As Claude Debussy famously said, "Music is the space between the notes."

This beautiful quote gets right to the heart of what makes silence so powerful. It's not just the absence of sound—it's what gives music its shape, meaning, and emotional depth. In a therapeutic setting, silence works as a counterbalance to the dynamic energy of the music that's used. It offers the space clients often need to process, reflect, and integrate their experiences. Without moments of silence, music can feel like an endless stream, losing some of its emotional punch. Used thoughtfully, silence becomes a tool to highlight the peaks and valleys of a session, making everything feel more intentional and grounded.

Sometimes clients even request total silence to explore deep meditative states with fewer interruptions. However, it's important to address this possibility well before the journey begins, preferably during the orientation. Let the client know that silence can be a powerful tool for connecting with their inner voice and healer but also check if they're comfortable with moments of complete quiet. Establishing this understanding in advance helps avoid surprises and ensures a sense of trust and safety during the session.

Silence can be most effective after a particularly intense or moving musical peak, giving space for emotions to settle and take root. That said, silence shouldn't feel jarring. Abruptly cutting off the music can create confusion or even disrupt the journey. Instead, ease into it—lower the volume gradually or transition to a track with long pauses or ambient textures before silence takes over. This way, the shift feels supportive and natural rather than sudden.

Negotiating the dance between sound and silence is both an art and a skill. No two clients will respond to it the same way, and part of your role as a guide is to read the room, trust your instincts, and adapt to the moment. Whether you're fine-tuning volume, adjusting transitions, or embracing silence, these subtle choices can turn the journey space into something truly profound.

Modern Soundscapes: Integrating Ambient, Electronic, and Neoclassical Music in Psychedelic Therapy

The DJ mix protocols referenced in this guidebook center on electronic ambient and downtempo chill-out, with touches of modern neoclassical music. I prefer the balance of emotional depth and flexibility this combination provides for psychedelic therapy sessions because it creates a personalized, immersive experience. While classical compositions once formed the backbone of therapeutic playlists for their structure and harmonic richness, my approach builds on that foundation by blending classical and neoclassical influences with the expansive, adaptive possibilities of ambient and electronic soundscapes. This evolution mirrors the principles of Psychedelic Soundtracking, integrating traditional harmonic depth with modern flexibility to enhance the therapeutic process. In my practice, the combination of these genres captures both the emotional depth of classical compositions along with the futuristic qualities of modern soundscapes.

For example, "Some Other Place" by Arcade Fire and Owen Pallett is a deeply cinematic piece with soaring strings and subtle electronics that evoke a sense of wonder and longing, creating a safe space for emotional exploration. Ludovico Einaudi's "L'Origine Nascosta" fosters heartfelt introspection with delicate piano melodies and swelling orchestration, culminating in a powerful crescendo. Tracks like Jóhann Jóhannsson's "Flight from the City (Vikingur Ólafsson Rework)," Hiatus's "For Now (Roaming Soundtrack)," and zakè and City of Dawn's "J'ai vu un ange" create an atmosphere of introspection and calm, supporting journeyers during tender, reflective moments.

Building on this, modern ambient and electronic music has become integral to contemporary psychedelic therapy. We honor the roots of traditional compositions while expanding into dynamic, evolving soundscapes. These contemporary genres provide an expansive range of textures, tempos, and layers that can be tailored to support every stage of the psychedelic journey. In live sessions, these soundscapes allow for moment-to-moment adaptation, enabling the therapeutic DJ to adjust seamlessly to the journeyer's emotional and energetic flow. From ethereal drones that mirror the spaciousness of inner exploration to intricate rhythms that evoke emotional catharsis, modern ambient and electronic music offers unparalleled flexibility for creating personalized, lively, transformative experiences.

For instance, "Autumn of Communion" by Autumn of Communion evokes a sensation of floating in boundless space through its delicate harmonies, shifting textures, and playful rhythms, fostering deep relaxation and inner peace. Similarly, Harold Budd's "Boy About 10" exemplifies ambient neoclassical mastery, blending ethereal piano melodies with soft, atmospheric textures for timeless introspection. These modern works guide journeyers through moments of calm reflection and emotional depth, complementing the fluid, boundary-dissolving nature of psychedelic states.

Unlike classical compositions, which often follow structured forms and focus on harmonic complexity, electronic soundscapes excel in their capacity to evoke emotional resonance through open-ended arrangements. These pieces emphasize spaciousness, repetition, and dynamic layering—qualities uniquely suited to altered states of consciousness. The immersive qualities of these modern soundscapes often lead journeyers to report experiences of synesthesia, vivid imagery, and deep emotions.

One of the most powerful aspects of ambient and electronic music is its ability to guide and anchor the journeyer through moments of intensity. Tracks with slow, evolving textures can offer a sense of grounding and continuity, while more dynamic compositions can propel the journeyer into moments of transformation or release. In this way, the modern therapeutic DJ becomes a responsive soundtracker—curating soundscapes that evolve fluidly with the journeyer's unfolding process. This practice combines the timeless qualities of neoclassical and ambient music with the fluidity of electronic soundscapes, resulting in a deeply adaptive and client-centric approach.

For the remainder of this chapter, we'll explore advanced techniques such as beatmatching and harmonic mixing, both of which deepen music's therapeutic potential during a client's journey. Rooted in the principles of Psychedelic Soundtracking, these approaches transform the therapeutic DJ into an intuitive guide—aligning music with the journeyer's emotional and psychological landscape.

Advanced Techniques

Before diving into these advanced techniques, it's important to remember that not every tool or method discussed here needs to be mastered or even utilized at all to create powerful and meaningful musical experiences in psychedelic therapy. These techniques are presented to inspire and empower you, offering ideas for deepening your practice if and when you feel ready. If you're new to Therapeutic Music Curation, feel free to skim or even skip this section for now—come back to it when you're excited about exploring more advanced methods.

This section expands on the concept of Psychedelic Soundtracking that was introduced earlier and offers tools and techniques for creating soundscapes that mirror the client's unfolding journey. These approaches, including beatmatching and harmonic mixing, are designed to help DJs and guides weave music into a cohesive, emotionally resonant flow, supporting the client's hero's journey through carefully selected and synchronized tracks. Think of this section as a resource: take what resonates, leave what doesn't, and trust that any step you take toward understanding music's potential is a step in the right direction.

Beatmatching: Synchronizing Rhythm and Flow

Beatmatching is a fundamental DJ technique for seamlessly blending two or more tracks by syncing their tempos (that is, their bpm). Traditionally, this skill involves manually adjusting song tempos to create smooth transitions and maintain rhythmic flow. When done right, it feels magical; when it goes wrong, it can sound like shoes tumbling in a dryer. Mastering beatmatching is a powerful tool, especially in dance-focused settings where a steady rhythm is key to sustaining energy.

One of my first real experiences with beatmatching was with Plastikman's *Sheet One* double-disc limited edition picture vinyl. Getting the tempos of both discs to align felt like magic—like weaving separate musical threads into one continuous storyline. There was a rush in knowing I could keep the musical flow going undisturbed. That moment sparked an insatiable drive to master the art of mixing records, with each transition an opportunity to deepen the journey's flow.

Beatmatching originally required daily practice on tempo-adjustable turntables and vinyl records, with DJs fine-tuning tempos by ear. Today, technology has made this process much more accessible. Programs like Traktor, Serato, Rekordbox, and djay Pro include features like "sync" and "auto mix," enabling bpm alignment at the touch of a button. Similarly, modern DJ turntable setups, such as the Pioneer CDJ series, allow users to adjust tempos digitally while offering a tactile experience similar to traditional vinyl. These tools open up beatmatching to newcomers, bypassing both the steep learning curve and cost of high-end equipment. While some argue that sync technology and advanced turntables take away the artistry, Richie Hawtin—a pioneer in electronic music—sees it differently. He believes digital tools can unlock greater creativity, especially in complex setups with layers and apps. That said, he still emphasizes the importance of ear-based skills for DJs who want full control over their mix.[4]

Beyond smooth transitions, beatmatching trains the ear to focus on blending separate musical sources, which builds sensitivity to music's subtleties. This skill is particularly valuable in Psychedelic Soundtracking, where DJs need to balance their attention between the music and the client, aligning the musical flow with the client's unfolding story. Learning to synchronize tracks encourages a deeper awareness of different songs' unique qualities, which can ultimately help DJs better respond to client cues as they come up and then match the music to the client's emotional state and journey.

In dance-floor DJing, where maintaining a consistent rhythm is essential for keeping energy high, beatmatching is foundational. In Therapeutic DJing, however, where clients are relaxed, inwardly focused, and not moving to a beat, seamless alignment is less important. Instead, the emphasis is on a more flexible musical flow that adapts to the client's emotional landscape. This approach allows the music itself to act as a guide, shifting organically to match the client's evolving inner experience.

While learning to beatmatch can deepen a psychedelic DJ's connection to music and its nuances, it's not a requirement. Many therapists may not have the time for or interest in mastering this time-intensive skill. Thankfully, as mentioned earlier, modern tools make it easier for beginners to experiment with expert-level transitions without getting lost in technical minutiae. Even without precise beatmatching, the ability to craft intentional transitions and maintain a cohesive flow is key to Psychedelic Soundtracking. The intention here is not to create a polished club mix but to curate an intuitive soundtrack that supports the client's inner world.

The mix that accompanies this book reflects this distinction. It's not a traditional beatmatched DJ mix. Rather, it demonstrates how thoughtful song selection and intentional transitions serve to create a cohesive musical journey. Whether or not you learn all the ins and outs of beatmatching, the primary goal here is to approach music curation with care and creativity, adapting your skills to the unique needs of therapeutic work. While yes, some dance-floor DJs may view sync technology as a shortcut, it's more important for our purposes to focus on the heart of Therapeutic DJing: connection, flow, emotional resonance, and, most importantly, thoughtful track selection. Whether you use advanced techniques or simple tools, what matters most is the intention behind the music and how it serves the listener's journey.

Harmonic Mixing: Enhancing Therapeutic DJing

Harmonic mixing is another powerful technique that has evolved out of traditional beatmatching and is commonly utilized in nightclub DJing. In a psychedelic therapy session, harmonic mixing assists practitioners in both curating playlists in advance and making real-time adjustments during a session by categorizing each song based on root notes, bpm, and overall energy. This technique, when integrated into the broader practice of Therapeutic DJing, enhances the emotional resonance and flow of the musical journey.

Harmonic mixing might sound complex, especially if you're unfamiliar with music theory or terms like G minor or F-sharp. But thanks to a tool called the Camelot Wheel, the process has been simplified into an intuitive numbering system that will allow you to think of it as "play by numbers" rather than needing to understand the intricacies of musical scales or chords. This system allows anyone, regardless of their musical background, to match compatible tracks and create smooth, emotionally resonant transitions. By following the numbers on the chart, you can harness the emotional power of harmonic mixing without needing to learn traditional music theory.

Even if this all feels unfamiliar at first, the process becomes intuitive once you get started. Modern technology takes care of the technical details so you can focus on creating playlists that flow beautifully and naturally. Think of it as a creative experiment—an opportunity to explore and learn as you go.

Harmonic mixing ensures that each piece of music blends seamlessly into a cohesive soundscape, preventing sudden changes or disruptions in continuity. It's a skill that provides practitioners with greater control over the atmosphere, mood, energy, and emotional impact of any given session, allowing them to evoke powerful memories, insights, and emotions throughout a client's psychedelic experience.

Before the advent of modern music analysis technology, finding the root key of a song was a hands-on process. My older brother Michael, a naturally gifted and classically trained musician with perfect pitch, introduced me to harmonic mixing. He taught me to recognize each song's root key by ear and mark it for compatibility using a customized, handmade circle of fifths chart tailored for my DJ sets. Early DJs often relied on tuning devices or instruments like pianos or guitars to identify a song's key and then would manually mark the key on the vinyl or CD sleeves.

World-renowned electronic and house music DJs Sasha and John Digweed were pioneers of harmonic mixing in the mid-'90s DJ world. By focusing on building cohesive musical soundscapes that flowed naturally, they amplified the emotional depth of their live sets and their studio albums like *Northern Exposure* and *Renaissance*. Their meticulous approach to matching keys allowed them to create seamless, atmospheric journeys that became their signature, setting them apart from their peers at the time. Their work, blending intuition with precision, inspired a generation of DJs to adopt similar techniques. Harmonic mixing has since become a cornerstone of my own practice, particularly in psychedelic therapy, where it deepens the emotional impact of the musical journey.[5]

Today, digital tools like the Mixed In Key program have transformed what was once a time-intensive process into something effortless. The software instantly identifies a track's root key, bpm, and energy level, making it easier to create playlists and craft musical journeys with the same intentionality and resonance as early manual efforts. These advancements have democratized harmonic mixing, enabling practitioners to focus more on curating meaningful and emotionally resonant playlists.

THE PSYCHEDELIC DJ

One of the most useful features of this system is the Camelot Wheel, which is a variation on the traditional circle of fifths diagram. This valuable tool analyzes each song for its root key and assigns it one of 12 numbers and letters on either the minor or major scales. The number and letter can then be used with the Camelot Wheel to find the best song, or groups of songs, to play next, helping create harmonious playlists for psychedelic therapy sessions. This method becomes especially impactful in Psychedelic Soundtracking, where smooth tonal transitions mirror the emotional shifts of the journeyer. Psychedelic therapists can use these selections to choose songs that will trigger specific emotions or, alternatively, to induce the opposite emotional effect, depending on the desired outcome.

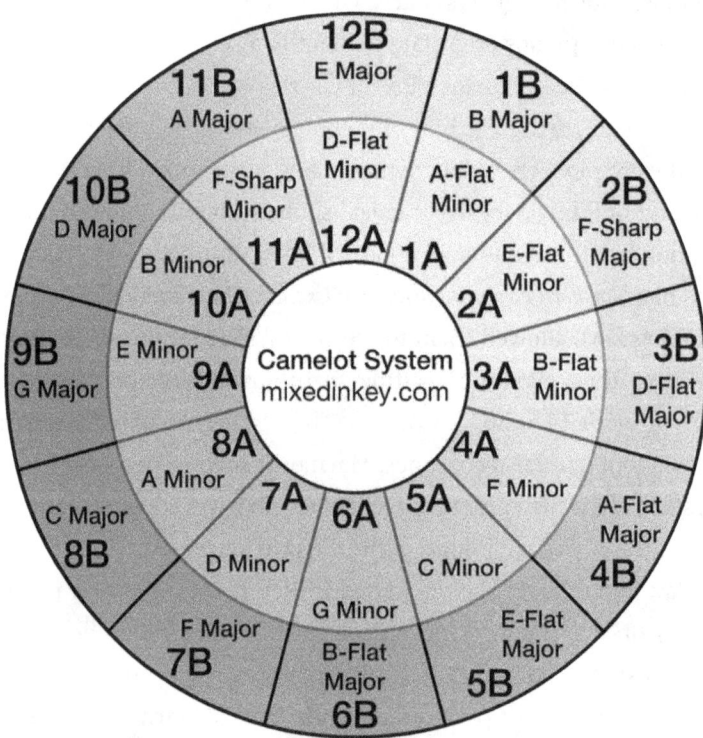

Courtesy of Mixed In Key, "The Camelot Wheel," https://mixedinkey.com/camelot-wheel/.

The first step in working with the Camelot Wheel is to analyze your tracks using the Mixed In Key app or the key analysis feature in your preferred DJ program. This step is simpler than it sounds and makes harmonic mixing easy to apply. By identifying and labeling the keys of your tracks, you're creating the foundation for smooth transitions and emotionally cohesive playlists.

Mixed In Key offers two options for analyzing and organizing music based on key: the original Mixed In Key software and the newly released Mixed In Key Live. The main program requires downloading MP3 or WAV files to analyze their root key, bpm, and energy level; this information can then be used to rearrange tracks in playlists manually. This is a fantastic option for those who prefer working with downloaded files. However, many people now rely on streaming platforms like Spotify, making the process of downloading music less common. For these users, Mixed In Key LIVE provides a new solution—it allows you to analyze tracks by simply playing them through your speakers, regardless of whether they are streamed or downloaded. With this feature, you can mark the root note manually, enabling you to create playlists based on key compatibility even without owning the files. This innovation simplifies the process of working with streaming playlists, making harmonic mixing more accessible than ever before.

Regardless of whether you're working with downloaded files or streaming playlists, identifying and labeling the root key of each track is an essential step in harmonic mixing. By understanding the tonal relationships between tracks, you can use the Camelot Wheel to create smooth, emotionally resonant transitions. This foundation supports the responsive nature of harmonic mixing, ensuring that playlists maintain the intended energy, mood, and emotional arc of the session.

The Camelot Wheel is a graphical representation of musical keys and chords, designed to simplify harmonic transitions once you've identified the root keys of your tracks. Each key is indicated by a number and letter combination, making it easy to visualize compatible transitions. The outer ring represents major chords, denoted by a number and the letter *B*, while the inner ring represents minor chords, denoted by a number and the letter *A*.

THE PSYCHEDELIC DJ

In my work with clients, I have found that major chord music tends to be lighter, more uplifting and approachable, creating comfort and digestibility for most psychedelic sessions. These qualities make major chords especially effective in fostering emotional openness and building trust, allowing clients to feel safe as they explore their inner landscapes. Major chords inspire lowered defenses, helping release emotions like love, hope, optimism, and gratitude. Compositions in A major (11B) evoke confidence and feelings of strength and courage, while D major (10B) feels victorious, as if an obstacle has been overcome. C major (8B) brings playfulness, innocence, and a simplicity that engages creative thinking and the inner child. F major (7B) can evoke calm, resolve, *or* regret, providing a paradoxical blend of emotions. Major keys can open the heart while providing an atmosphere for reflection, forgiveness, and completion.

Minor keys, on the other hand, tend to be darker, moodier, and more introspective, bringing the focus to the shadowy aspects of the self. These qualities make minor chords invaluable for guiding clients through challenging emotions and unresolved inner conflicts, helping them process and release difficult feelings. Minor keys are effective at addressing and releasing emotions like resentment, insecurity, anger, fear, hate, rage, anxiety, or grief. For example, C minor (5A) conveys introspection and longing and feels a bit like gazing out a window on a rainy day. A minor (8A) resonates with vulnerability and deep sadness, while F minor (4A) has a brooding, mysterious quality that invites exploration of the darker shadows within. By confronting these emotions, clients often uncover buried insights and find pathways to healing.

The next element that's central to harmonic mixing is key matching. The Camelot Wheel is a simplified representation of musical keys designed to make harmonic transitions more intuitive, even for those unfamiliar with music theory. Each key is assigned a unique code—like "8A" for A minor—making it easy to map compatible tracks visually. Adjacent keys on the wheel share similar tonal characteristics, enabling smooth transitions, while major and minor keys with the same number (e.g., 8A and 8B) share a tonic note, creating a natural mood shift. This

THERAPEUTIC DJING

system not only simplifies the process of crafting playlists but also ensures that transitions between tracks feel seamless and emotionally coherent.

If you're playing a track in 8A, the simplest approach is moving to another 8A track, maintaining flow and consistency. From 8A, you can move to keys 7A or 9A, which are adjacent on the wheel and share common notes, creating a natural and cohesive mix. You can also transition from 8A to 8B (the corresponding major key) because they share the same tonic—the central note, or "home base," of a key. For example, in G minor (6A), the tonic is the note G, which is also the foundation of its relative major, B-flat major (6B). This connection allows for a subtle shift in mood while maintaining harmonic compatibility. Tracks in G minor (6A), for instance, may evoke tension and feel like an approaching storm; this effect can be used intentionally to amplify emotional intensity but may also feel overwhelming for less experienced journeyers.

A	Perfect match	Energy boost +	++	+++	Energy drop -	--	---	Mood change
1A	1A, 12B	1B, 2A	10A	3A, (8A)	12A	4A	11A, (6A)	4B
2A	2A, 1B	2B, 3A	11A	4A, (9A)	1A	5A	12A, (7A)	5B
3A	3A, 2B	3B, 4A	12A	5A, (10A)	2A	6A	1A, (8A)	6B
4A	4A, 3B	4B, 5A	1A	6A, (11A)	3A	7A	2A, (9A)	7B
5A	5A, 4B	5B, 6A	2A	7A, (12A)	4A	8A	3A, (10A)	8B
6A	6A, 5B	6B, 7A	3A	8A, (1A)	5A	9A	4A, (11A)	9B
7A	7A, 6B	7B, 8A	4A	9A, (2A)	6A	10A	5A, (12A)	10B
8A	8A, 7B	8B, 9A	5A	10A, (3A)	7A	11A	6A, (1A)	11B
9A	9A, 8B	9B, 10A	6A	11A, (4A)	8A	12A	7A, (2A)	12B
10A	10A, 9B	10B, 11A	7A	12A, (5A)	9A	1A	8A, (3A)	1B
11A	11A, 10B	11B, 12A	8A	1A, (6A)	10A	2A	9A, (4A)	2B
12A	12A, 11B	12B, 1A	9A	2A, (7A)	11A	3A	10A, (5A)	3B

B	Perfect match	Energy boost +	++	+++	Energy drop -	--	---	Mood change
1B	1B, 2A	2B	10B	3B, (8B)	1A, 12B	4B	11B, (6B)	10A
2B	2B, 3A	3B	11B	4B, (9B)	2A, 1B	5B	12B, (7B)	11A
3B	3B, 4A	4B	12B	5B, (10B)	3A, 2B	6B	1B, (8B)	12A
4B	4B, 5A	5B	1B	6B, (11B)	4A, 3B	7B	2B, (9B)	1A
5B	5B, 6A	6B	2B	7B, (12B)	5A, 4B	8B	3B, (10B)	2A
6B	6B, 7A	7B	3B	8B, (1B)	6A, 5B	9B	4B, (11B)	3A
7B	7B, 8A	8B	4B	9B, (2B)	7A, 6B	10B	5B, (12B)	4A
8B	8B, 9A	9B	5B	10B, (3B)	8A, 7B	11B	6B, (1B)	5A
9B	9B, 10A	10B	6B	11B, (4B)	9A, 8B	12B	7B, (2B)	6A
10B	10B, 11A	11B	7B	12B, (5B)	10A, 9B	1B	8B, (3B)	7A
11B	11B, 12A	12B	8B	1B, (6B)	11A, 10B	2B	9B, (4B)	8A
12B	12B, 1A	1B	9B	2B, (7B)	12A, 11B	3B	10B, (5B)	9A

63

Keys are considered compatible when they share common notes or tonal structures. This creates an auditory experience that feels natural and smooth, like blending complementary colors on a painter's palette. For example, 8A (A minor) and 7A (D minor) share overlapping notes, making transitions between them intuitive and seamless. Similarly, 6A (G minor) and 6B (B-flat major) share the same tonic note (G), creating a mood shift that feels harmonious and balanced. By understanding these relationships, you can guide the emotional arc of a session with transitions that feel both intentional and effortless. By understanding these relationships, you can use harmonic mixing to create playlists that align with the emotional and energetic needs of the session, providing a structured yet flexible framework for guiding clients through their journey.

Treating music as its own form of medicine is essential. I've learned to apply the same "go slow and dose low" approach you would use with administering a psychedelic substance to understanding clients' music preferences, needs, and tolerance. Each person has unique reactions to different keys, so honoring these differences is crucial. Minor chords often push clients to confront emotions directly, stirring up anger, fear, or resentment, which can clear paths for the emergence of suppressed love and vulnerability. Major chords, by contrast, invite pleasure and warmth, softening defenses and allowing emotions to flow freely. After clients face challenging emotions brought out by minor chords, transitioning to a major chord can provide a sense of relief, resonance, and resolution. Major chords guide clients into their hearts, while minor chords delve into the deeper, shadowy realms of the psyche. Engineering a skillful mix of major and minor chords can be a form of "sonic surgery," helping a client to uncover buried emotions, confront their shadows, and ultimately experience emotional release.

You can explore these advanced techniques—beatmatching and harmonic mixing—to bring greater depth and nuance to the emotional and sensory landscape of a psilocybin journey. These methods craft a soundtrack that feels truly alive, adapting to the unique energy of each client's experience. By aligning the music with the evolving emotional arc of the journey, practitioners create a dynamic story that mirrors the unfolding hero's journey, guiding clients through both challenges and breakthroughs with intention and care.

As we move into the next chapter, we'll take a closer look at the psilocybin experience itself—its physical, psychological, and sensory effects, and how music becomes such a vital companion on this transformative path. We'll explore the timeline of a mushroom journey, showing how these musical approaches unfold from preparation to integration.

Take your time—there's no need to master everything at once. Each small step you take with these tools builds your confidence and creativity, helping you craft meaningful, transformative experiences for yourself and those you guide.

4
THE PSILOCYBIN EXPERIENCE

As we transition from advanced musical techniques to the psilocybin experience itself, it's important to acknowledge that working with this medicine comes with both immense potential for positive transformation and the possibility of awakening significant cultural and personal baggage. Psychedelic therapy can be an intense, deeply transformative process. Understanding how psilocybin interacts with the mind and body is essential before diving into this profound work. Let's take a closer look at psilocybin's physical, psychological, and sensory effects to understand how they intertwine with the therapeutic process and musical soundscapes throughout.

Physical Effects

The effects of mushrooms typically last around six hours, which is less than half the duration of other classic psychedelics like LSD and mescaline, both of which last 10 to 12 hours. Psychedelic mushrooms, commonly known for their mind-altering effects, can cause a variety of physical reactions, most commonly the dilation of pupils. At higher doses, these mushrooms can lead to a slight increase in heart rate and blood pressure.[1] However, it's important to note that these effects are transient and dose-dependent, typically requiring no medical intervention.[2]

Consumption of raw mushrooms can result in physical discomfort such as nausea, vomiting, or diarrhea for some individuals. However, these side effects are less common for those who ingest synthetic psilocybin. The onset of nausea is typically reported shortly after consumption as the stomach begins to metabolize the substance. Any nausea experienced during later stages of the journey is often attributed to emotional or energetic purging, given that the substance has likely been fully digested by this point. Fortunately, there are established preparation and delivery protocols designed to minimize these unpleasant physical reactions. By following these protocols, it's possible to significantly alleviate, or even completely eliminate, symptoms of digestive upset. Later in this chapter, I'll outline these protocols in detail, providing practical steps to help ensure a smoother experience.

Other physical effects of consuming psychedelic mushrooms can include muscle spasms, electric-like shocks, tremors, shaking, dizziness, and fluctuations in body temperature. The intensity of these effects can range from mild to strong, depending on the dosage and the individual's response. These symptoms may also indicate a release of trauma from the body and would be considered normal in that case.

The sense of touch can also be greatly impacted, resulting in overall increased sensitivity, mild to strong boosts of bodily energy, unique tingling sensations, unexpected hot and cold flashes, or even mild to strong bouts of numbness. It's crucial to remember that these effects are temporary and will dissipate as the influence of the mushrooms wears off. As with any substance, it's essential to be informed and cautious when using psychedelic mushrooms.

Psychological and Sensory Effects with Music

In most cases, psychedelic mushroom experiences bring a mix of both positive and challenging moments as the subconscious opens up, releasing biographical material and realizations about family and important relationships. Profound shifts in consciousness, thought processes, and sensory perceptions are at the heart of the signature psychological effects of psilocybin mushrooms. Journeyers often report seeing closed or open-eye visuals of intricate geometric patterns, stained glass-like images, and other vibrant scenes that seem to dance across surfaces, giving everything a sense of altered reality. Natural materials, like wood or fabric, might appear to be alive and shifting, and some even notice faces in inanimate objects.

Plants and stones may seem to breathe, exuding a life force that feels more palpable than usual.

Auditory hallucinations may also affect the perception of sounds and music. Journeyers have reported that sounds become vibrant and feel alive, as if they are communicating in a unique language that transcends spoken words. Subtle nuances and background noises become more pronounced, with notes stretching and melodies weaving together into a larger multi-dimensional tapestry of colorful sounds as different instruments merge together. Some clients have described sounds as transforming into faces or appearing as supportive beings alive within them. Others can feel as though they are witnessing the music being created from inside themselves, as if they have become the source of the sounds.

As I reflect on a moment when mushrooms profoundly affected my own perception of music, I am immediately brought back to the first psychedelic experience I had after a 15-year hiatus. This moment took place in Joshua Tree National Park, after my wife and I had consumed a Thanksgiving gift of Lovedrop chocolate mushrooms. As the effects began to settle in, I climbed up a giant boulder and played one of my all-time favorite albums, *Lifeforms* by the Future Sound of London.

As the album began, I was in awe of what I was "seeing" with my ears. The sounds seemed to come alive inside my mind, projected onto an internal screen inside my head or behind my eyelids. Each sound was its own unique being, yet all of them danced together in harmony, forming a single entity that spoke to me as if from the very studio where the music was recorded in 1993. The sounds became so palpable that I could almost reach out and touch them. They felt familiar, as if I had met them before, which I had many times in the past, but not in such a lifelike capacity. The music took on a language of its own, one that spoke not just through the sounds themselves but through the spaces in between.

When I opened my eyes to take in the sunset, my altered perception convinced me that I was either the first or last person on Earth, surrounded by the abstract beings embodied by the music. As the album continued, I felt an overwhelming rush of emotion, breathing heavily and expressing my astonishment with audible sounds of wonder. My wife watched over me from a distance, and when we finally locked eyes, it was as if I were meeting her and all humans for the first time.

Perhaps an hour later, we found ourselves listening to Jon Hopkins's masterpiece, "Light Through the Veins." The sheer beauty of the ascending music opened my heart, unleashing an intense wave of joy that culminated in a cathartic release of tears—a level of emotional purging I had never previously experienced in such a capacity. This profound moment flowed seamlessly into listening to the mixed album *Live at CoSM* by Tipper. Like *Lifeforms*, this album seemed to become a living being within my mind, dancing through my thoughts and body. It guided me into deep-seated childhood trauma, bringing it to the surface as I instinctively placed my hands on my chest, massaging my heart with empathy and compassion as I communicated directly with it and my inner child, offering comfort and understanding as the music wrapped around me.

As the medicine began to descend, we turned to the Icelandic dub-techno masterpiece "Rigning" by Yagya. The soft and deeply reflective music provided a soothing backdrop as the full moon rose over the desert horizon, washing over me with rays of white light that cleansed my mind and body. The entire experience was a symphony of sound, emotion, and healing, one that stayed with me long after the music had faded. I was humbly reminded yet again that mushrooms and music were more than recreational substances of my youth; instead, they were truly medicines.

As psilocybin and psilocin rewire perception, senses can cross paths in an extraordinary way known as synesthesia, where journeyers might hear colors or see sounds. This sensory blending can feel magical and is often met with astonishment. It can be experienced as positive or overwhelming, depending on the client's mind-set, expectations, and overall state. For many, the right piece of music can act as a steady anchor, offering comfort and safety. For others, music may intensify emotions, both the joyful and the challenging.

For those seeking a gentle and calming atmosphere during powerful or challenging stages of a journey, certain tracks can provide a sense of tranquility and introspection while maintaining the ability to tickle the senses. Selections such as "Childhood Dreams" by Purl, "The Present

Moment (Still Version)" by Lav & Purl, "Witness" by Inquiri, "Distant Ray Collector" by Saphileaum, "Us, Inside" by Arovane & Mike Lazarev, "Whispers of Our Ancestors (Tylepathy Remix)" by Liquid Bloom, and "Moonlight Saptah" by Shaman's Dream create an environment conducive to relaxation and deep reflection.

Therapeutic Benefits and Challenges

Other than creating ineffable mystical experiences that often defy explanation, psilocybin has been shown, both historically and more recently, as effective in the treatment of alcohol and nicotine addiction.[3] Research has also proven that psilocybin is an effective treatment for drug-resistant major depressive disorder, for reducing existential anxiety in advanced-stage cancer patients, and for the treatment of OCD and headaches.[4] Most studies of the psilocybin in psychoactive mushrooms have shown that this substance is helpful in improving mood, shifting negative perceptions, and altering brain activity in the amygdala, where challenging emotions are processed in a way that impacts conscious decision-making.

As for safety, recent studies have concluded that psilocybin mushrooms, especially when used in a controlled setting, are relatively safe and result in few adverse effects.[5] Despite that assurance, psychedelic mushroom experiences can be powerful and may instigate elevated levels of anxiety. As a result, people receiving treatment for cardiovascular disease should be mindful of the possible risks and always check with their doctors before taking any psychedelic substances.

Research into high-dose psilocybin sessions reveals how mushrooms can open doors to mystical experiences, leading to profound emotional states that feel timeless, connecting users to a vast sense of unity with the universe that often defies description.[6] High-dose sessions, however, can also lead to frightening experiences of perceived death or infinite psychosis, resulting in intense fear, paranoia, anger, anxiety, agitation, panic, confusion, and disorientation—all of which will dissipate once the effects subside. In high-dose sessions, clients may also unexpectedly experience ego dissolution, leading to disorienting beliefs that nothing is real or that they've gone crazy. This can be very disorienting both during and after the experience if proper support, normalization, and integration are not provided. These effects underscore the importance of selecting the appropriate dose, as more does not always equal better.

Regardless of dosage, unpleasant material can appear during a session and is often exacerbated by attempting to resist what unfolds. To address this possibility, it's helpful to teach clients breathing techniques during prejourney preparation sessions before diving into the actual mushroom journey. If intense releases and unforeseen challenges occur in ways the client was not expecting, unexpected feelings of acute stress, discomfort, and confusion may arise. These feelings may also persist over time and require additional follow-up counseling to help the client ground, make sense of, and integrate whatever psychological or somatic material is still emerging.

Choosing music that encourages grounding and emotional closure is key for this integration. Tracks like "Prana (Soundscape Mix)" by For the Good of All, "Sane" by Iyakah, "We Control Everything" by Charlie May, "Dimensions" by Arcade Fire and Owen Pallett, "Kangaru" by Jóhann Jóhannsson, "Brockley" by Totally Enormous Extinct Dinosaurs, and "Saved" by RxGibbs offer uplifting yet centered soundscapes that can help tie together the threads of the experience.

All that said, proper preparation is perhaps the best method for preventing challenging psychedelic experiences in the first place. Understanding the substance, the dosage, the mind-set, and the setting is essential for safe and effective psychedelic travel, as is choosing a quiet, private, safe, comfortable, and friendly environment free from worry or unwanted interruptions. Staying informed and aware of potential effects and making the best arrangements to provide support if and when needed can also make or break the quality of a psychedelic journey. This includes the preparation and selection of music that is pleasing and easily accessible, which helps prevent disruptions during the peak of the experience.

It is equally important that you, as journey guide, are grounded, understanding, nonjudgmental, relaxed, loving, and supportive. As mentioned earlier, psychedelic mushrooms (like other psychedelic substances) will more than likely lower the boundary of the subconscious and push vast amounts of unknown material to the surface. Because of this, it is essential for the journeyer to be mindful when scheduling the timing of their journey. Planning for a journey during times of significant instability, extreme stress, acute grief, or other challenging life occurrences has the potential to unnecessarily intensify emotions and add stress to an already complicated time in one's life. There is no need to create more problems in an attempt to solve others.

Safe and effective psychedelic work is best achieved when the client is as grounded and emotionally stable as possible. Though psychedelic work can be incredibly helpful at times, the power of these substances can also lead to unexpected, unintended, and unnecessary levels of instability, confusion, and disintegration if not properly timed. Being a responsible facilitator means always considering factors that could contribute to the experience and outcome, for better or for worse.

Broad Dosage Guidelines

The alkaloids present in psychoactive mushrooms are psilocybin (4-PO-DMT), psilocin (4-HO-DMT), and baeocystin (4-HO-NMT), with psilocybin being the most stable of the bunch. Swiss chemist and LSD pioneer Albert Hofmann first isolated psilocybin in 1957 from a *Psilocybe mexicana* strain cultivated from mushrooms obtained by R. Gordon Wasson during his famous expedition to meet with Mazatec shaman María Sabina. Studies have shown that once ingested, psilocybin is then converted into psilocin, and that equal amounts of both produce similar subjective effects. So even though psilocybin is considered the more stable of the two, psilocin is actually most responsible for the psychoactive effects.

The potency of psilocybin mushrooms varies based on species and variety, as well as how they are grown and stored. It has been found that such common varieties of *Psilocybe cubensis* and *Psilocybe semilanceata* contain approximately 6 to 10 milligrams of psilocybin per gram of dried mushroom, whereas other varieties such as *azurenscens* can contain much higher amounts, some as much as 1.78 percent per gram when dried.[7]

It's impossible to know how much psilocybin is contained within any single mushroom just by touching or looking at it. In my experience, eyeballing the mushrooms almost always leads to a wildly different result, one that is often neither expected nor desired. Best practice is to know your grower or grow them yourself so that you will know exactly what they are and if they were grown properly.

Beyond that, it's helpful to investigate user reports about each strain, the reported psilocin and psilocybin content, and the commonly reported duration and effects. Once you have that information, one reliable method for evenly dispersing the amount of psilocybin to be ingested is to blend all the mushrooms using a coffee grinder and then weigh the resulting mass with a digital scale that can measure milligrams in order to accurately calculate the dosage.

When considering dosages, be aware that individual sensitivity varies based on a number of personal factors including body weight, past experiences with the substance, and mind-set going into the journey, along with the specific mushroom strain used. Various online mushroom dosage calculators, such as those from Zamnesia and Mushly, can help determine appropriate doses based on body weight.[8] Using a precise digital scale is crucial for safe and accurate dosing, so be sure to invest in a good one. You can find many affordable options online. While precision in dosing is crucial, I have found it best to avoid complex methods such as brewing tea or using acidic juice; instead, I prefer to let the mushrooms do their work with as little interference as possible. In this context, less is indeed more.

When it comes to the kind of synthetic psilocybin that's typically used in legal research studies, dosages for oral ingestion are as follows:

- Microdose: <4 mg
- Small dose: 4–8 mg
- Medium dose: 6–20 mg
- Large dose: 20–35 mg
- Extra large "heroic" dose: >35 mg

Dosages for actual mushrooms are less accurate and vary based on factors including what variety and type they are, how they were grown, their age, how they were preserved, and whether they are dried or not at time of consumption. The typical dosages, in grams, for the most commonly used strains are as follow:

- Microdose: <0.25 g
- Low dose: 0.25–1 g
- Medium dose: 1–2.5 g
- Large dose: 2.5–5 g
- Extra large "heroic" dose: >5 g

For *microdosing*, recommended dosages range from 0.001 to 0.002 grams per kilogram of body weight. For example, a person weighing 70 kilograms would take between 0.07 grams (70 mg) and 0.14 grams (140 mg). Microdosing should be subperceptual, meaning there are no consciously noticeable effects. Basically, if you can feel it, you aren't microdosing.

Low dosing, intended for mild effects, ranges from 0.005 to 0.01 grams per kilogram of body weight, which would translate to 0.35 to 0.7 grams for a 70-kg individual. A moderate dose, producing noticeable psychedelic effects, ranges from 0.01 to 0.03 grams per kilogram of body weight. For a 70-kg person, this is 0.7 to 2.1 grams.

A *medium dose*, offering strong psychedelic effects, is 0.03 to 0.05 grams per kilogram of body weight, or 2.1 to 3.5 grams for someone weighing 70 kg.

Large doses range from 0.05 to 0.07 grams per kilogram of body weight, resulting in 3.5 to 4.9 grams for a 70-kg person.

Heroic dose is the popular term for an extra large dose that often provides ego dissolution or other profound mystical experiences. This is defined as 0.07 or more grams per kilogram of body weight, meaning 4.9 grams or more for someone weighing 70 kg. Heroic dose mushroom sessions can result in a lack of resistance from the client due to the intensity and strength of the dose. This lowered resistance can in turn lead to a deeper and more profound experience. However, with such intensity also comes a greater chance of strong, uncontrollable emotional or psychological releases that may appear unusual or even present as psychotic. As the ego dissolves, clients may lose control of their conscious mind along with the ability to make rational decisions that ensure their own safety. If an individual becomes overwhelmed by the intensity and creates an unsafe situation for themselves, it's crucial to provide calm emotional support. In extreme cases, physical restraint might be necessary to ensure the client's safety.

So, though they are incredibly powerful and potentially beneficial, I do not recommend heroic doses for most clients, especially new clients, first-time users, highly sensitive individuals, or budding guides and therapists newly stepping into psychedelic journeywork. For all sessions, I use a titrated dosing schedule—a slower, more controlled approach that starts with either a medium dose or a dose somewhere in between medium and high, which is primarily based on body weight though also considers the client's current mind-set and past psychedelic experience. This method follows the guiding advice to "go slow, dose low" and the principle that "you can always take more, but you can't take less," allowing us to ease into the process and assess sensitivity and response. If a booster dose is deemed appropriate, one can be added at the 55-to-60-minute mark during the basecamp bathroom and booster break. In my experience, it's most effective to consume the booster dose before the 75-minute mark to ensure maximum effectiveness without unnecessarily extending the overall duration of the experience.

While larger dose sessions aren't out of the question, both in the initial dose and any potential booster, these are best considered after trust and rapport have been established between the client and guide. Even in these cases, a titrated dosing schedule remains the most effective approach.

Surprisingly, the impact of low dose psilocybin mushroom sessions can be equal to or greater than popular higher dose journeys. Renowned psychedelic researcher Myron Stolaroff has noted that low doses can bring uncomfortable feelings to the surface, and that this process is actually essential for personal growth:

> The most infallible guide to Shadow material is our uncomfortable feelings. Many do not like to use low doses because these feelings come to the surface. Rather than experience them, they use larger doses to transcend them. But these uncomfortable feelings are precisely what we must resolve to free ourselves from the Shadow, gain strength and energy, and function more comfortably and competently in the world. By using smaller amounts and being willing to focus our full

THE PSILOCYBIN EXPERIENCE

attention on whatever feelings arise and breathe through them, we find that these feelings eventually dissolve, often with fresh insight and understanding of our personal dynamics. The release of such material permits an expansion of awareness and energy. If we work persistently to clear away repressed areas, we can enter the same sublime states that are available with larger doses—with an important additional gain. Having resolved our uncomfortable feelings, we are in a much better position to maintain a high state of clarity and functioning in day-to-day life.[9]

Dosing Delivery Methods

In my client work with psilocybin mushrooms, I've experimented with several preparations to optimize the experience. To minimize stomach discomfort, I advise that clients refrain from consuming solid food for at least four hours before taking the substance. An empty stomach reduces the chance of upset and enhances the psychedelic experience.

Chewing raw mushrooms is not recommended due to potential digestive issues caused by the effort required to break down the substance. Instead, I suggest grinding the mushrooms into a fine powder using a coffee grinder and soaking the powder in room temperature water for 10 to 20 minutes. This process softens the mushroom powder, facilitating digestion and ensuring even distribution of psilocybin for accurate dosing.

Although I do not personally recommend them, other common methods include brewing the mushrooms in hot tea or soaking them in acidic liquids such as lemon or orange juice. The "Lemon Tek" technique involves soaking the mushroom powder in an acidic juice for 10 to 20 minutes. This method can intensify the psychedelic experience and speed up onset. However, it should be used cautiously, especially with highly acidic juices, as it can lead to a more intense and rapid onset, sometimes resulting in anxiety. While brewing tea might be popular, it can be messy and time-consuming, while also potentially degrading the psilocybin due to excessive heat. If you do opt to use the tea-brewing method, be sure to advise your client to consume the liquid as well as any remaining mushroom material left behind in the cup in order to receive the full benefits of the active ingredient.

5
PSILOCYBIN MUSHROOM JOURNEY PROTOCOL

A common misconception is that psychedelic therapy revolves solely around the journey itself, with counseling added as an afterthought. In reality, psychedelic therapy is first anchored in counseling, with the psilocybin journey acting as an enhancement to the deep work already begun. To set the stage for the chapters that follow, here is an overview of my psilocybin-assisted therapy protocol. This step-by-step approach ensures a structured, supportive, and deeply transformative experience.

Initial screening. The process begins with a 60-minute video session designed to assess a client's mental and physical readiness. This session helps build rapport and gives us space to discuss personal intentions for the journey, review key agreements that establish trust, and set expectations for the process. This thorough assessment also identifies any contraindications and ensures a safe foundation for the upcoming experience.

Prejourney preparation. The client participates in at least two or three 90-minute preparation sessions that focus on deepening the therapeutic relationship, exploring personal history, and setting clear, meaningful intentions. These sessions create a safe and informed space for the client to get ready for their journey mentally and emotionally, while also giving us more time to discuss practical considerations and address any additional questions or concerns.

Journey day. This pivotal 10-hour session is divided into several stages. There is a full hour allotted for arrival, which allows the client to acclimate and settle into the space. Then, there is an hour for orientation and ceremony, when intentions are reinforced and a calm mind-set is established. The heart of the day is the four-hour guided journey supported by live curated music that aligns with the client's goals and evolving experience. The final three to four hours are dedicated to returning to baseline, processing initial reflections, and concluding with a closing ritual to anchor the day's insights.

First and second follow-up calls. These 30-to-60-minute calls take place on the first and second days following the journey. They provide immediate post experience support, offering space for the client to share early reflections, ask questions, and begin the integration process. This step helps clients navigate any residual emotions from the session itself and reinforces their sense of safety and connection.

Postjourney integration. At least two or three 90-minute integration sessions are conducted in the two weeks following the journey. These sessions aim to help clients process and incorporate their insights into daily life, to explore any unexpected themes that emerged, and to develop actionable steps for long-term growth and change. Integration is essential for allowing the journey's revelations to flower into meaningful, lasting transformation.

Third follow-up call. Another 30-to-60-minute call is conducted 30 days after the journey to assess progress, provide further guidance, and address any final questions or needs. This final touchpoint ensures that the client feels supported as they move forward and helps evaluate the impact of the journey on their personal development.

The following sections (and chapters) will dive into each of these stages in more depth to provide more thorough understanding for both practitioners and clients.

Screening and Journey Preparation

To begin, I base my pay rate on the totality of my services, which currently include a minimum of 15 to 17 hours of therapeutic contact time, assorted administrative tasks, and overhead expenses like rent, food, and music. Typically, participants commit to one medicine journey that is supplemented by at least two preparation and postjourney integration counseling sessions.

My protocol for journeys is a streamlined adaptation of the well-known eyeshade-and-music approach to psychedelic therapy sessions. That said, these protocols are flexible and can be adapted further, based on the client's needs and the practitioner's preferences. While I find two preparation and two postjourney sessions beneficial for most, adding or reducing sessions is entirely up to the client and practitioner, allowing for individualized care. Practitioners should also remain mindful that additional sessions come with increased costs. Given that psychedelic therapy can already be expensive, it's important to find a balance that works for the client and their budget. I encourage practitioners to customize their own approaches to suit the specific circumstances of their clients.

I also believe it's important to respect how each session unfolds. Every journey is unique, and the client and I are both impacted by the dynamic flow of that experience. By staying open to the evolving nature of the process, I can adjust my approach in real time based on feedback from the client and the journey itself. This flexibility ensures that the experience remains attuned to the client's current needs and energies, which can shift with each session. As clients develop greater self-awareness, they can better assess their readiness for future journeys that will allow us to explore emerging material or address new insights from previous sessions.

Flexibility in customizing protocols ensures individualized care based on each client's unique needs. Research on psychedelic therapy, particularly with psilocybin and MDMA, demonstrates that multiple journeys, combined with thorough preparation and integration counseling, can lead to profound and sustained benefits for individuals with complex mental health conditions like major depression and PTSD.[1] Though I rarely recommend more than one journey upfront, I may mention the possibility of additional sessions during the initial screening if the client presents significant issues that would be considered treatment resistant in other contexts. In such cases, I am mindful of the sensitivity required, ensuring the client's vulnerability is not exploited. Additional journeys can also be offered if an experienced psychonaut expresses a strong interest and understands the commitment involved. Regardless of the number of journeys booked, additional prejourney and postjourney counseling sessions may be needed and can prove beneficial, as they continue to build rapport and allow the client to process insights and deepen self-awareness.

Operating on a journey-by-journey basis also contributes to a deeper understanding of the evolving client-counselor dynamic. Each journey becomes a stepping-stone toward further growth and increased self-awareness. Taking a deliberate, unhurried approach allows me to honor the power and potential of the current journey. It also provides valuable insights into each client's unique preferences, their response to the medicine, their musical sensitivities, and any other feedback they may have about the process or the overall protocol, all of which can evolve as the client progresses through their journeywork.

This slower, more individualized approach becomes even more important when working with first-time clients, as guide and client venture into the unknown together. The development of mutual trust takes time to grow in the delicate garden of vulnerability and collaboration, though even a single session can be profoundly transformative. In such cases, the client may find that they no longer require my services or anyone else's, if they learn to rely on the wisdom that resides within and with which the medicine allows them to become better acquainted. Essentially, my goal is to counsel myself out of a job and empower my clients to tap into the resourcefulness and resilience of their own inner healer.

Intentional psychedelic journeywork is best guided by the ethical principle of "first, do no harm," prioritizing safety at all times. The safest approach begins with a comprehensive screening—the first line of defense against unintended consequences. Due to the transformative nature of psychedelic medicines and the power they have to lower a client's defenses, the relationship between client and guide requires a deep level of trust and safety.

Many people fear the unknown and may feel vulnerable embarking on a long journey with a stranger with whom they can expect to explore and express repressed emotions or memories. During the initial screening, clients take the first step toward sharing sensitive information about their past and present lives, and the practitioner, who serves as a witness to these hidden aspects, must do their best to be sensitive to and aware of this vulnerability to ensure a sense of comfort and trust as the client moves forward. The rapport established during screening and prejourney counseling sessions deepens the client's willingness to eventually surrender control and trust the process when their ego defenses are lowered. In this profound exploration, the subconscious opens, allowing for suppressed shadow material to emerge.

Beyond building trust, thorough screening is essential to psychedelic therapy because it ensures that clients do not bring mental or physical health conditions to the process that would contraindicate with their chosen psychedelic substance and subsequent therapy. Of course, providing mental health assessments without adequate training and experience can lead to misdiagnosis and serious consequences, so it is crucial that professionals undergo proper training to conduct these evaluations safely and effectively. Reputable sources such as the Coalition for Psychedelic Safety and Education (CPSE), the Icahn School of Medicine at Mount Sinai, and platforms like Psychedelic Support offer trainings. For additional information, consider reviewing the extensive resources on mental health and psychedelics available on Dr. Ben Malcolm's website Spirit Pharmacist.[2]

To prevent dangerous reactions, clients should be carefully evaluated for the following:

- Bipolar 1 (classic manic depression)
- Schizophrenia
- Psychosis
- Borderline personality disorder
- Acute or prolonged high-risk substance use disorders
- Past or current suicidal or homicidal ideation
- Active eating disorders
- Active OCD or other self-harming behaviors, such as cutting

In cases where these contraindications are present, the client must be informed about the associated risks and dangers; they may be ruled out for treatment or referred to a higher level of care for further assessment. Physical health issues must also be considered. A history of seizures, heart conditions, high blood pressure, asthma, or other conditions may impact treatment. Current medications should also be assessed; prescriptions related to SSRI, SNRI, SPARI, DNRI, TCA, MAO-A, and MAO-B can negatively interact with or block the effects of psychedelic substances.

THE PSYCHEDELIC DJ

Once any undisclosed issues have been ruled out, the client then undergoes a thorough assessment of their past history and current experience with psychedelics and other drugs. This inquiry serves multiple purposes: it gauges the client's level of familiarity with psychedelic substances and spaces, and it often yields key information about sensitivity and tolerance. These insights are crucial for adjusting doses and treatments effectively. Beyond this, the assessment explores the client's motivation for treatment and is a chance for you as the therapist to ensure that the client grasps the importance of following up with pre- and postjourney realizations, recommendations, and assignments. It's essential to emphasize that psychedelics are not a cure and that the client's own motivation before and after the journey plays an essential part in their achieving both short- and long-term treatment goals. Additionally, the assessment explores the client's support system. Are family members or partners supportive of the client's goals for psychedelic treatment? Is the home environment conducive to their pre- and postpsychedelic work?

Expectations around the role of music at each stage of the journey can also be clarified during the screening process. It's a good time to provide more in-depth explanations of how the psychedelic soundtrack is designed to support the client through the experience. I will explain that my extensive background as a DJ enhances my ability to curate a nuanced mix of ambient-electronic music that aligns with the stages and emotional landscape of the journey. Since the music as used here is less about personal preference and more about supporting the journey's natural rhythms, clients are encouraged to trust the curated flow. While I occasionally incorporate specific requests if the track aligns with the session's goals and avoids identifiable vocals, most clients find it beneficial to surrender to the overall musical experience. However, this discussion provides the client with the opportunity to determine if the musical style aligns with their preferences, allowing us both to make an informed decision to opt out of working together if my approach isn't the right fit.

Confidentiality agreements are also discussed, and the client acknowledges the practice's policies and procedures. Furthermore, the client is informed that the counselor actively participates in the therapeutic process by posing challenging questions or inviting the client to engage in thought experiments that explore presenting issues, clarify goals, or raise awareness, thereby enhancing the overall effectiveness of treatment.

Subsequently, the client is invited to engage in a brief discussion about their treatment goals or intentions. During this dialogue, they express how they believe counseling and the psychedelic substance can address their specific issues. The counselor then thoroughly explains the entire protocol so the client can offer informed consent. This includes what to expect during the psychedelic experience itself, as well as the pre- and postjourney counseling sessions. If no issues have been identified and both the client and counselor establish a strong connection, a journey day is selected along with preparation and postsession dates and times.

A confirmation message is promptly sent containing all relevant information. Once payment is received, the client gains access to a confidential, encrypted, HIPAA-protected online client portal. Here they complete all necessary legal documents, including intake and intention-setting forms. This process marks the beginning of self-exploration and can be challenging for some, as it may bring to light aspects of themselves they have learned to cope with or avoid throughout their lives.

Prejourney Writing

Prejourney writing and preparatory counseling sessions are foundational for meaningful therapeutic work. Journaling prior to the psychedelic session allows the client to articulate their thoughts, feelings, and intentions in greater detail. This practice cultivates access to previously hidden aspects of themselves and aims to provide a cathartic release that will bring unresolved emotions and needs to the surface—an especially powerful tool on the day of the journey.

The writing process begins with a comprehensive intake form completed shortly after the client gains access to the online portal following a successful screening. This intake form provides insight into the client's intentions for therapy, along with their personal and family histories. Following the intake, clients complete a prejourney intention-setting form focused on their goals, concerns, and anticipated challenges for the upcoming session.

The intention setting assignment is typically submitted the night before the first preparation counseling session. By allowing the client additional time for their reflections to evolve after the initial screening, this writing encourages greater self-awareness, increases motivation, and enhances the quality of preparation work. Sample questions include:

1. What are your goals or intentions for this work?
2. What concerns or fears do you have about this journey?
3. Do you believe this will be enjoyable or challenging?
4. What do you believe will go right? What do you think could go wrong?
5. What kind of healing do you desire?
6. What is your biggest hurdle to personal growth?
7. What fears or beliefs are holding you back?
8. What internal blockages do you want to clear or remove?
9. What internal material can the medicine help to decompose or transform?
10. What positive traits would you like to magnify as a result of this journey?
11. What action(s) can you take to best prepare for your journey?
12. How can you begin to live as if the journey has already occurred?

Reflecting on these questions helps the client gain greater clarity about their intentions, more effectively preparing them for the journey ahead. The client also has the opportunity to process their journal entries in the first session, sharing any insights or emotions that arose during their writing.

Preparation Counseling Sessions

When a client seeks treatment, they usually want to enhance their overall well-being and address unresolved issues from the past. I often use a gardening metaphor to illustrate the entire psychedelic journey, helping clients understand the role of each stage. Preparation shines light on the weeds and roots within their subconscious, bringing hidden aspects to the surface. During the journey itself, these roots are fully dug up and decomposed, and the seeds of transformation are planted. Finally, in the postjourney integration, these seeds are carefully nurtured and watered, allowing new insights to take root and flourish over time, supporting lasting change.

Once the client completes the intake and prejourney writing tasks, they have their first 90-minute prep counseling session, usually about 10 days before the journey. This vital session helps build rapport and clarify their journey intentions. I will check in to see if any goals or intentions have changed since the initial screening. The client is encouraged to delve into their issues and think about how to integrate the changes they hope to achieve. I remind them that actions taken before the journey reinforce what they gain from the experience, making it easier to adopt new behaviors, goals, and perspectives afterward.

During these sessions, I introduce exercises and interventions that encourage deeper awareness of material that may surface or intensify during the journey. One potent exercise, inspired by Gestalt therapy, invites the client to envision their future selves after the journey and engage in a dialogue with this version of themselves, amplifying self-awareness and identifying steps toward change. This exercise, along with other preparatory practices, lays a meaningful foundation for the journey and the integration work that follows. Guiding questions for this exercise might include:

1. How does your future self appear postjourney?
2. What do you feel upon meeting your future self?
3. What do you notice is different about this version of yourself?
4. How did your future self get to where they are now?
5. What specific actions did your future self take to achieve this transformation?
6. What can you start doing now to make that happen?

This immersive exercise encourages the client to amplify self-awareness and integrate disowned parts of themselves—those aspects they may have suppressed or rejected. Through this exploration, they can create an action plan for the journey, beginning to embody the traits they admire in their postjourney selves, building momentum even before the journey begins. This approach also proves valuable during postjourney integration counseling as the client reflects on their prejourney intentions and shares insights from the days or weeks following their experience.

The client will often start making gradual changes between sessions as previous counseling and writing assignments invite increased awareness. If additional journal entries have been submitted, subsequent preparation sessions provide an opportunity to process that material. Common feelings of nervousness and excitement can be utilized to deepen the preparation process. The client is encouraged to dialogue with parts of themselves that may feel apprehensive, practicing a mind-set shift from worry toward envisioning positive outcomes. This practice supports a resilient prejourney mind-set and is equally valuable postjourney when awareness is heightened, enabling the client to balance opposing inner voices.

In addition to building rapport and clarifying intentions, preparation counseling sessions are an opportunity to learn more about the medicine clients plan to bring to the session, discussing its source, strain, and cultivation methods, if known. We explore how the medicine works, its history of safe use, and how it aligns with the client's goals and intentions. I may provide additional resources, such as psychedelic documentaries like *Fantastic Fungi* by Louie Schwartzberg and *How to Change Your Mind* by Lucy Walker and Alison Ellwood, or books like *Your Psilocybin Mushroom Companion* by Michelle Janikian, *The Psychedelic Explorer's Guide* by James Fadiman, and *The Psychedelic Handbook* by Rick Strassman. However, I caution clients that online content can be highly subjective or sensationalized and that consuming too much media before the journey can lead to worry or confusion. Mindful consumption of such materials is encouraged in the lead-up to the journey.

This is also a good time to discuss the possibility of experiencing ego dissolution or ego death—a profound state where the client might temporarily lose their boundaries or sense of self. During such moments, their sense of agency may be diminished, so discussing safety protocols in advance is helpful. The client should be informed that, in the rare instance they attempt to leave the journey space or unknowingly put themselves in harm's way, gentle and minimally invasive restraint may be used as a last resort if nonphysical methods are not effective. These methods are outlined further in the Crisis Intervention Plan section, which emphasizes compassionate approaches and techniques to safely guide clients through challenging experiences.

The client is further briefed about the stages of the journey, the associated music selections, dietary recommendations, and the importance of rest in the days before and after their journey. I also provide pictures of the journey space to help clients feel more comfortable and to reduce prejourney anxiety by easing any uncertainties.

The client is encouraged to ask any questions about me as their guide, including my views on psychedelics, my experiences with previous journey sessions, and the benefits I've observed or heard about through psychedelic work. This dialogue offers the client insight into my approach and helps establish trust.

Two or three days before the journey, a final 90-minute preparation session is recommended where we can review any journal addenda and provide space for new insights that may have emerged since the first session. During this time, we finalize journey day logistics, address any last-minute questions, and go over practical recommendations for the night before and the morning of the journey. With intentions set and questions answered, the client is encouraged to slow down, mentally prepare, and reach out if further support is needed leading up to the journey day.

Dietary and Activity Suggestions

I do recommend that the client eats as healthily as possible in the days leading up the journey, as this prepares the body for the high energy demands of psychedelic journeywork. Healthy eating is often subjective, so I simply encourage the client to choose light, easy-to-digest, nutrient-dense foods high in amino acids, vitamin D, and other antioxidants that can support neurotransmitter and hormone functions. My recommendations include organic whole grains, nuts, seeds, fresh salads, organic vegetables, fruits, smoothies, or lean meats such as chicken or seafood. Foods to avoid would be heavy, highly processed fast foods loaded with sugars, salts, and hard-to-pronounce preservatives. I also recommend eliminating alcohol for a minimum of one week (or even longer) as well as reducing caffeine intake. These dietary guidelines are essential to adopt in the three to five days leading up the journey; during that time I recommend clients better manage their eating habits both to prepare their bodies and brains to receive psychedelics as well as to prevent any unwanted disruptions to their sleep cycles.

Just as the journeyer must consider what they are feeding their bodies before a session, it is also wise to consider what they are feeding their mind and nervous system prior to an experience. I usually recommend avoiding all highly triggering social media, news, television, politics, violent movies or shows, and pornography for as long as possible to help cleanse the mind and body of any experiences or memories they would not want showing up during a psychedelic journey. Simply put, a client should not consume anything prior to the experience that they don't want showing up during the journey.

I have worked with clients who, despite my recommendations, decided to watch violent superhero movies or consume highly charged political news, discussion, or podcasts before a session. As a result, clients return from the journey reporting strong images of famous television stars, movie characters, or contentious political personalities hijacking their attention and otherwise distracting them throughout much of the medicine journey. This outcome can be easily prevented by practicing discipline and avoiding forms of entertainment that differ from the kinds of material they might be attracted to following their journey.

In lieu of consuming triggering media, I recommend creating art, listening to music, dancing, practicing yoga or meditation, reading, journaling, or exercising in the days before a session. Even taking a simple walk in a beautiful location can be beneficial. During these activities, the client can take time to practice their breathing skills, connect with the spirit of the mushrooms, or engage with parts of themselves that have been lost or newly discovered during the writing or preparation sessions. Many believe the effects of the medicine begin to work long before consumption, so these aspects often do come flooding into the client's awareness.

PSILOCYBIN MUSHROOM JOURNEY PROTOCOL

Prejourney Considerations for Practitioners

As a guide, I recognize that my own preparation is as important as that of the journeyer. In the days leading up to the journey, I take time to review and play music selections in the journey space to warm up, cleanse, and fill the room with supportive frequencies. This is akin to prepping a canvas before it is painted. While the journey music plays, I dust, vacuum, empty the garbage, and thoroughly clean the adjoining bathroom. This is not only respectful to the client but also contributes to clearing the space for this sacred process.

To avoid unnecessary rushing on the journey day, I gather all my tools and prepare the space the night before. I set up the 38" x 80" twin XL journey bed on the floor, adjacent to the DJ booth and meditation seat. The booth is placed on a small floor table that's close enough to offer support yet far enough away to provide a protective space for both the client and myself. I continue to prep the space by adding two boxes of tissues for each side of the bed, two pairs of Mindfold eyeshades, one water bottle for the client, two glass cups for the initial and booster doses, two spoons, a one-milligram scale, two pens, one clipboard, one lighter, and one butane torch for lighting candles, sage, or other items. Additionally, I gather remotes to control the lighting fixtures, ceiling fan, air conditioning, and heating units.

I thoroughly test the computer and run a disk utility program to ensure stable operation and prevent crashes. I make sure the sound system and related DJ controller are tested and working properly. I place shakers and sound bowls nearby for use during the prelaunch ceremony and the breathwork following ingestion. I gather the ceremonial sage bundle and tobacco for prejourney energy clearing and protection in the shamanic realm. I gather sweetgrass, palo santo, yerba santa, cedar, or sprays containing essential oils, which, if agreed in advance, might be used sparingly, if at all, during the journey. I then place all tools around the DJ booth for easy access and print out the completed intake and prejourney forms, addenda, and journal entries and attach them to a clipboard along with progress notes for documenting the session.

On the morning of the journey, I focus on resourcing myself with self-reflection and meditation. I usually wake at 6 or 7 am to begin my morning routine, which includes a quick hike up the mountain to push out any grogginess from the previous night of sleep. I prepare a breakfast of foods that regulate my blood sugar. In my experience, caffeine can be helpful later in the day, but I consume it sparingly before the journey as it can misalign my energy with that of the journeyer. After showering, I review my intentions for the day and connect with my inner spiritual guidance. I communicate with the medicine about the client and their intentions for treatment. I offer a prayer for assistance to allow for the greater will of either Love/God/Spirit/Creator/Higher Self or Medicine Spirit to flow through me with limited interruption. I express intentions for a clear mind, an open heart, physical energy, wisdom, empathy, compassion, guidance, patience, flexibility, forgiveness, and strength to hold the space throughout the long day ahead. Most importantly, I express gratitude for the honor of supporting and guiding another soul through their inner world in what has the potential to be one of the most vulnerable and awe-inspiring experiences of their lives.

Journey Day Supply List

Here's an organized list of recommended supplies that practitioners might need to gather before a psychedelic therapy session:

1. Digital Watch with Stopwatch: This is crucial for maintaining accurate time throughout the entire session. It helps in monitoring the timing of initial and booster doses, noting timestamps on progress notes, and timekeeping during instances of significant emotional releases or unexpected crises. It also eliminates the need for frequent smartphone checks, thus reducing distractions.

2. Session Essentials: Gather a few items before the session, including:

- Phone and charger
- Milligram scale
- Two cups and spoon
- Extra eyeshades
- Water bottle
- Headphones
- Noncrunchy snacks
- Tea, coffee, or other warm beverages
- Clipboard for client paperwork and progress notes
- Extra pens
- Lighter or torch
- Blankets
- Pillows
- Tissues
- Lined receptacle for tissues or purging
- Towels for accidents
- Journal
- Book
- Warm layers
- Socks
- Slippers
- Remotes for fans, air conditioning, and lighting
- Stones, crystals, or any other personal comfort items

3. Prepared Lunch: Have your lunch prepared before starting the session. Choose quiet foods that aren't loud or crunchy, don't have a strong smell, and aren't wrapped in noisy plastic or paper bags. Your client's senses will be significantly magnified during the journey, and every sound and smell can become a distraction during sensitive moments.

6
JOURNEY DAY—
CREATING A SAFE SETTING

Welcome

Journey day begins with the client's arrival between 8 and 8:30 am. After I welcome them, we take a tour of the land and journey space. I open our conversation by naming and acknowledging any feelings such as anxiety or excitement. It's wise to be mindful of small talk, however, because the time can easily fly by if not managed properly. Simple acknowledgment, normalization of their experience, and inviting them to slow down to connect with their breath and body are helpful for clearing their minds and calming their prejourney nerves.

Before entering the journey space, the client is invited to pause at the outside altar for a brief prejourney energy clearing practice. Here, we burn sage, sweetgrass, palo santo, or tobacco as a way to release any lingering prejourney energies, offering a moment of grounding before stepping into the experience. This practice is also an invitation to call in support and protection from a higher source—be it a personal spiritual connection or simply a mindful breath of gratitude.

It's also important to recognize the diverse perspectives clients bring, so these practices are always optional. Asking for explicit consent to perform and discussing the appropriateness of these prejourney rituals during screening or preparation sessions both foster respect for each individual's comfort level. If spiritual rituals feel out of step with the client's preferences or personal history, taking a simple moment to pause with acknowledgment or express a quiet offering of gratitude is sometimes all that's needed to mark the powerful threshold before beginning.

Upon entering the journey space, the journeyer is welcomed with a selection of longform, drone-style ambient music in major chords that is uplifting, hopeful, peaceful, and serene. Examples include "Sun" by Purl and Deflektion, "LA12," "LA17," or "LA5" by Moby, "Eternal Resonance 1" by zakè and City of Dawn, "Conference of Morning Birds at the Happiness Research Center" by Music for Sleep, and "Narcissus Dream" by Ishq. This music, also effective as a gentle background soundtrack during the landing/process stage, is best played at a very low volume—just enough to fill the space softly without becoming overly activating or distracting from the sensitivity of the moment. Some clients may prefer silence before beginning their journey, so it's essential to check in with them about personal preferences.

After a small tour of the grounds, the facility, the journey bed, and bathroom, the client is encouraged to settle in and connect with their breath, their body, and the present moment as orientation begins.

Orientation

Orientation provides an opportunity to slow down, bring mindful presence to the moment, create a safe environment, and establish guidelines for the day ahead. It's a crucial time to review both the process and protocol, as well as the roles and responsibilities of the journeyer and guide, ensuring I can effectively support the client if needed. This part of the journey typically starts at 9:00 am and takes between 30 and 45 minutes, depending on the amount of information shared.

During this time we review the consent and agreements previously discussed during the preparation sessions. This helps create a grounded and safe environment for the journey. The client is asked to acknowledge their choice to consume a psychedelic substance and their reasons for doing so and to confirm that they have not been coerced by the guide or anyone else. Establishing this is crucial, particularly in cases of ego dissolution where rational thinking may be compromised, leading to potential paranoia about the substance and its source.

To prepare for potential challenges, it's helpful for the client to acknowledge the safety of their surroundings and their trust in the guide.

JOURNEY DAY—CREATING A SAFE SETTING

They agree to follow all instructions, without question, during the session for their own safety and benefit. The client commits to remaining in the room, on the bed, with eyeshades on for the four-hour music set and will not attempt to go outside until the guide approves. The client explicitly agrees to allow the guide to "keep them safe no matter what," which includes using gentle physical intervention as a last resort if they lose agency and attempt to leave the room or engage in self-harm. This is meant to ensure their safety above all else. They are reminded that my role is to keep them safe, even if that means physically guiding them back to the space when all other methods fail. This agreement is discussed openly to ensure transparency and understanding. The client also agrees to refrain from asking to make phone calls or send emails during the session—a surprisingly common occurrence in some higher dose sessions. To further prevent this possibility, the client agrees to surrender their phones, shoes, and car keys before the session begins. If a client attempts to alter these established rules, the guide will gently remind them of their prior agreements.

The client is encouraged to reach out for assistance if they are struggling so I can offer support or recommendations, though I will not initiate engagement unless prompted. I will refrain from engaging in back-and-forth counseling dialogue or related exercises during the journey to avoid creating unnecessary distractions. Instead, my role is akin to that of a lifeguard, offering support, reassurance, and normalization but only when requested during challenging moments.

Once all agreements are met, I introduce the concept of using simple mantras and breathing techniques to manage symptoms like anxiety, physical discomfort, nausea, or confusion. For example, a client may say (or think) "trust and surrender" (trust on the inhale, surrender on the exhale). The client is encouraged to request bathroom breaks as needed and is advised that ignoring such needs can be distracting, deplete valuable energy, or lead to accidents.

The rules concerning physical boundaries and touch are reviewed, emphasizing that any touch will always be consensual and never sexual and that boundaries will remain unchanged regardless of the client's state. Physical touch may be appropriate in specific instances, such as holding a hand through challenging experiences (only if requested), assisting with bathroom trips, managing long hair during purging, or preventing self-harm. However, physical touch will generally not occur, especially in male/female dynamics, to ensure safety and respect.

If the client has consented to a guided meditation, they are then offered the option to partake in a 10-to-12-minute sitting following the consumption of the psychedelic. The practice may include gentle breathing exercises or chakra-activation techniques as well. If the meditation has been declined, the client can specify how they would like the journey to begin, perhaps by quietly listening to music as the medicine takes effect or by requesting silent presence.

The client is reminded about the stages of the music journey, what to expect in terms of style and energy, and the potential for synesthesia. They are encouraged to lean into challenging thoughts or feelings triggered by the music and to share their experiences if needed. The importance of volume adjustments is discussed, and the client is encouraged to collaborate with me on volume adjustments to support or instigate reactions as needed.

Finally, the client is invited to connect with the medicine energetically and to acknowledge their intentions for the day, either verbally or silently, as they prefer. After this, they are encouraged to release all stated intentions and expectations, trusting that the medicine will provide the experience they need. With all agreements in place, they are now fully prepared to embark on their journey. At this point, my role as the guide shifts toward holding space while remaining mindful of key elements that contribute to a stable and supportive session: tracking time, ensuring internal focus with proper eyeshade use, and monitoring for physical comfort with recommendations for mindful bathroom use when necessary. These foundational elements allow the client to fully surrender to the experience once the ceremony begins.

Timekeeping

As the guide, it is my responsibility to keep accurate track of time, as the journeyer's perception of time may be significantly, if not entirely, altered. Maintaining proper timekeeping helps establish structure and safety while respecting the previously agreed-upon expectations for how the session will likely progress. However, arriving at a session with a rigid agenda can be counterproductive, as it doesn't allow for the evolving needs of the journeyer's present experience. It's best for the process to remain firmly tracked yet adaptable whenever possible.

For instance, during the later stages of the experience (during the late summit or the descent), some journeyers may feel that the effects of the medicine have worn off or that the journey has ended. Ending the session prematurely could result in the journeyer missing the valuable insights that often surface during these less intense but deeply impactful stages. In my experience, some of the most significant breakthroughs and realizations occur just after a journeyer reports that the medicine has supposedly worn off. In these instances, I've found it beneficial to encourage them to stay the course and continue engaging with whatever arises during this crucial phase of the experience.

Another key aspect of time management is preventing the journeyer from extending their journey beyond the agreed-upon endpoint. When sessions extend past the planned duration, the client may experience thought loops or struggle to request assistance in concluding their journey. Exceeding the agreed-upon time does not respect informed consent and often drains energy already exhausted during the four primary stages of the musical journey. For both journeyer and guide, energy diminishes throughout the day, and focus wanes as the journeyer continues to descend back to baseline sobriety.

Eyeshade Use

Carl Jung once wrote, "Who looks outside dreams; who looks inside awakes," while some shamans have simply stated, "It's easier to see in the dark." Thus, the use of eyeshades in psychedelic therapy allows us to amplify certain senses and minimizes others by introducing the element of darkness. This helps focus the client's attention inward and prevent both distractions as well as the tendency to avoid challenging material that may emerge in the mind's eye.

Eyeshades help create a blank canvas where subconscious material can be presented. It can also help calm the nervous system by decreasing brain activity resulting from subject/object relations. This process helps lessen the external stimulation that often creates significant feelings of overwhelm during the peak strength of the medicine. All these concerns are explained to the client prior to launch. So for this specific protocol, the client agrees to wear eyeshades for the duration of the four-hour musical journey.

It is natural for a client to want to remove the eyeshades at times, whether to satisfy a moment of curiosity or simply for convenience when visiting the bathroom. Brief eyeshade breaks are totally understandable. However, the client is notified prior to launch that I will gently encourage them to put the eyeshades back on whenever possible, as doing so makes for a much more focused and less challenging experience. If eyeshades become saturated by sweat or tears, a client can request a fresh pair at any time. If a client resists the use of eyeshades prior to launch, it might be a sign they are not ready to dive deep yet. In such cases, this might be a good time to reconsider the initial dosage in order to better match the client's mind-set and avoid situations of overwhelm. If the client still resists after the initial dose, avoiding the booster dose might be a good choice to prevent any further issues. If the booster dose is administered and the resistance to wearing the eyeshades occurs afterward, the client may be struggling to surrender to the experience as it is unfolding within them. In this case, the removal of the eyeshades may suggest they are attempting to hold onto reality. To assist with this, it's helpful to take a friendly, lighthearted, noncombative stance and roll with their resistance; check in with them concerning any emerging material that could be creating a need to remove the eyeshades. With the client's sensitivity likely at its highest point, you as guide may also consider further darkening the room instead and/or lowering the volume or intensity of the music to prevent any additional feelings of overwhelm. In most cases, the client will simply require a friendly, grounded, compassionate reminder to return to using the eyeshades for their own comfort.

Bathroom Use

Using the bathroom when the need arises is essential for avoiding unnecessary discomfort, distraction, and accidents. Ignoring such basic needs creates physical discomfort that depletes essential energy that could otherwise be spent exploring emerging material. However, to help prevent unnecessary trips to the bathroom, it is wise to recommend that the client arrives to session on an empty stomach. You should also encourage them to drink just enough to assist with dry mouth (though of course never to the point of causing unnecessary dehydration). Preventing multiple trips to the bathroom will also help to reduce the possibility of accidents that result from the client attempting to navigate their way to the bathroom while under the influence of psychedelics. This is only a recommendation, however, and one that is to be followed loosely and on a case-by-case basis, as physiological needs can vary from person to person. If a client either forgets to ask to use the bathroom or mistakenly believes they have already done so, they may accidentally soil themselves and the journey bed. If that occurs, remain calm, lighthearted, and nonjudgmental as you tend to the accident.

Ceremony

Music has long held a central role in ceremony, acting as a bridge between the physical and spiritual realms. Beyond just sound or background noise, it's a tool that can help establish sacred space and allow clients to both ground their intentions and guide them through the experience. For ceremonial purposes, the most effective music often consists of hypnotic, droning, ambient sounds accompanied by some form of nondescript vocal chanting. These kinds of compositions encourage inward focus and evoke a powerful, spiritual sensation of openness, depth, and self-reflection. The repetitive and cyclical nature of droning sounds or chants reflects the rhythms of nature, drawing attention inward and allowing the client to move beyond the noise of everyday life. Music helps open the door to deeper emotional and spiritual layers, creating an environment conducive to personal transformation and insight.

The ceremonial process can and should be tailored to the individual's needs. It can range from simple to complex, depending on the guide's skill and the participant's personal and cultural preferences. Incorporating elements of each participant's own spiritual or religious beliefs can, with the client's explicit consent, add a deeply personal and potent layer of meaning to the journey ahead.

When leading a ceremony, I begin by honoring the spirit of breath. Recognizing its role as a life-sustaining force that anchors and supports the journey, I invite the client to engage in deep, mindful breathing in order to sustain energy and consciousness throughout the process. Following my invocation of the spirit of breath, I use a brief, nondenominational, shamanic prayer, inspired by the Celtic traditions of my heritage, that calls in and honors the cardinal directions. In Celtic and other shamanic traditions, honoring the four cardinal directions is a common practice in prayer and ceremony. Often referred to as "calling the corners" or setting up a "medicine wheel," this practice is rooted in ancestral lines and is used to create sacred space for spiritual work. The medicine wheel typically includes the four primary directions—East, South, West, and North—along with a central point or axis. Some traditions also recognize "Above" and "Below," viewing the central axis as inherently connected to these two spaces. The directions can also be associated with different qualities, gifts, elements, and power animals.[1] This beautiful framework acknowledges the qualities of the natural world and the powers and traits associated with each of the seven directions:

- East (Fire/Spring): Sunrise, clear vision, new beginnings
- South (Earth/Summer): Inner child, joviality, playfulness
- West (Water/Fall): Sunset, endings, darkness, mystery, shadow, death/rebirth
- North (Air/Winter): Inward reflection, hibernation, clear judgments, inner knowing
- Above: The universe, Father Sky, stars and galaxies, infinite possibilities
- Below: Mother Earth, ancestors of the land, food, water, shelter, safety, medicine
- Within: The Body Temple, the spirit vessel

Offering this framework not only provides support and meaning but also pays homage and respect to all shamanic cultures that have used such prayers for ceremonial practices. In psychedelic ceremonies, the use of cardinal directions can also help create a controlled and safe environment. Initiating the journey by calling the directions, or with another appropriate

JOURNEY DAY—CREATING A SAFE SETTING

and meaningful ritual, can prepare the mind, body, and spirit for the psychedelic experience. This process often parallels the spiritual and emotional purification that one seeks by taking the journey. This also expands the prayerful imagination to include the universal principles of diversity, particularity, interiority, and communion.[2]

After calling the corners, I then call upon the spiritual realms, whether perceived as real or symbolic. This part of the prayer welcomes any spirits, allies, ancestors, or guardian angels who may wish to offer wisdom, guidance, support, and protection. This prayer often particularly resonates with journeyers who hold a strong spiritual background or seek connection with lost loved ones.

Next, I invoke the spirit of music and honor its medicinal powers, its universal frequencies and vibrations that not only evoke emotions and trigger memories but also provide a sacred and supportive container for transformation and healing.

Then, I honor the mushroom spirit, the great decomposer who illuminates and transforms that which no longer belongs into fertile soil for new growth. I thank this spirit for being a profound teacher and ally who harmonizes the energies of mind, body, spirit, and sound into a cohesive, healing experience. I invoke its ancient wisdom and invite it to guide a powerful yet gentle journey filled with love, peace, clarity, and deep healing.

Lastly, the client is invited to close the ceremony by providing any additional thoughts, feelings, intentions, prayers, or statements they deem appropriate based on their personal preferences, religious beliefs, or cultural practices.

During the ceremony, I may reinvoke the stated intentions of the journeyer, whether it's for protection, gratitude, healing, or grounding, as it helps to personalize the experience and inspire the journey with greater meaning. Past clients have reported such prayers provide a sense of grounded support, expansiveness, peace, and deeper understanding of the journey ahead.

It's important to note that specific ceremonial practices and interpretations can vary widely depending on the culture and the individual practitioner. Consent is always foundational to this process. If you're interested in incorporating a seven-directional prayer into a ceremony, you might consider creating one that resonates with your own spiritual beliefs, lineage, and connections to the natural world. For clients who prefer to forgo ceremonial elements, they can be invited to honor the experience in their own way—whether through silent reflection, a personal ritual, or simply by consuming the medicine, laying back, and preparing to embark on the journey. That said, the ceremonial process can be deeply personal and transformative during a psychedelic journey, enriched by the incorporation of music, prayer, and the honoring of cardinal directions. It invites us to connect with the natural world, our ancestors, and the deepest parts of ourselves. Whether you and your client choose to incorporate these elements or simply follow the musical journey, remember that the experience is yours to shape. The power of the ceremony lies not only in the rituals performed but also in the intentions behind them.

Crisis Prevention: Proper Dosing, Music Adjustments, and Preparation

When working solo with clients choosing to partake in psychedelic therapy—especially with medium to higher doses that could result in ego dissolution or an unexpected psychotic break—clear preparation and safety measures are of utmost importance. The potential for intense experiences makes it essential to have a well-defined plan to manage any challenging situations that may arise, including the rare need for physical intervention.

Above all, screening, preparation, and proper dosing are essential for creating a safe journey. This includes resisting the temptation to dose clients excessively simply because of popular trends extolling the supposed benefits of high-dose ego death. While deeper experiences can certainly be transformative, they should be approached with respect for each individual's mind-set, sensitivity, readiness, and current needs. Proper dosing minimizes risks and ensures that the journey remains within the client's capacity for handling such an experience.

Screening for factors including the client's height, weight, age, and sex is likewise crucial for ensuring safety during sessions. These considerations are particularly important when there are significant physical differences, such as in certain male/female dynamics. Proper assessment can help the

JOURNEY DAY—CREATING A SAFE SETTING

practitioner determine if there's a risk of being physically overpowered and may influence the decision to have additional support available.

Informed consent and clear communication create a solid foundation for this approach. During the preparation and orientation process, I thoroughly brief clients on my safety protocols, including what it means for me to "keep them safe." This discussion covers the possibility of physical intervention if the client poses a risk to themselves or to me—for instance, if they attempt to leave the safe space while disoriented or engage in any form of self-harm. Clients are told that physical intervention is always a last resort, utilized only when verbal de-escalation and grounding techniques are insufficient to ensure their safety.

I make sure to set clear boundaries around physical contact, emphasizing that the primary goal is always to calm and reassure them using nonphysical methods first. Grounding techniques, such as offering guided breathing exercises, suggesting a refocus on positive imagery, and maintaining a calming presence, are prioritized to help clients reconnect with their bodies in the present moment. If physical intervention becomes necessary, it is done gently and with the utmost respect for the client's dignity, with the goal of guiding them back to a safe space rather than using forceful restraint.

Additionally, musical adjustments can play a significant role in maintaining a balanced setting. Grasping the impact of each musical piece is crucial for understanding how it affects the client's experience. If I assess that the current music is contributing to a challenging situation, shifting from more activating or intense tracks to calming and relaxing pieces has been shown to ease the client's experience.

For higher-risk cases—such as those involving high-dose journeys or clients with a history of trauma or sensitive psychiatric conditions—having a cofacilitator or someone trained in de-escalation and physical safety present can be very helpful. Making sure that a trusted friend or colleague who is aware that journeywork is occurring will be available by phone and can come by if extra support is needed provides an added layer of safety. Additionally, having a plan and consent to contact emergency services if the situation escalates is a key aspect of crisis preparation as it further ensures the client's well-being the top priority.

Ultimately, the focus remains on prevention—selecting the right clients, creating a calm setting, and using music, breathwork, and grounding practices to maintain a sense of safety and stability. Thorough preparation helps minimize the need for physical intervention, allowing for a smoother and more supportive journey. My role as guide, similar to that of a lifeguard, is to monitor the client's state, offer reassurance and support, and intervene only when absolutely necessary to maintain safety.

For those offering solo psychedelic therapy sessions, it is highly recommended to seek specialized training in nonphysical de-escalation techniques and, when appropriate, physical safety interventions focused on ensuring client well-being. Such training equips guides with the skills needed to manage challenging situations safely and compassionately, further ensuring the well-being of both clients and practitioners.

Ego Death

Ego death, also known as ego dissolution, is a profound experience where a person feels their sense of identity or "self" dissolve. This can manifest as a disconnection from personal memories, the perception that time and space no longer exist, or even a sense that the individual or their loved ones never existed at all. These effects occur due to changes in the levels of glutamate, the most common excitatory neurotransmitter released by nerve cells in the brain. These changes, occurring between the cortex and the hippocampus, are thought to be linked to how a person perceives their psychedelic experience. The default mode network (DMN), a network in the brain associated with self-referential thoughts, becomes less active during a psychedelic experience, potentially contributing to the dissolution of the ego. A 2020 study also found that the claustrum, a part of the brain involved in sensory integration, was less active under the influence of psilocybin.[3]

The concept of ego death has been discussed for centuries in religious and spiritual traditions such as Zen Buddhism. In Zen, ego death is often seen as a necessary step toward enlightenment, referred to as *satori* or *kenshō*. Zen teachings emphasize that the ego, or the false sense of a separate self, creates suffering by fostering attachment to fleeting thoughts, desires, and perceptions. Through practices like meditation (zazen), practitioners seek to dissolve the illusion of the self and realize the interconnectedness of all existence. Ego death in this context is not something to be feared but is embraced as a gateway to awakening, where one can experience the world without the filter of personal identity. This parallels the experience of ego dissolution during a psilocybin journey, where clients may encounter a similar release from the confines of the ego, allowing for a broader, more expansive awareness.

Experiencing ego death can be either frightening or deeply illuminating, depending on the person's level of readiness and the environment they are in. It's essential that clients are in a safe and supportive space and are given the context for what they might encounter during this phase of the journey.

If a client begins to experience a challenging ego death, they may feel as though they are losing their identity, forgetting key aspects of who and where they are; they may even believe they have died or lost touch with reality. This can lead to feelings of panic or a desire to stop or change the experience. One common sign of a client struggling with ego dissolution is a repeated attempt to remove their eyeshade, often during the more challenging climb and summit stages of the journey. By attempting to take off the eyeshade, they may be seeking to reestablish a sense of control or to distract themselves by engaging with the external environment. However, this can disrupt the natural flow of their inner process and overwhelm them with sudden visual stimuli.

In these instances, gentle guiding and reassurance can make a significant difference. Encouraging the client to return to the eyeshade for comfort, guiding them through slow, deep breaths, and normalizing their experience can help them reengage with their inner journey. Inviting the client to share what they are feeling in their body and what they would like to express can offer them a way to process the experience without attempting to escape it. Additionally, adjusting the music can be helpful. If you assess that the current piece of music is contributing to the intensity of the experience, consider switching to a track that uses major chords or has a gentler tone to soften the emotional weight.

If the client continues to make requests to stop the trip or engages in actions outside of the agreed-upon parameters—such as going for a walk or using their phone—it's important to gently remind them of the agreements made beforehand. A calm, confident, and grounded approach reassures the client that what they are experiencing is a natural effect of the substance and will eventually pass. Reminding them of their safety, the purpose of the journey, and their ability to trust the process often helps them refocus.

In rare cases where the client is completely unable to follow directions due to a loss of agency, maintaining a soft, friendly yet firm presence can help. Lightheartedly rolling with any resistance, normalizing their subjective experience, and providing reassurance can assist the client in navigating what they are going through. Encouraging them to remain on the bed, keep their eye shades on, and breathe deeply—perhaps using the mantra "trust and surrender"—offers a practical approach to help them work through the challenging material that is emerging.

If the client appears to be looping (repeating the same thoughts or actions), they can be reminded that the effects of the medicine will eventually wear off and that their sense of agency will return during the return/descent stage of the journey. Keep in mind that ego dissolution such as this is more common during high-dose sessions but can also occur in lower doses when paired with particularly powerful pieces of music.

The ability to work through ego death smoothly often depends on the foundation of trust and rapport built during prejourney preparation. If the client has been properly screened and oriented, they are more likely to tap into their inner strength, breathe through the challenges, and request support as needed. Successfully navigating ego death can be one of the most profound experiences of their life and may provide lasting benefits long after the journey is complete.

Crisis Intervention Plan

Here are some approaches to consider when a client loses agency as a result of an ego death during a journey.

1. Reassurance: The guide should remind the client that they are alive and well, that their body is safe, and that they are in a secure environment. They can be reminded that what they are experiencing

is a temporary effect of the psychedelic they consumed. Most importantly, the practitioner should reassure them that all is well and that they are there to ensure their safety.

2. Supportive Presence: The guide should stay close to the client, providing a calm, grounded, confident, supportive, and friendly presence, both in demeanor and voice. The guide should acknowledge, validate, and reflect the client's feelings and experiences without judgment. If supportive hand-holding was agreed upon during preparation and orientation, this is a good time to offer it, without any pressure or expectations for the client to accept. Always be mindful to respect physical space and obtain approval in the moment before initiating any physical contact. However, if the client loses agency and attempts to leave the safe environment or engage in self-harm, physical intervention may become necessary. This is only used as a last resort, with the sole purpose of ensuring the client's safety.

3. Grounding Techniques: The guide can use grounding techniques to help the client reconnect with the present moment. This could involve focusing on their breath and guiding them through deep, slow breathing exercises with a simple mantra like "trust and surrender." The guide can also invite the client to feel the weight of their body on the bed or to describe what they are seeing or feeling in the present moment.

4. Guided Imagery: If experiential support is deemed appropriate, the practitioner can use guided imagery to help the client navigate their experience. This could involve the instruction to imagine a safe place or a calming scene, such as floating down a river like a leaf on the surface of the water.

5. Physical Safety: In situations where nonphysical approaches do not suffice, such as when a client is attempting to leave the room, gentle physical intervention may be needed to ensure they do not hurt themselves or enter an unsafe environment. This intervention is used only after verbal reassurances and grounding efforts have been exhausted. The client is reminded of the agreements made during orientation, emphasizing that this measure is taken to ensure their well-being.

6. Focus on Careful, Nonforceful Action: Any physical contact is applied calmly, gently, and respectfully, aiming to guide the client back to a safe position rather than restraining them forcefully. This approach is always executed with the intention of minimizing discomfort and distress for the client.

Crisis Support: Nonphysical Guiding Intervention

In almost all cases, the safest and best approach is to guide a client *through* their experience, rather than *down from it*. This involves recognizing the heightened sensitivity of the psychedelic experience and remaining a compassionate presence throughout. Being mindful means creating a safe space for the client, actively listening to their needs, staying present and adaptable, and maintaining a nonreactive awareness. Subtle and mindful intervention not only fosters trust but also allows for a more effective and transformative journey, though advanced-level guiding and counseling techniques should only be used by those who have the appropriate training and experience.

Here's a brief example of what a nonphysical crisis intervention might look like from a body-centric, Reichian/Somatic Experiencing approach:

Client: I . . . I can't see myself . . . I'm scared . . .

Therapist: I understand that you're feeling scared right now. Thank you for speaking up and letting me know. It's OK. You can't see yourself because you're wearing an eyeshade. This helps maintain calm and keeps your focus inward, so please keep your eyeshade on. Remember, you're in a safe space and I'm here in this room to support you through this.

Client: I . . . I don't know who I am anymore. I feel like I've lost myself or that I died. Am I alive?

Therapist: I completely understand that you're feeling overwhelmed. Yes, you are alive and your body is safe. What you're experiencing is

JOURNEY DAY—CREATING A SAFE SETTING

an ego death from the mushrooms you took a little while ago. I know things are intense right now, but just remember it's a temporary and normal part of the journey. Let's focus on your breath for a moment. Start by taking a few long, slow, deep breaths. I'll do it with you. Now, let's focus on your body for a moment. Can you feel the rise and fall of your chest as you breathe? What sensations are you feeling right now?

Client: I feel . . . numb. And there's a tightness in my chest. Actually, I don't feel like I have a body sometimes. Am I alive?

Therapist: Thanks for sharing that. Yes, you are alive and everything is safe here, so don't worry. Let's try taking a few more deep breaths to help release that tightness. Breathe in . . . hold . . . and breathe out . . .

Client: OK, I'm trying . . .

Therapist: Excellent. You're doing great. Now, perhaps imagine that tightness in your chest as a block of energy. Visualize it. What does it look like?

Client: It's . . . dark and heavy . . . I just want to scream!

Therapist: (*Setting a boundary.*) It sounds like you're really angry. Feel free to express yourself with your emotions but please stay on the bed and refrain from any violence.

Client: (*Screams loudly and pounds hands on bed.*)

Therapist: Very good! Let that out. Now take a deep breath. Imagine a warm light surrounding that block of energy, softening it, opening it, making it lighter. Continue slowly breathing and visualize that heavy block slowly dissolving with each breath. And as you breathe, remember the mantra we discussed: "Trust on the inhale, surrender on the exhale." Repeat that to yourself as you breathe. Let's do it together . . . breathe in "trust," breathe out "surrender." One more time, nice and slow . . .

Client: The tightness . . . it's lessening.

Therapist: Good. You're doing really well. Let's continue the breathing exercises to help you through this. I'm now going to play a piece of calming music. Let the music guide you into that opening. Allow it to fill your mind and body, helping you navigate through this experience as you trust and surrender with your breath.

Client: I . . . I think I can do this . . .

Therapist: You're doing great. Remember, this is a powerful journey, and it's OK to feel overwhelmed. It's only temporary and it will fade. We're here together, and we'll navigate through this. If you need to hold my hand, just let me know, but no pressure. Otherwise, let's keep focusing on your body sensations and remember, you're safe here, everything that's happening is OK and part of the healing process.

Crisis Intervention: Training and Resources
Sara Gael from the MAPS Zendo Project has authored an excellent resource on assisting clients with challenging psychedelic experiences, describing how to create a safe space, sit with clients instead of guide them, talk through complications, and understand how difficult moments aren't necessarily bad. Her guide was initially designed for peer-to-peer harm reduction support at festivals but can be readily adapted for therapeutic psychedelic sessions. The principles of nonphysical intervention remain foundational, but in solo practice, additional safety measures, including the potential for physical restraint, must be considered and discussed ahead of time.[4]

For those seeking to deepen their skills in managing challenging situations during psychedelic therapy, training in de-escalation and crisis intervention can be invaluable. Organizations such as NEST Harm Reduction, Zendo Project, Crisis Prevention Institute (CPI), Mental Health First Aid (MHFA), and Somatic Experiencing Trauma Institute (SETI) offer training that equips practitioners with both nonphysical and physical intervention techniques. These resources help ensure that psychedelic guides are prepared to respond safely and compassionately, creating a more secure journey for all involved.

Postcrisis Integration

After the session has ended, helping the client integrate their experiences is essential, especially if the journey involved an ego death or a crisis-based event. Begin by reviewing the session with transparency and empathy. If physical intervention was required, ensure that the client understands why it was necessary and invite them to share how it felt for them. This mutual understanding can help ease any lingering discomfort or confusion about the experience.

For clients who lost agency or encountered intense emotional or physical sensations, integration may need to focus on reestablishing safety and meaning. While much of the process involves normalizing the experience and identifying insights, additional steps might include:

- **Processing Intense Emotions:** Some clients may carry lingering emotions such as fear, shame, or frustration. Encourage them to articulate these feelings during the session or to journal about them between sessions. Validate their experiences and offer reframes that highlight the courage it took to navigate the challenging moments.
- **Somatic Integration:** Incorporate grounding practices to help reconnect the client with their body. Gentle stretching, breathwork, or a body scan meditation can help address any residual physical tension or dissociation that arose during the crisis.
- **Finding Meaning from the Challenge:** Guide the client to reflect on how the challenging moments contributed to their overall journey. Ask open-ended questions such as, "What did this experience reveal about what you're working through?" or "How might this challenge inform how you approach similar situations in your daily life?"
- **Self-Care Practices:** For clients feeling emotionally or physically raw, suggest restorative activities such as connecting with loved ones, spending time in nature, or practicing mindfulness. Tailor these

suggestions to their preferences and needs, keeping their comfort level in mind.
- **Reviewing Agreements and Boundaries:** If physical intervention was required, revisit the safety agreements made during the preparation phase. Reflect on how these agreements functioned to maintain safety and discuss any adjustments for future sessions.
- **Follow-Up Support:** For particularly intense journeys, consider scheduling additional integration sessions or check-ins. This extra support can help the client process any unresolved elements and provide a structured space for further reflection.

Integration after a crisis-based experience requires sensitivity to both the client's emotional landscape and the physical intensity of the session. By focusing on reassurance, meaning making, and collaborative reflection, the guide can help transform the challenging experience into a source of growth and empowerment.

7
STAGES OF A MUSHROOM JOURNEY

When explaining the stages of a psychedelic journey to clients, I often use the metaphor of climbing a mountain. This analogy helps clients understand what to expect at specific intervals. I also remind them that each journey is unique and that the effects of the medicine can differ, sometimes considerably, from person to person, day to day, journey to journey, and substance to substance.

With this mountain-climbing metaphor in mind, I consider myself (the guide) as a sherpa or mountaineer who has traversed this path many times and has the tools to navigate the terrain, anticipate potential challenges, and provide support as needed. This analogy emphasizes the importance of trust, communication, and mutual respect within the guide-client relationship.

Timeline of Psychedelic Effects and Journey Stages

As soon as the psychedelic mushrooms are ingested, the expedition up the mountain commences. The first effects can usually be felt within 15 to 30 minutes, which differs from LSD and mescaline, whose first effects often don't begin for 45 to 60 minutes following the initial dose. Of course, in some cases, the onset can vary by as much as 30 minutes in either direction. I have also learned that adjustments in the overall setting can also impact the duration and/or reported effect of the medicine along the timeline. However, the journey typically progresses in this sequence:

THE PSYCHEDELIC DJ

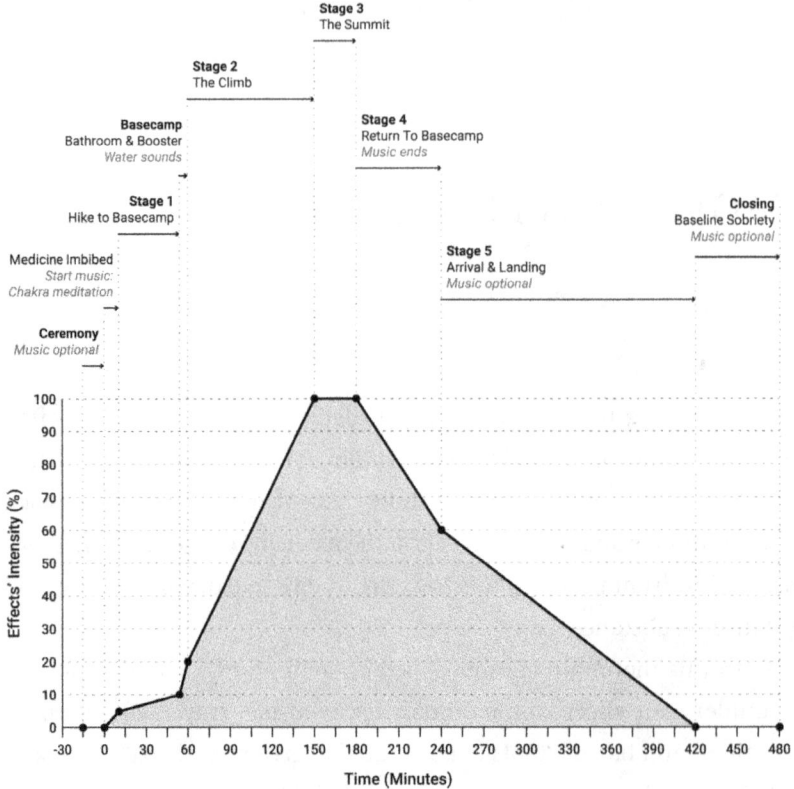

Trailhead: The Imbibing Ceremony (-10–0 mins)

As discussed in the previous chapter, before consuming the mushrooms, the journey is initiated with a 10-minute ceremonial prayer directed toward the seven cardinal directions. This practice helps create a safe container, focus the client's intentions, and invite spiritual support for navigating other realms of consciousness, though it is always presented as optional, pending the client's consent.

Musical Approach and Clinical Observations

This initiation ritual is enhanced by spiritually infused music that features soft chanting or droning soundscapes, which guides attention inward. Examples include *Ascension Harmonics* by Jonathan Goldman or *The Eternal Om* by Robert Slap. These soundscapes create a hypnotic atmosphere,

STAGES OF A MUSHROOM JOURNEY

facilitating deep introspection and the opening of spiritual portals.

During this stage, clients often begin a deep and introspective process, connecting to themselves, the medicine, and the journey ahead. Common emotional responses include nervousness, excitement, or anticipation. Some clients may experience tears of joy as they reflect on their intentions or connect to a sense of gratitude or divine presence. Others may display physical responses, such as trembling or shaking, which are often tied to feelings of anxiety or the release of nervous energy. In such instances, the pace of the ceremony can be gently adjusted to address their concerns. Guided breathing exercises may be offered to help clients ease their nerves, ground themselves in the present moment, and regain a sense of readiness before continuing with the process.

Clients also frequently use this time to communicate their intentions and hopes, either silently to themselves or to the medicine or aloud to the room. Occasionally, clients bring personal prayers or rituals to the ceremony, which they may perform privately or share with me. This can enhance the ceremonial atmosphere and deepen their connection to the process.

In some cases, clients report feeling the effects of the medicine even before consuming it, describing subtle shifts in their perception of energy or an otherwise heightened sense of awareness. This phenomenon is often attributed to the anticipatory state of mind, the ritualistic nature of the ceremony, or the profound psychological preparation involved. Once the medicine is consumed, it is common for clients to request a brief pause to visit the bathroom before settling in to begin breathwork or meditation.

This phase provides a powerful opening to the journey, setting the tone for what lies ahead. The guide's role is to hold space with calm presence, offering reassurance and allowing clients to ease into the experience at their own pace.

Stage One: Hike to Basecamp (Onset, 0–55 mins)

After the ceremonial opening, the journey begins in earnest as the client embarks on their metaphorical hike to basecamp. This initial phase, after consuming the substance, is often filled with anticipation as the client acclimates to the medicine and awaits its effects.

Musical Approach and Clinical Observations

The introduction and meditation is accompanied by soothing tracks such as "Singing Bowl (Ascension)" by Jon Hopkins or "Butterfly Breeze" by Ishq. These tracks create a calming soundscape that encourages relaxation and focus, supporting the client's transition into the journey.

As the so-called hike commences, clients are invited to lie down, put on their eyeshade, and, if consent has been previously obtained, engage in a 10-to-12-minute guided breath, body, and chakra-activation meditation. This practice helps center their awareness, relax their body, and prepare them for the initial effects of the medicine.

The meditation, informed by the Chakra Awareness Guide by A.M.I., incorporates the qualities, traits, and affirmations associated with each energy center. This meditation is tailored to the individual client and is based on their presenting issues, therapeutic goals, and intentions as discussed during their preparation sessions.

The Meditation

Opening Breaths: The meditation begins with several deep breaths into the entire body. The client is guided to feel the breath travel throughout their being, shifting their focus from their thoughts to their physical sensations. This grounding step fosters safety and presence.

Lower Body Awareness: The client is encouraged to breathe deeply into their feet, legs, and lower body, anchoring themselves in the physical and creating a sense of grounding and stability.

Chakra Activation Sequence: Moving sequentially from the Root Chakra to the Crown Chakra, the meditation incorporates:

- **Visualization:** At each chakra, the client is invited to envision its associated color and element (e.g., a red light at the Root Chakra or a violet light at the Crown Chakra). These visualizations help them connect with each energy center.
- **Positive Traits (Inhale):** On each inhale, clients call in positive traits and qualities aligned with the chakra, such as stability, creativity, or intuition.
- **Negative Traits (Exhale):** On each exhale, they release associated challenges, such as fear, guilt, or self-doubt.

STAGES OF A MUSHROOM JOURNEY

- **Affirmation:** Each chakra ends with a simple, empowering "I" statement affirmation tailored to the client's unique goals and issues. For example:
    - **Root Chakra:** "I am grounded. I am safe."
    - **Throat Chakra:** "I have a voice. I speak my truth."
    - **Crown Chakra:** "I am spirit. I am infinite."

Tailoring the Meditation

The qualities, traits, and affirmations selected for each chakra are customized based on the client's expressed intentions or challenges. For example:
- A client working on overcoming anxiety may focus on grounding qualities in the Root Chakra and emotional flow in the Sacral Chakra.
- A client exploring creative expression may emphasize creativity in the Sacral Chakra and communication in the Throat Chakra.
- A client desiring to address feelings of isolation may focus on love and connection in the Heart Chakra and spiritual unity in the Crown Chakra.

This individualized approach ensures that the meditation resonates deeply with the client's intentions and supports their therapeutic journey.

Closing Integration

After the Crown Chakra affirmation, the client is invited to take several deep breaths into their entire body, integrating the positive qualities of each chakra and releasing any residual tension or negativity. As they do this, I gradually fade out the accompanying meditation track, guiding them into a state of stillness. This moment of quiet is often mirrored by my own steady breathing, which many clients naturally follow, helping them settle further into calm and balance.

Gong Ritual

To seal the practice, a Tibetan singing bowl is gonged three times:
- Once overhead, representing connection to spirit and the Crown Chakra.
- Once over the Third Eye, symbolizing intuition and inner vision.

- Once over the heart and body, grounding the client in love, compassion, and their own physical presence.

The bowl's natural resonance creates a gentle closure, allowing the meditation's energy to ripple through and settle.

The Transition

Once the meditation is complete and the effects of the mushrooms begin to take hold, I select light, uplifting music to gently ease the client into the experience. This music, which is minimally active or percussive, is played at a low volume to create a pleasant, nondistracting background as the client metaphorically strolls toward basecamp. The chosen tracks are soft, expansive ambient soundscapes in either supportive major or mellow minor keys. Tracks like "L'abitudine di tornare" by Music for Sleep, "Weightless" by Marconi Union, "Vespers" by Anita Tatlow & Salt of the Sound, and "Planatia" by Neel offer an unobtrusive yet expansive atmosphere. As the energy remains minimal for the remaining 45 to 50 minutes of this stage, pieces like "Penumbra" by Helios, "Take Me by the Hand (Acid Dream Version)" by 36 & awakened souls, "000607053 OTS3 [Solar]" by zaké, "Nanyei" by Iyakuh, "Astral Realm (Extended Öona Dahl Ritual Mix)" by Öona Dahl & Giddyhead, "Wildlife" by Warmth, "Evenings" by Damm, and "Winds" by Pulse Emitter gently accompany the client's journey inward.

As the client approaches the scheduled bathroom break, the energy progresses slightly, and tracks such as "Migration," "Certainty of Tides," or "Passing Dreams" by awakened souls & From Overseas offer a subtle yet intentional lift. To wrap up this stage and bring things home for a landing, I turn to delicate, grounding tracks like "Lotus Garden Spaces" by Desert Dwellers, "Us, Inside" by Arovane and Mike Lazarev, "At the Gates of Dawn" by Poemme, "Hiking with Eve" by Halftribe, or "If/Then" by BT. These selections gently draw the client's awareness inward, setting the stage for deeper introspection as they arrive at basecamp, ready to embrace the next phase of the journey.

Clinical Observations

Throughout the onset phase, I observe the client's reactions to both the music and the medicine, watching for changes in breathing, emotional releases, shifts in facial expressions, or physical effects such as shaking, tremors, or frequent position adjustments. Clients often report seeing geometric shapes, recalling memories, or gaining realizations about their lives. Even clients that remain quiet or are seemingly asleep may be experiencing profound internal effects, while others might feel few or no effects at all.

These observations help me gauge the client's tolerance to the experience, assess whether a booster dose might be appropriate during the upcoming break, and determine which musical selections will best support the client's ascent to the summit phase of the journey.

Basecamp: Bathroom and Booster Break (55–60 mins)

The client is now offered the opportunity to visit the bathroom before the ascent and, if desired, consume a booster dose to deepen, intensify, or support the challenging climb ahead.

Musical Approach and Clinical Observations

At this juncture, the effects of the mushrooms are likely being actively experienced, so it's crucial to be mindful of the client's sensitivity during any direct engagement. I use a soft, whispering voice when gently checking in, and I also lower the volume before transitioning to soothing, nonmusical selections like field recordings of nature sounds such as ocean waves or spacy, looping effects. Bringing in soundscapes during this interval aids in maintaining sensory continuity while preventing significant activation. Some clients have reported that underwater soundscapes evoke deep-seated feelings, memories, or experiences of being in the womb—often described as warm, nurturing, and deeply comforting. Selections such as "Jellyfish Atmosphere" or "Under the Rough Oceans" by Disneynature Soundscapes, "Drifting (Part 1)" and "Drifting (Part 2)" by Henrik B, "Seraphim III" by How to Disappear Completely, and "Under Water" by Dreamfish are particularly effective.

Clients often report heightened effects at this time, due to the additional stimulation from changing their position from lying down to standing up, as well as the shift in setting from the journey bed to the restroom and back again. During this time, they often comment on the strength (or lack thereof) of the mushrooms and may express surprise at the passage of time, the extent of their experiences, or how the journey so far has diverged from their expectations. While some clients may feel a need to process, I support their sharing while also gently guiding them back to the subject of the booster dose and the overall experience to prevent them from becoming overly distracted.

At this point, if the client expresses a desire to delve deeper and both the guide and client deem it appropriate, a booster dose is administered. The client consumes the booster, lies down, puts on the eyeshade, takes a few deep breaths, and commences the ascent to the summit as the climbing music begins.

Stage Two: Climbing the Mountain (Ascent, 60–150 mins)

During this phase, the effects of the initial dose significantly increase. If a booster dose was taken, its effects will be most noticeable approximately 30 to 45 minutes into this stage.

Musical Approach

As the effects of the medicine intensify throughout the body, it's an opportune moment to synchronize this energy surge with an increase in the soundtrack's tempo, rhythmic structure, melodic complexity, and chord progressions. This synchronization can escalate emotions, visions, and psychedelic experiences. As this powerful phase unfolds, tracks like "Domain" by the Future Sound of London, "When I'm with You" by Endless Melancholy, "Stay (with Be Still the Earth)" by Salt of the Sound, "Odyssey (Intro)" by Saphileaum, "We're All in the Dark Looking for a Light" by Slow Dancing Society, "Summit" by James Bernard, "Whispering Goodbye" by awakened souls, "Welcome" by Jon Hopkins, "Breaker (Impossible Color)" or "The Ocean Inside" by the Seven Fields of Aphelion, and "Photosensitive" by Archivist can be especially effective in mirroring this dynamic shift that immediately follows the booster dose and bathroom break. Modern neoclassical compositions such as the opening to Richard Wagner's "Das Rheingold Vorspiel (MX Custom Edit)," "Safe" by Juliana Barwick, or "Tree Strings" by Jonny Greenwood are also powerful tools to kick off the ascent. For a more rhythmic, immersive, and emotional experience, following up with songs like "Youth" by Hiatus, "Milano" by Jens Buchert, "Light Through the Veins" by Jon Hopkins, and "Wanderer (Alex Rize Remix)" by the Unique Matter can balance movement and melody as energy increases.

As with all stages, music selections for this phase of the climb can be geared toward the client's goals, intentions, and sensitivity that were determined in the prejourney counseling sessions. If sensitivity is established and addressing anxiety is the stated goal, meeting that anxiety with uplifting and playful music might be helpful; consider tracks such as "Skygazer" by Alucidnation, "Forest Groove" by Brian Mayhall, "Collaborative Survival" by Lav, "Dr Dream" or "You and I" by Melorman, or "Dream as Memory" by Tycho.

Music can also be a powerful ally in addressing specific emotional or psychological blockages that arise during this stage of the ascent. If clearing grief and achieving a state of contentment is the goal, mild agitation via sublimation could be helpful; the right music can create a disruptive counterbalance that presents a challenge, resulting in catharsis and restful satisfaction. "Forever in a Moment" by Black Swan & Endless Melancholy, "Lost Time Archive 10 (Bass Guitar & Pedalboard)" by James Bernard, "Amidst the Tall Grass" by Hollie Kenniff, "Lunar Landscape" by Sacred Seeds, "Auberge" by Grandbrothers, "Fields" by Synkro, "The Land of Three Moons" by about : forest, "Guidance" by Synkro & Indigo, "Seventh Act" by ASC, "Evighetsblomma" by Purl, "Love Theme" by Martin Roth, "Empty City" by Sophie Hutchings, "part viii - nothing is lost" by Jon Hopkins, "Miss You" by Trentemøller, and "Life Field" by Syzygy can provide a sad but beautiful tension and release.

If accessing blocked creativity is the client's goal, playing pleasant yet somewhat challenging music directly at the anxiety or tension that's creating the block, such as "Lose You" or "I Can Chase You Forever" by

THE PSYCHEDELIC DJ

John Beltran, "Dream on Wagogo" by Treeboga, "Azarca (Synkro Remix)" by Alaska x Synkro, or "Resonating Heart" by Bluetech, might help effect a clearing.

For those who resonate with more uptempo, steady yet propulsive rhythms, the kind of hypnotic undercurrent these sounds provide can be particularly effective in unlocking creative flow. Tracks at this tempo provide both a grounding beat and a spacious atmosphere for the mind to wander. If a client is drawn to such styles—something you will typically assess in advance—dub and hypnotic techno tracks like "Alhambra" and "The North Path" by Primal Code, "Lemurian (Kryss Hypnowave Remix)" by Eamo, "Högre" by Evigt Morker, "Need Your Light (awakened souls – Influx Dub Version)" by 36 & awakened souls, "Ring Cairn Aurora" by Arkaean, "D'Arc" by Illuvia, and "8 a.m." by Melorman blend this rhythmic depth with atmospheric space. These tracks gently engage the mind while maintaining a meditative pulse to inspire breakthroughs.

In more challenging cases, where emotional stagnation or resistance requires a stronger push, a darker and more confrontational piece of music can provide the necessary intensity to directly engage with and clear the internal obstacle before reaching the summit. Tracks such as "I Eat Air (Marcel Dettmann Remix)" by Mathilde Nobel, "The Call for Total Surrender" by Byron Metcalf & Steve Roach, "Jaguar Dreaming" by Liquid Bloom, "Redacted" by Spinger, "The Desert White" by Peter Benisch, "Gethen (ft. Yaima)" by Bluetech, "Outermost Structure" by Martin Nonstatic, "Dave's Alley Metafizz" by David Last, "Breathless" by 36, "Symmetry" by Speedy J, "Northern Nights (Peter Benisch Remix)" by Mick Chillage, "Anchialine Pool" by Jonas Margraf, and "So Far Out of Love" or "One Life" by Malibu can be potent tools in creating a disruptive counterbalance that facilitates catharsis and emotional release.

As the journey ascends toward its peak, approaching the summit where the medicine nears full strength, "Out (Poemme Remix)" by Ed Harrison or "Iliad" by Malibu stand out as invaluable tools for healing. These compositions are among the most beautiful pieces of ambient electronic music in my collection, easily some of the most powerful I have ever used in therapeutic sessions. Their profound emotional depth and intricate

STAGES OF A MUSHROOM JOURNEY

soundscapes shape an environment that is both delicate and powerful, fostering self-reflection and transformation—perfectly suited for this stage of the climb.

Nearing the final stretch of the ascent, with the summit in sight, selections like "Barefoot" or "Early" by Chicane, "Midnight Sun (Helios Remix)" by Synkro, "Holograms" by M83, or "Sun in Your Eyes" by Above and Beyond can be great choices for the hugely uplifting effects the client may be experiencing. Meanwhile, "Clouds" by Carbon Based Lifeforms, "Movement" by Synkro, "Dreams Within Dreams" by Deepchild, and "Enveleau" by Matt Robertson offer ethereal, expansive, melancholic soundscapes that are ideal for self-reflection in these final moments before transitioning into the summit.

Clinical Observations

Clients at this stage often display heavier breathing patterns, physical shaking or trembling, major shifts in body posture, sobbing, giggling, or laughing. These effects can increase with particular musical selections. Clients may also verbalize to the guide, themselves, ancestors, God, the medicine, or other beings they may encounter within themselves or within the transpersonal spirit realm or share powerful realizations about their life, patterns of behavior, current or past interpersonal conflicts, unrealized or unresolved traumas, past memories, or spiritual truths. They often report spiritual visions or other images such as geometric shapes, structures, colors, and archetypes.

To help with the intensity that arises during this stage, clients may request assistance from the guide who can offer support in the form of simple acknowledgment, hand-holding, normalization of the present healing process, invitation to engage in gentle breathing exercises, or letting clients know it's safe to trust the process and surrender.

As the guide, I remain mindful not to interrupt the client's experience with subjective interventions or mindless chatter. If the client is able to surrender to the experience on their own, the guide can focus on other tasks such as music curation, appropriate volume adjustments, taking notes, or other space-holding or self-resourcing activities.

THE PSYCHEDELIC DJ

Even though the client hasn't actually left the bed for more than a bathroom visit, they have exerted a lot of energy and effort working through the intensity of the medicine and whatever powerful subconscious material is being released during this stage. Therefore, it's important to stay attuned to any energy shifts during this time, as the client approaches the equally powerful Summit stage.

Stage Three: The Summit (Peak, 150–180 mins)

Here the client crests the top of the mountain to reach the highest peak of their experience. At this point they are usually wide open, often experiencing some form of ego dissolution, especially with larger doses. At this stage, the client may still be navigating through some significant psychological, emotional, and physical releases and engaging with a range of wild visual imagery or otherworldly transpersonal interactions.

Musical Approach

At the Summit, the client is deep into their psychedelic journey and is likely exploring spaces beyond this earthly realm. Musical selections can now be quite large and expansive, or else deeply meditative with a bit more movement and spaciness than the similar hike/onset music selections. Awe-inspiring, hypnotic, droning soundscapes with limited chord movements can match the vastness of the client's inner experience and self-reflection. Long-form compositions with sweeping arrangements, such as "Weightless" by Eternell, "Childhood Dreams" by Purl, "Zauberberg 7" by GAS, "Eternal Resonance 3" by zakè & City of Dawn, "With the Changing of the Leaves" by Poemme, "Ascend" by Inquiri, "I Will Comfort You" by marine eyes & zakè, "Tragic" by Lapsed Pacifist, "Regen" by Valentino Mora & Ligovskoï, and "part vii – dissolution" from Jon Hopkins, leave lots of room for the imagination to explore, evoking the sense of reaching a summit and beyond. Such pieces may unfold across the visual spectrum, providing a canvas for the vast amount of emerging material and projections that continue to flood out of a client's uninterrupted subconscious during the peak psychedelic effects.

As the strength of the medicine does its work, you may also consider featuring music selections containing fascinating organic sounds that offer less activation. Tracks like "Interbeing (Tylepathy Remix)" by Liquid Bloom and TRIBONE and "Moonlight Saptah" by Shaman's Dream offer the right balance, avoiding too much distraction or interference in the client's process so there is greater space for their imagination to soar. For a client seeking or requiring a more otherworldly or mesmerizing experience during the peak, tracks such as "Evocazione/Contatto/Risveglio" by LF58, "V 3.2-3.4" from Waveform Transmission, "Vaporware 01" by Donato Dozzy, "Annie's Diaries" by Primal Code, "School of Fish" by Dreamfish, or "Electron Central" by Pulse Emitter provide the perfect blend of trippy and expansive qualities to satisfy even the most demanding of psychonauts.

Clinical Observations

During this phase, clients have both been observed and have self-reported communicating with God, their ancestors, other parts of themselves, their inner child, and people from their past or engaging in various forms of voluntary (or even involuntary) physical self-healing techniques, such as using their hands to move energy or clear body trauma. They may cry heavily, laugh at themselves, profess realizations, or simply lie completely still. In some instances, I have witnessed clients making hand gestures or performing movements that resemble Vitarka Mudras, which are commonly associated with both Hindu and Buddhist deities. Interestingly, clients often subsequently report that these movements occurred without any conscious awareness or prior knowledge of these specific symbols, further emphasizing the depth of subconscious processing in their journeys. It's possible these gestures are drawn from the collective unconscious, reflecting universal archetypes that emerge in altered states.

At this point, the medicine is typically at its strongest. This is when ego dissolution is most common, causing large amounts of shadow material held within the subconscious to be released without interruption. Some clients will surrender, while others may feel afraid or overwhelmed by the loss of identity. They may begin to resist or try to stop the experience by sitting up and removing the eyeshade, which in many cases actually increases the energy and intensity of these already powerful effects.

When guiding a client through challenging moments of ego dissolution or heightened intensity, it's important to focus all your attention on assisting the client through these powerful experiences of rebirth. Normalizing the effects and providing reassurance of safety are essential interventions. If unreasonable requests arise, such as a desire to go for a walk or contact a friend, the client can be gently redirected and invited to share what they are feeling in their body or how the request relates to their experience.

Inviting the client to take slow and concentrated breaths can help, and you may also adjust the music if needed. If the current selection is too intense—particularly if it features minor chords—switching to a track with major chords or a softer tone may help reduce the emotional weight of the experience. Long-form tracks can also be beneficial at this point for maintaining a consistent emotional theme without sudden or drastic shifts in mood.

When clients are struggling to stay engaged with the journey—whether by removing the eyeshade, attempting to call a friend, or requesting to leave—careful curation of the music becomes essential. Softer, more grounding tracks with slower tempos can help recenter the client within their own experience. Tracks that emphasize natural sounds like water and wind, or even light drumming, may create a sense of familiarity and safety, encouraging them to reengage with their internal world. However, be mindful to avoid abrupt or overly stimulating changes in the music, as this can further escalate feelings of disorientation. Instead, opt for soundscapes or ambient pieces that promote a sense of calm and allow the client to ease back into the flow of the journey.

In cases where the client is unable to follow instructions or seems overwhelmed by the experience, remaining calm and grounded as the guide is essential. This may be a good time to provide support by reminding the client where they are, who they are with, and that the experience is temporary. Gently encouraging the client to trust your guidance and their own inner strength is key to helping them navigate through resistance.

Stage Four: Return to Basecamp (Descent, 180–240 mins)
As the peak effects of the mushrooms begin decreasing, the client's agency slowly returns as they begin their descent to basecamp.

STAGES OF A MUSHROOM JOURNEY

Musical Approach

Having ascended to and explored the expansive summit, they are now ready to return to their bodies and reality. Unlike the climb, the descent is a more relaxed period of gentle self-reflection—a downhill hike that, while easier in some regards, carries its own power and moments of challenge.

At this stage, the client is still experiencing the effects of the medicine. The increased awareness from breaking through internal blockages can now be redirected to the new material occupying the open spaces within them. Their mind, heart, and body have been cleansed, offering greater clarity regarding the subconscious material they've witnessed and the realizations that have come to light. Some of the biggest realizations of the journey often occur during this phase, particularly in the final 30 minutes, when the selected music resonates with the soft and tender moments unfolding.

In this phase, the primary themes are closure and conclusion. I often select a soundtrack that stirs memories and evokes a sense of homecoming, signaling the bittersweet end of a long, beautiful, and challenging journey. These types of soundtracks, emotionally resonant and steeped in nostalgia, can be tailored to the client's experience if the guide has reviewed the music beforehand and has taken the time during the prejourney preparation to understand the effects that might be triggered. This helps ensure the music aligns with the client's intentions and therapeutic goals. At this point—similar to yet distinct from the ascent—music with more movement, energy, and dynamic chord progressions becomes suitable again. Tracks like "El Pequeño Zorro Colorado" by Federico Durand, "Goodfellowship" by Goldmund, "Stay (with Be Still the Earth)" by Salt of the Sound, or "Kangaru" by Jóhann Jóhannsson will welcome the client down from the summit, while pieces such as "All at Sea" by Alucidnation, "Upstream Dream" by Slow Meadow, "Expand" by Endless Melancholy, "Belfast (Anna Remix)" by Orbital, "Another Halcyon Day" by State Azure, "Child's Play" by Another Fine Day, "Fake Magic is Real" by Slow Meadow, "Halving the Compass (Rhian Sheehan Remix)" by Helios, "Ripples Through Time (Haquin Revibe)" by Liquid Bloom, Tylepathy & Divasonic, "Stones Throw" by Lusine ICL, and "Pareidolia" by Slow Meadow might follow. These tracks offer the perfect balance of warmth, nostalgia, and melancholy, stirring feelings of humility, gratitude, relief, and resolution. In my experience, there is no finer piece of music to close such powerful journeys than "Immunity" by Jon Hopkins—it's a true masterpiece of psychedelic sound.

Clinical Observations
As the medicine's effects diminish, the client's agency returns, sometimes bringing heightened energy and excitement as their inner burdens lighten. Occasionally, this lightness can trigger a premature urge to wrap up the journey, talk about insights, or engage in idle chatter. When appropriate, I gently encourage clients to remain immersed in the experience, directing their attention back to the music and the emerging nonverbal cues. Some of the most profound realizations often happen in the final 30 minutes of the journey, especially when the selected music resonates with the delicate and tender moments as the story draws to a close and the client returns to their senses.

Stage Five: Basecamp (Landing and Processing, 240–420 mins)
This is a stage of rest and relief. As the effects of medicine continue to rapidly decrease, the conscious integration process begins either through meditation or verbal expression.

Musical Approach and Clinical Observations
As the first four stages of the journey come to an end, a sigh of relief often signifies the transition into a new phase of integration. At this point, the client's senses are highly attuned, requiring a quiet setting and gentle presence from the guide. The journeyer may feel tired upon returning to basecamp, but they may also experience a sense of relaxation. During this period, it's advisable for the guide to exercise patience and step back, allowing each client to return at their own pace.

Many clients may choose to continue their journey in silence behind the eyeshade, as they are still under the effects of the medicine. If the client is open to guidance, you can gently check in after 20 to 30 minutes to assist them in concluding the eyeshade portion of the experience. If agreed upon, the client can be invited to slowly remove the eyeshade, allowing their eyes to adjust to the change in visual stimulation. Once the client has adjusted, it's recommended that you maintain a friendly yet mostly quiet presence for at least the next 30 to 45 minutes. This allows the client to focus on their own mind and body as the effects of the medicine continue to diminish and their agency returns.

Once the client has regained agency and safety is confirmed, they can be invited to change the setting by either using the bathroom or stepping outside for some fresh air and a view of nature. If they choose to remain inside, they can be invited to either return to the bed to rest, move to the couch, or stretch out on the floor.

To ensure the client is properly rehydrated after the reduced consumption of fluids during the journey, you may now offer them water, coconut water, juice, or tea. You can also provide a variety of healthy and easy-to-digest snacks such as fruit to help the client return to a refreshed yet grounded state of presence.

At this juncture, it's preferable to steer clear of intellectual processing. Instead, the focus should be on promoting nonverbal somatic awareness. If the client wishes, they can engage in gentle drawing or other art making. If the client opts to remain in silence, you can take a step back, provide a supportive environment, and trust in the natural progression of the process. It's important to remember that each client has their own unique way of processing the experience they've just been through. Some may want to verbally comment on their experiences in great detail, while others may adopt a quieter, gentler approach that is more centered on the body.

If a client expresses a wish for more music after removing their eyeshade, it's crucial to select warm, welcoming, mellow tracks that encourage introspection. These selections should typically be positive, uplifting, and rewarding, if slightly melancholic. Warm and understated vocals can be appropriate, but care should be taken to avoid promoting a specific agenda. To respect the client's sensitivity and prevent overstimulation, it's beneficial to maintain a low volume in the background. Soft, supportive background music at a barely perceptible volume is ideal, so as to avoid interfering with their reflections.

THE PSYCHEDELIC DJ

Using DJ mixes, full albums, or personal playlists can alleviate the need to select individual tracks, allowing you to concentrate entirely on the client as they process their experience. Powerful DJ mixes such as "Savasana" (Vol. 1, 2, or 3) and "Ambient Impressions" (Vol. 1, 2, or 3) by Gelka are excellent choices for background processing. Full-length albums like *We All Have Places That We Miss* by Hollie Kenniff, *Elegant, Golden* or *Cloud Dreaming and Shadows* by Halftribe, and *Drift* by RxGibbs are also fantastic options.

As the effects of the mushrooms continue to diminish, the conscious mind reengages and the client's sense of control returns. The clients will often find themselves comparing their actual experiences with their initial expectations, noticing significant differences. As they transition back to a normal waking state, feelings of astonishment, humility, exhaustion, and gratitude are commonly reported. Many clients report being "blown away" or "shocked," often expressing themselves with simple phrases like, "Wow," "Oh my God," "I'm speechless," or some variation of "This was one of the most powerful, beautiful, and challenging experiences of my life." On the other hand, many may find it challenging to articulate their experiences, which is understandable given that most of what transpired involved nonverbal material surfacing from their subconscious. It's also not uncommon for clients to refrain from processing their experience immediately, as it may defy their understanding. For clients who do wish to reflect on and articulate what they have seen, felt, and experienced, it's crucial to remain flexible, open, and attentive as they attempt to make sense of the ineffable. This is an opportune time to normalize their experience and provide space for the continued expression of thoughts through more conscious, verbal processing, which can aid in their understanding and integration of these experiences.

Opinions differ on what is best to do during this time. Some guides prefer to step out of the way and not engage much in processing, instead inviting the client to practice quiet presence, remain with their somatic process, and connect with their inner voice/inner healer. Other practitioners use this time for psycholytic therapy (medicine with processing) while the brain is activated and in a malleable state, making the exploration of nonverbal material even more impactful during the client's postjourney life.

In most cases, I encourage breathing and quiet presence. However, if the client chooses to process, I will mindfully and gently engage with them. My approach uses sensitive moments of awareness to increase the effectiveness of experiential therapeutic interventions. As with most counseling, each client and each moment calls for an individualized approach with varying degrees of interaction. In all cases, it's best to be sensitive, move slowly, and follow the client's lead.

You may invite your client to explore what emotions or body sensations they notice emerging as they delve into describing their experiences. This approach helps avoid overintellectualization of the experience and keeps clients aware of and connected to their bodies and emotional states. It's advisable to stay flexible and patient and to maintain a delicate presence so the client's process can come forward while the background music both supports and gently influences this concluding stage of the journey.

Stage Six: Closing Ceremony (Baseline Sobriety, 420–480 mins)

Effects of the substance will continue to subside and be replaced with feelings of exhaustion, astonishment, humility, gratitude, and celebration.

Musical Approach and Clinical Observations

With reverence for and in honor of all that unfolded during the day, the client may leave this profound, shared experience of transformation with a sense of exhaustion and a unique sensation some have described as an "emptied fullness." If the client reports any lingering psychedelic effects, this stage can be extended until they return to baseline sobriety.

They may expect to feel a sense of fatigue, irritability, or raw sensitivity for the first two to three days as their mind and body readjust. Disrupted sleep, headaches, and other symptoms are par for the course but are thankfully temporary, rarely if ever extending beyond the next four to five days. Clients are encouraged to allow themselves time to rest and should aim for at least three good nights of sleep before becoming overly concerned about any residual discomfort they may be experiencing.

Encourage them to keep in mind that postjourney symptoms are fleeting, much like waves gradually receding from the shore. It may be helpful for the client to envision themselves as a flexible surfer, skillfully riding the waves of change toward the shore of their new normal, embracing both the highs and lows without fixating on any specific outcome. They have undergone a profound psychological, emotional, physiological, and spiritual journey, akin to undergoing major surgery. Advise them to rest and avoid making any major life decisions immediately afterward. On an interpersonal level, it's best for the client to establish boundaries with others and steer clear of conflicts while continuing to integrate their experience.

Clients will be highly sensitive to music at this stage, so I usually avoid it altogether and instead encourage silence or a focus on the breath to allow time for quiet reflection. This helps to honor the exhaustion and rawness clients may feel. However, if music is used, it is crucial that it remains nonactivating and is played at a very low volume, fading into the background where its presence is barely noticeable. The use of gentle ambient soundscapes with soft, mellow percussive elements or environmental field recordings is preferable. Tracks from earlier in the welcome stage, such as "Sun" by Purl and Deflektion, can also be looped back into the closing stage to create a sense of continuity. For more whimsical, environmental sounds, "Butterfly Breeze" by Ishq is another ideal selection to bring back again. A carefully chosen soundscape ensures a soft and supportive comedown without overwhelming the client's sensitivity at this point in the journey. In most cases, though, silence is more than enough to support this stage.

It is recommended that the client resists the temptation to tackle weighty discussions or unresolved issues right away. Ideas and realizations need time to fully integrate. They can use this integration period as an opportunity to explore life with fresh senses and renewed energy levels while taking note of the changes within themselves and reflecting on what patterns have shifted or emerged. Clients are further encouraged to embrace the concept of self-care so that they can prioritize their own recovery and well-being over the needs of others during subsequent integration. This is a good time for clients to consider how they will water and nurture the seeds of insight that have emerged from their journey.

You may also recommend that your client make at least one or two brief journal entries the night of and the morning after the journey. Beyond that, brief bullet points noting any significant changes they experience in the first few days following the experience will suffice. This integration writing practice is particularly helpful given that what they remember about the journey will change day by day, as will their memories of what has occurred in the days that follow. Keeping such notes will also be helpful for completing the postjourney summary prior to the follow-up integration sessions that will occur seven and then fourteen days after the journey.

As a closing practice before the final ceremony, the client is invited to engage in a Gestalt therapy exercise where they communicate with their prejourney self from the perspective of their postjourney self. During this exchange, they can see more clearly what they looked like before the trip, what their prejourney self expected to experience, and what they learned during the experience. This experiential integration practice has proven quite powerful at raising awareness, confirming plans for change, and bringing about closure.

After completing this exercise, the client is guided outside to the altar to engage in a closing cardinal direction ceremony, similar to the one conducted prior to imbibing, which is followed by the same sage cleansing and tobacco blessing that was conducted prior to entering the journey space.

Following the ceremony, the baseline sobriety of the client is fully assessed. If the client and guide agree that baseline sobriety has been reached and that the client feels safe to depart, arrangements are made to return the client to their place of residence where they can take a shower, eat some food, and get the much-needed rest they desire and deserve. Remind your client that they can reach out to you for support at any time and be sure to contact them the next day, or the day after, to hear their voice, make sure they are feeling OK, answer or help process any questions, or simply provide as whatever support they need following such a powerful life experience.

THE PSYCHEDELIC DJ

TABLE OF STAGES: TIMELINE AND RECOMMENDED MUSIC

Timeline	Stage	Type of Music
0–55 min	Hike to Basecamp (Onset)	Background, quiet, warm, welcoming, spacious, expansive, meditative chants, bells, beatless ambient music, minimal rhythms (if any)
55–60 min	Basecamp: Bathroom/Booster	Field recordings, nature sounds, background for continuity
60–150 min	The Climb (Ascent)	Foreground, increased energy and movement, rising effect, chord changes, rhythm structures, music for motivation
150–180 min	The Summit (Peak)	Background, softer energy, less movement, introspective, expansive, spacy, hypnotic, droning, awe-inspiring, beatless ambient, music for imagination
180–240 min	Return to Basecamp (Descent)	Foreground, moderate energy and movements, soft, welcoming, self-reflective, nostalgic, melancholic, heart opening, music for remembering
240–420 min	Arrival and Landing (Process)	Nondistracting, deep background, low volume, soft, warm, uplifting, supportive, accomplished, resolved, introduction of minimal vocals
240–480 min	Closing Ceremony— Baseline Sobriety	Silence, breath, gentle shamanic instruments

8
PSYCHEDELIC AUDIO PRESENTATION—A TECHNICAL GUIDE TO JOURNEY SPACE SETUP

In psychedelic therapy, sound is not just a background element—it is an integral part of the setting. Just as the physical environment influences the journey, so too does the quality and delivery of sound. Sound moves air, shaping and manipulating the setting, which in turn has a profound impact on the immersive quality and depth of the psychedelic experience. Thoughtfully curated audio presentation—balanced with intentional moments of silence—creates the foundation upon which the journey unfolds, influencing emotional, mental, and spiritual states. This interplay between sound and silence deepens the client's connection to their inner experience and amplifies the transformative potential of the session.

As discussed earlier, while sound and its overall volume play a central role in shaping the journey, moments of silence can be equally powerful. Silence offers a space for clients to pause, process, and connect with their inner experience without external influence. This balance between sound and silence transforms the auditory setting into a dynamic and responsive environment, amplifying the therapeutic potential of both elements.

The audio equipment you select can significantly influence this experience, whether it's for personal enjoyment or professional journeywork. With a myriad of options available on the market, it can be daunting to navigate and select the best tools for your therapeutic needs. This chapter aims to assist you with the process, spotlighting some of the top-quality speaker options, the advantages of modern DJ setups, and the considerations for different connection methods.

DJ Software

DJ software, like djay Pro by Algoriddim, is particularly effective for those new to the practice. This user-friendly program allows music and playlists to be pulled directly from popular streaming platforms like Apple Music, Tidal, SoundCloud, and Beatport. (However, please note that if you want to use a Spotify playlist, you'll have to do so via the Spotify app itself, as it's not currently available within any professional DJ apps.) djay Pro's Automix function is a great feature for those uninterested in professional mixing techniques but still seeking control over the music environment. The djay Pro iPhone app is also a convenient tool, offering Automix capabilities both on its own or in conjunction with a computer-based setup.

For those not ready to venture into the world of DJ programs quite yet, the music subscription apps you're likely already familiar with can work well, provided you download your playlists before a session to avoid Wi-Fi or latency issues. Most streaming services allow users to customize playlists on the fly, which is helpful when adjusting to the flow of the session. Experimenting with the "blend" or "transition" settings can help create smoother transitions between tracks, maintaining the emotional and energetic continuity that's so crucial in psychedelic work.

While DJ software provides enhanced controls, elegant transitions, and more powerful playlist management, keep in mind that the speakers you pair with your system are responsible for bringing the music to life. Whether you're working with Bluetooth speakers for a simple setup or high-end monitors for a professional experience, the choice of speakers is a critical component of the overall journey.

Speaker Recommendations: Creating the Foundation for Immersion

The speakers you choose can dramatically shape the auditory component of the psychedelic therapy experience. They are foundational for delivering music with the clarity, depth, and emotional resonance needed to support the journeyer's unfolding process. While the specifics of your setup will depend on your goals (and your budget as well), there are a few key considerations to keep in mind when selecting speakers for your journey space.

First, prioritize speakers that produce a balanced and immersive sound. Look for options that offer excellent dynamic range and clarity, ensuring that subtle details in the music come through without distortion. Speakers with a wide stereo field can create a sense of spaciousness, surrounding the journeyer with sound in a way that feels natural and supportive.

In my personal practice, I've gravitated toward Adam Audio speakers, as they consistently deliver exceptional quality. Their ribbon tweeters are particularly noteworthy, producing crisp, high-definition sound that pairs beautifully with ambient, neoclassical, and electronic compositions. This level of detail enhances the music's emotional impact, helping clients immerse themselves more deeply into the experience. While Adam Audio offers professional-grade options suited for advanced setups, they also provide consumer-friendly models at a range of price points, making them accessible for different needs. Though ultimately, your choice of speakers will depend on the space you're working in and the type of sound experience you want to create.

Beyond the speakers themselves, experiment by testing different placements in the room. For instance, try positioning your speakers closer to the journey bed for increased intensity or farther apart for more spaciousness, and then evaluate how different music genres resonate. The key is to trust your ears and adapt to what feels most supportive for the journeyer.

Because every journey space is unique, the remainder of this chapter will explore the possibilities for different configurations—ranging from basic, affordable solutions to professional, immersive setups. To start, we'll take a look at how my own journey space is arranged. My setup is designed to maximize immersion and emotional resonance and offers just one example of what's possible for those seeking a professional-level experience. Afterward, we'll explore simpler and more accessible options for those just starting out.

My Journey Space Setup

My audio setup is currently equipped with a Macbook Pro M4 laptop, boasting 32GB of RAM and 2TB of hard drive space. The laptop runs Native

THE PSYCHEDELIC DJ

Instruments Traktor Pro 4 DJ software, played through an Apogee Duet 3 DAC (digital audio converter, or "sound card"). This setup is managed by an Allen & Heath Xone:K2 USB mixer that controls a four-turntable layout with various internal effects units offering additional creative options. As I mentioned, my setup features a pair of Adam Audio S3V mastering-grade monitors. These speakers, positioned at head level on either side of a twin XL floor mattress, form the cornerstone of my setup, essentially creating a large pair of "headphones" that immerse my clients in a more natural and dynamic audio experience for psychedelic journeywork.

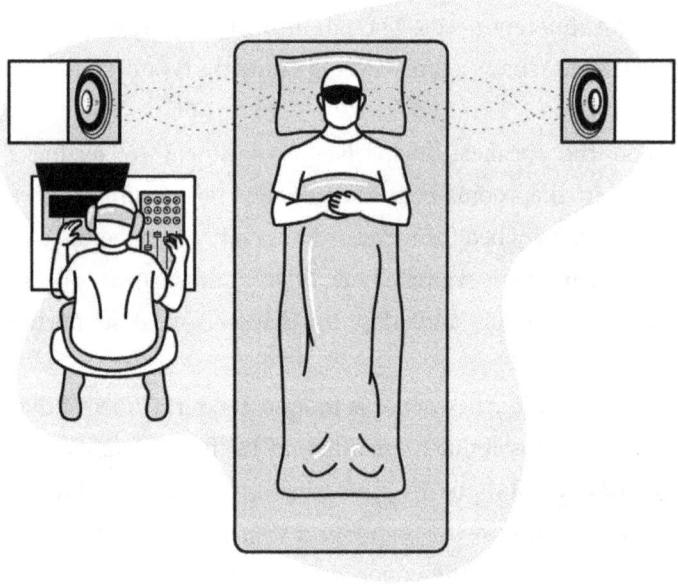

While my journey space setup is tailored for professional-level therapy, not every session requires this level of equipment. For those just starting out or working with simpler needs, here are some more accessible options for creating an effective setup.

Basic Setup: Simplicity and Affordability

For those just starting out or on a tighter budget, it's possible to create a quality audio experience using minimal equipment. The goal here is simplicity and ease of use, utilizing tools you may already have.

Laptop, Smartphone, or Tablet: You can use any laptop, iPhone, iPad, or Android device to play music directly from your MP3 library, device browser, or streaming apps such as SoundCloud, Apple Music, Tidal, or Spotify. Just make sure to download any playlists or tracks ahead of time to avoid interruptions due to Wi-Fi or internet connectivity issues.

Speakers: Bluetooth or Wi-Fi–enabled speakers are a great starting point. Some affordable and reliable options include the RIVA Concert or RIVA Stadium; JBL Flip, JBL Charge, or JBL Xtreme series; Ultimate Ears Boom, Megaboom, or Wonderboom series; and the Bose SoundLink series. When choosing Bluetooth speakers, it's best to select a brand with True Wireless Stereo technology, allowing you to pair two speakers together to create a left/right stereo field, which can significantly enhance the listening experience.

Considerations: A limitation of this basic setup is the inability to cue to (or preview) the next track before playing it. This means you will need to rely on your memory when switching between tracks or playlists. Despite this, the setup remains simple, portable, and effective for personal or small group sessions.

Intermediate Setup: Balancing Performance and Control

For those ready to move beyond the basics, this setup allows more control and a deeper sound experience, without requiring the high-end gear of a professional studio.

Laptop: A MacBook or similarly powerful laptop with at least 16GB of RAM is recommended for running DJ software like Traktor Pro 4, Serato, Pioneer Rekordbox, or djay Pro. These programs provide advanced control of music, playlists, and effects for tailoring the audio experience to the journey's needs, making them an excellent upgrade for smoother, more dynamic sessions.

THE PSYCHEDELIC DJ

DAC (Digital Audio Converter): Incorporating a DAC like the Apogee Groove, Focusrite Scarlett 2i2, or Komplete Audio 6 will greatly enhance sound clarity. This component is essential when working with high-quality monitors or speakers to deliver professional-grade audio.

Speakers: Upgrading to Adam Audio A7X, Genelec 8010A, KRK Rokit G4, or Yamaha HS5 studio monitors will enhance the depth, clarity, and dynamic range of the sound, providing a more immersive experience for your clients. These monitors are particularly well-suited for environments where sound quality and depth are paramount.

MIDI Controllers and Mixers: Pairing DJ software with a USB controller such as the Allen & Heath Xone:K2, Traktor X1 MK3, or Traktor Kontrol Z1 allows for real-time music adjustments. This setup enables you to adjust transitions, add effects, and seamlessly maintain the flow of the session, ensuring an adaptive and intuitive experience.

Advanced Setup: Immersive and Professional

For those who want the most immersive, fine-tuned audio setup, this section explores top-tier options. This is ideal for professional guides or for those looking to replicate the deepest sound immersion possible.

Laptop and DJ Software: At this level, I recommend a powerful laptop like the MacBook Pro M4 (32GB+ RAM), running Traktor Pro 4, Pioneer Rekordbox, djay Pro, or Ableton Live for more complex soundscapes. Any of these software options will provides endless creative flexibility for looping, layering, and adding live effects.

Speakers: The Adam Audio A77X or H, Adam Audio S3V or H, or Genelec 8351B monitors paired with an Apogee Duet 3 DAC or Universal Audio Apollo Twin X DUO Gen 2 provide studio-grade sound, creating a vast soundstage. Any of these speakers would be ideal for larger spaces or environments where sound quality needs to be impeccable. Note that adding a subwoofer from Genelec, Adam Audio, or JBL deepens the low-end frequencies and adds richness to the sound and feeling, enhancing the physical and emotional depth of the journey.

MIDI Controllers and Mixers: With a setup like this, an advanced mixer/

controller like the Allen & Heath Xone:96, a Pioneer XDJ/DDJ unit, or a Native Instruments Traktor Kontrol system provides flexibility and precision. You can experiment with different mixing techniques or use it to incorporate live instruments and samples throughout the journey.

As with any journey space setup, it's essential to experiment, observe client reactions, and adjust accordingly. Every journey space is unique, and whether you're working with a basic, intermediate, or advanced setup, the key is to stay attuned to the energy in the room, observe the journeyer's responses, and trust your instincts. By experimenting with your tools and allowing the music to guide the experience, you can create a soundscape that enhances the client's healing process.

Headphones Versus Speakers: Preparing the Sound System

In psychedelic therapy, the setting is just as important as the substance itself, as it shapes the journeyer's experience. Music is a central component of this setting—not just as background sound but as a dynamic force that moves through the air, filling the space and creating an atmosphere that supports the journeyer's unfolding process.

While headphones can deliver music more directly into the ears, they also create a more closed-off and intense experience. This can feel restrictive and may lead to sensory discomfort, whether that's ear pressure, increased body temperature, or limited freedom of movement. Any of these factors can interfere with the journeyer's ability to process intense emotional or physiological material.

In contrast, a left/right stereo speaker setup provides an open-air environment that surrounds the journeyer with sound in a way that feels natural and expansive—like lying inside a large pair of headphones. With speakers placed on either side of the journeyer's body, sound can flow freely through the room, engaging the entire space. This setup allows clients to feel the music physically, beyond just hearing it, as the air and acoustics carry the sound and bring it to life. The open configuration also allows the journeyer to move around easily while staying grounded and to hear their own voice and any supportive prompts from the guide as well.

To create this spacious open-air environment, place two speakers on either side of the bed at head level. Point each speaker toward the journeyer's ears, maintaining three to four feet of distance on each side. This positioning creates a natural and balanced soundscape: moving the speakers closer intensifies the sound, while placing them farther away softens it, allowing the sound to breathe. Experiment until you find the right spot, ensuring the sound fills the space without overwhelming it. By fine-tuning the setup, you create an environment that's open, supportive, and perfect for a deeply personal journey.

Using Headphones: Ensuring Redundancy

Headphones have long been a staple in psychedelic therapy. Like eyeshades, they help create a more internally focused, controlled, and isolated setting. However, if you and your client decide to use the traditional headphone method, it's crucial to pair the headphones with a set of speakers. This setup ensures redundancy and continuity in case the client abruptly removes the headphones at any point during the session.

To achieve this, consider purchasing a basic DJ mixer or headphone amplifier that offers both a headphone connection and speaker output. This will enable you to split the sound between the headphones and speakers (or another related amplifier), maintaining seamless playback in both.

Bluetooth and Wi-Fi Audio

While Bluetooth and Wi-Fi audio solutions like AirPlay or Chromecast offer convenience, they are generally less reliable and lower in sound quality compared to traditional wired setups. Wireless systems are also prone to audio dropouts, particularly if the connection isn't strong or the signal is obstructed by a person or object.

However, if you only have access to a single Bluetooth or Wi-Fi speaker, place it approximately two to three feet directly above or near the listener's head to simulate a stereo effect. Proper positioning also helps ensure the sound remains clear and immersive. Be sure to keep your phone, laptop, or other playback device as close to the speakers as possible to prevent glitches or connectivity issues.

PSYCHEDELIC AUDIO PRESENTATION

Your Personalized Audio Environment

The journey to creating an enhanced audio experience is a personal one, influenced by your specific needs, preferences, and the environment in which the music will be played. Whether you're a professional seeking to present the highest quality sound reproduction in a session or simply a psychonaut looking for a rich and immersive auditory experience, the right combination of speakers, sound card, and connection method can significantly elevate the listening experience, making it worthy of a life-changing psychedelic therapy session. Remember, while wireless options offer convenience and are more affordable, they may compromise sound quality and reliability. A wired setup with a sound card and active speakers can potentially be more expensive or challenging to learn, but it often provides a superior and more reliable audio experience during altered states of consciousness. Ultimately, the choice is yours. Use this guide as a starting point, explore the options, listen to different setups if possible, and choose what sounds best to you and your client. After all, in the realm of audio playback, your ears are the best judge.

Testing Your Setup: Audio Mixing

Testing your setup is the next essential step in order to ensure the sound environment aligns with the needs of the journey. The way you mix, transition, and set volume levels can significantly influence the client's experience, creating a setting that supports emotional depth, introspection, and healing. Just as therapists in training benefit from experiencing therapy, it's incredibly helpful for psychedelic guides and therapeutic DJs to try out their journey protocols by either guiding or being guided by a friend or colleague. Experiencing these skillsets firsthand deepens understanding of how volume and silence can shape a journey. Feeling the impact of these elements personally will help practitioners approach future sessions with greater empathy and intuition, making it easier to fine-tune the volume to genuinely support each client's unique experience.

While getting the technical aspects of audio presentation just right is essential to crafting a robust psychedelic setting, it's only part of the picture. The real magic in creating a transformative journey space lies in the interactions between sound, silence, and the music itself. You don't need to have everything figured out or invest in the most advanced equipment right away. Take your time, start with what feels manageable and suits your current needs, and let your setup evolve as your confidence and experience grow.

Once you've got the basics in place, the next step is building a music collection that aligns with your therapeutic goals and personal style. In the following chapter, we'll explore practical ways to source and curate tracks, blending the convenience of digital tools with the tangible experience of physical media. Whether you're uncovering rare vinyl or CD treasures or crafting thoughtful streaming playlists, this chapter will inspire you to approach music collecting as both an enjoyable art and a practice, guided by curiosity, creativity, and care.

9
THERAPEUTIC MUSIC COLLECTING

All DJs seek to amass quality music to fill their professional toolbox, otherwise known as a "record box." This term originates from the time when DJing involved playing and mixing two vinyl records together to create a sonic experience greater than the sum of its parts. A DJ's record box still serves many purposes. It fuels personal enjoyment, sparks creativity, provides professional support, stirs up dance floors, and, for our purposes here, helps craft meaningful psychedelic journeys. Having the best tools enables DJs to create intentional and impactful musical experiences that are tailored to the emotional and energetic flow of each session.

So where can you find the absolute best sonic tools for your therapeutic record box? First, look within. Connect with your inner music fiend. Call upon your internal music detective. Unleash the part of you that absolutely *must* discover and learn as much about music as possible: how it works, where it came from, the course of its evolution, and what inspired its creation. Once tapped into that motivation, start hunting around like a squirrel collecting acorns and gather tracks as if your practice and the healing of your clients depended on it—because in many ways, it does.

Building Your Record Box and Digging Deep

The current and most convenient method for sourcing music is digital downloads, preferably on Bandcamp or directly from the artist or label's own website. Platforms like Bandcamp stand out for their artist-centric model, which allows for direct support of and engagement with the musicians themselves. Other sites to explore include Beatport, Juno

THE PSYCHEDELIC DJ

Download, Boomkat, Bleep, and Traxsource, as well as iTunes, SoundCloud, and Mixcloud. DJs today are fortunate to have access to an expansive digital landscape when searching for music. Many online music shops have weekly or monthly newsletters that can be customized based on your preferences. These newsletters, combined with algorithm-based suggestions on sites like Bandcamp and other digital platforms, help you discover songs or albums similar to your previous purchases or those favored by like-minded customers. Social media platforms like Instagram and YouTube are also invaluable tools for music discovery. I follow music pages including @astrangelyisolatedplace, @orbmag, @deepbreakfastseries, @dj-maggie, and @overthemoontunes on SoundCloud and @overthemoon.music, @arturia_official, and @chillbeats_music on Instagram. These accounts feature a variety of new and classic tracks and albums and often share them as full-length releases, short clips, or even curated DJ mixes. Algorithms on these platforms then suggest similar tracks, artists, or pages that post related content, creating an infinite rabbit hole full of unexpected gems.

Streaming music sites use sophisticated recommendation algorithms to open up a vast range of possibilities tailored to your preferences. Platforms like BNDCMPR, Apple Music, Tidal, Spotify, and Pandora offer curated playlists and recommendation systems. These applications feature publicly shared playlists curated either by algorithms or by users who have already navigated the overwhelming array of choices for you. For instance, many psychedelic musicians mentioned in this book—including Jon Hopkins, Desert Dwellers, Liquid Bloom, Bluetech, Marine Eyes, and Tycho—have curated playlist stations on Spotify and BNDCMPR, as does the psychedelic music artist East Forest and author Steven Gelberg, whose book *Tuning In* is paired with companion playlists. As you explore these playlists, the algorithm will suggest new artists, songs, albums, and playlists, drawing you deeper into the expansive world of music that sonic detectives know and love. While there are many great options available online, you don't need to explore them all—just pick a few that resonate with you and dive in from there.

Engaging in online DJ forums or browsing curated playlists can also lead to unique discoveries. Music blogs are another excellent resource—

THERAPEUTIC MUSIC COLLECTING

they provide insights from well-informed writers who often receive advance copies of upcoming releases and share expert opinions that can help you sift through the overwhelming universe of music. Recommended music blogs include A Strangely Isolated Place, Cloud Collecting/Women of Ambient, A Closer Listen, Headphone Commute, Resident Advisor, XLR8R, Boomkat, Bleep, Electronic Beats, FactMag, Electronic Sound, Trancentral, and Dancing Astronaut.

It's also a great idea to join email lists and apps such as Bandsintown and Songkick, which are devoted to notifying music lovers when artists or bands they know and love are coming to town. Joining the email lists of DJs, artists, labels, blogs, retail stores, or online stores is also a great way to stay in the know about new tracks and albums as well as shows coming to your area.

Beyond digital platforms, current print magazines (and their related websites) such as *Fact*, *DJ Mag*, *Mixmag*, *Groove*, and *Electronic Sound*, also provide valuable insights into the music world and can guide your search for unique tracks.

Tapping into older physical media, like vinyl, CDs, and even cassettes, can unlock treasures that streaming platforms simply don't offer. These formats hold rare or out-of-print tracks that can bring a unique character to your therapeutic sessions. While classic record stores are always a great place to start, they're becoming harder to find, and even when you do find them, the options might be limited or prices might reflect the rarity of certain items. Luckily, online platforms like Discogs, Hard To Find Records (HTFR.com), Amoeba Music, Juno Records, and Deejay.de make it easier to track down those hidden gems. For those willing to dig a little deeper, thrift stores, record fairs, and specialty record shops are also worth exploring—there's something magical about the thrill of finding that one perfect track. Whether you're hunting through crates of records or exploring online platforms, the discoveries you find during your explorations can easily become part of your playlists.

Once you've found what you're looking for, ripping CDs into a digital format is an easy way to incorporate older music into your playlists. Programs like iTunes (macOS/Windows) and Windows Media Player

(Windows) allow you to rip CDs into high-quality formats such as WAV or AIFF, as well as compressed formats like MP3 or AAC. For more advanced control, tools like X Lossless Decoder (XLD) for macOS let you rip into a range of lossless formats, including FLAC and ALAC. Lossless formats preserve the full sound quality of the original recording, ensuring the highest possible fidelity—an important consideration for immersive and therapeutic settings. On the other hand, compressed formats like MP3 reduce file size but lose some audio detail, making them better suited for casual listening. Ultimately, you don't need to explore every tool or format—start with what fits your workflow and the needs of your sessions.

Exploring physical formats is about more than just finding music—it's a chance to connect with the music on a deeper level. Flipping through records, chatting with shop owners, or discovering a forgotten CD at a thrift store can spark inspiration and lead you to tracks that feel truly special. These experiences often bring a personal touch to your collection, adding stories and meaning to the music you'll share with clients.

When building your collection, it's vital to think about the energy and emotional arc that different tracks bring to a set or session. Consider the thematic and sonic qualities that align with different stages of a psychedelic journey—from grounding, ambient soundscapes for onset to more dynamic, cathartic compositions for peak experiences. A curated selection will make your record box not just a source of music but an intentional space out of which you can create memorable and healing experiences.

When thinking about music collecting, the most important thing is to not be afraid of getting started. Be curious and excited about the plethora of incredible pieces of music readily available for your enjoyment and the enjoyment of your clients. Become addicted to music and all it can inspire in your life. Don't settle. Go out of your way to learn as much as possible and to find all of the hidden gems you never knew existed. Share those pieces of music with your clients, friends, and colleagues, and you'll feel a sense of pride in having discovered something that nobody you know has ever heard of.

By thoughtfully sourcing and collecting music, you enrich your craft and ensure that your work as a guide is both intentional and respectful to the artistry behind each track. As we transition into a discussion of the sustainability and ethics of music curation, it's important to remember that this practice not only deepens your connection to the music but also supports the artists and the industry that make this transformative work possible.

Sustainability: Purchasing Music Versus Streaming

Unlike the vinyl purchases and downloadable digital music of the past, new technology has facilitated a change from purchasing music to renting it. Because it costs so much less for the consumer, most artists now also earn much less than they did when physical media like cassettes, vinyl, and CDs ruled the day. The primary issue here is that the compensation models for most streaming platforms pay artists only a fraction of a fraction of each penny the company itself earns. As a result, artists are now required to receive millions of plays to earn anything resembling a sustainable income to continue producing music. Coupled with the inescapable power of the algorithms, this model heavily favors mainstream artists and leaves emerging artists struggling to make a living from their art. Based on my research, here is the shocking compensation structure for various music streaming services from highest to lowest payout per stream:[1]

Streaming Service	Payout Per Stream in 2024 (US$)
Napster	0.019–0.021
Qobuz	0.022
Tidal	0.01284
Apple Music	0.0056–0.0078
Deezer	0.0064
Amazon Music	0.004
Spotify	0.003–0.005
Pandora	0.0013
YouTube Music	0.00069

THE PSYCHEDELIC DJ

As Harry Jackson notes at Whipped Cream Sounds, "These are averages and the payout per stream can vary depending on a number of factors such as location of stream, length of the stream, whether the stream is from a free or paid user, the deal [the] distributor/label has with the DSP, and more."[2] And as Mikalya Howard writes for the *Ohio State Technology Law Journal* blog, "for every 1,000 streams on Spotify, an artist will generate $4.37, $7.83 on Apple Music, and $4.02 on Amazon Music."[3]

For DJs, streaming has likewise introduced new challenges. While it has vastly increased access to music, it has simultaneously complicated the search for that unique needle in the haystack. Not to mention, not all music available on streaming platforms can be used during psychedelic sessions due to licensing restrictions or lack of access within popular DJ programs.

As a result, it's becoming increasingly important to purchase an artist's music directly through their personal websites, their record labels, or their platforms on sites like Bandcamp. Unlike streaming services, Bandcamp allows artists to retain the majority of their revenue by selling their music directly to fans. As of 2025, Bandcamp pays out approximately 82 percent of each sale directly to the artist or label, with the remaining amount covering Bandcamp's revenue share and payment-processing fees. This money usually reaches the artist within 24 to 48 hours of the sale.[4]

For DJs especially, purchasing music through Bandcamp has several advantages. It allows you to directly support the artists you love, contributing to the sustainability of diverse music scenes. It also provides access to high-quality downloads, which are crucial for professional DJing. Bandcamp's wide range of music, often from independent and emerging artists, offers a rich source for unique tracks that can set you, as a DJ, apart from others.

When you use music in your sessions as a psychedelic guide, you are using other musicians' work as a tool for healing. Therefore, it's only fair and respectful to make an effort to purchase the music you are using. At minimum, consider donating to the artist in some capacity, whether directly to the artist themselves or via the record label that represents them. If you truly love a piece of music and recognize its power for transforming lives, wouldn't you want to extend your gratitude directly to the artist? Instead of a fraction of a penny through a streaming service, a direct purchase or donation acknowledges the real value of their work and the impact it has.

The act of purchasing music pays homage to the artists and acknowledges the value of their work. It's a way of saying thank you to the artists who create these powerful musical tools. By actually purchasing music, psychedelic guides contribute to the overall sustainability of the music industry, ensuring that artists are compensated fairly for their work. When artists are fairly compensated, they can continue creating music that supports healing sessions and enriches lives. Supporting artists by purchasing their music is a strategic move that benefits the entire community, whether you are engaged in a lively dance party or a therapeutic psychedelic experience. After all, without artists, there would be no music. Life wouldn't be nearly as beautiful, and our therapeutic record boxes wouldn't be nearly as effective.

10
ASSEMBLING THE PARTS—
GESTALT THERAPY AND MUSIC IN POSTJOURNEY INTEGRATION

In this chapter, we'll explore the definition of integration, along with recommendations and questions for self-reflection in the days that immediately follow a journey. We'll also explore how Gestalt therapy's experiential methods provide a powerful foundation for integration, helping clients reconnect with disowned parts of themselves and resolve unfinished processes. Then we'll examine the role of music in integration work, uncovering how the soundscapes from the initial journey can be revisited as tools for further emotional release, self-reflection, and healing. We will see these principles in action thanks to real-life vignettes, where theory and practice come together to illuminate the transformative potential of psychedelic integration counseling. Finally, we discuss follow-up and future journeys, highlighting the importance of continuous client feedback and its role in refining the therapeutic process.

Psychedelic Integration

Integration has quickly become a mainstay in the current wave of psychedelic therapy and research, often described as the true heart of the practice. It is a process of "resting and digesting," making sense of the realizations that occur before, during, and after a psychedelic journey. It brings together the psychological, emotional, biological, energetic, and spiritual pieces of the puzzle into a greater whole, weaving extraordinary insights, revelations, and benefits back into the fabric of everyday life.

For many clients, this phase holds the potential to transform fleeting moments of clarity into lasting change. However, integration is not a linear path; it is a delicate and dynamic process that invites curiosity, patience, and intentional practice. With this foundation in mind, let's delve into specific recommendations and strategies to support clients during the integration process.

Immediately following a journey, clients are advised to relax, rest, and avoid strenuous activities for at least 72 hours. This helps prevent any unnecessary disruption in their systems while their bodies continue to off-gas subconscious material as they return to homeostasis and begin to integrate their experience. In the days that follow, clients are encouraged to make short journal entries or bullet-point notes about their thoughts, feelings, and initial reactions. This practice is valuable because what clients remember on day one after the journey often quickly evolves with each passing day. Writing these notes serves as a helpful self-awareness exercise, and the notes themselves are particularly useful when clients need to submit a final summary, typically before the final postjourney integration session. This final writing assignment encompasses all the client's experiences, starting from before the screening, through the journey, and beyond.

At the conclusion of the protocol, clients will have access to all their submitted writing assignments, which allows them to review their progress, remember all the lessons they've learned, and develop intentions for any future journeys.

Guiding Integration: Methods and Best Practices

Imagine dropping a giant boulder into a calm pond: the initial splash represents the psychedelic journey's profound impact, while the ripples symbolize waves of adjustment and realignment that occur during postjourney integration. The experience itself, a significant upheaval, is followed by subsequent waves of rebalancing as the client's brain, body, and emotions adapt to the new insights. This process can also be likened to a sine wave: starting at baseline, peaking dramatically, and gradually settling back into equilibrium. Each person's journey and its aftermath are unique and varying greatly from one individual to the next.

Common Reactions

- **Energy Fluctuations:** Many clients report a surge of energy the day after their journey, often followed by a dip the next day, or vice versa.
- **Emotional Sensitivity:** Clients might feel tired, irritable, or emotionally raw as their system reorients and seeks homeostasis.
- **Sleep Disruptions:** The first night's sleep can be restless, with difficulties falling asleep or frequent waking. Most clients find their sleep normalizes by the third night.
- **Headaches:** About 50 percent of clients experience postpsychedelic headaches. Encourage them to address this with their preferred comfort measures, such as hydration, rest, or over-the-counter remedies.

Best Practices

- **Allow Time for Adjustment:** Encourage clients to give themselves at least 72 hours, or what I call "three sleeps," to let their system find balance—a metaphor for allowing sufficient time for physical, emotional, and mental realignment.
- **Acceptance:** Help clients embrace all postjourney symptoms, whether they are pleasant or challenging. As Arnold Beisser's "Paradoxical Theory of Change" (which you'll read more about in the Gestalt Experiential Integration section) suggests, the best way to facilitate transformation is through fully accepting one's current state.
- **Self-Care:** Advise clients to treat this period as one of "selfish self-care." Remind them to honor the profound psychological, emotional, physiological, and spiritual shifts they've undergone. As such, it's important for them to prioritize rest during this time.
- **Boundaries:** Similarly, encourage clients to protect their time and space. It's OK to set boundaries with others who may be eager to hear about their journey before they feel ready to share about their experience.
- **Gradual Action:** Suggest that clients delay any major decisions or discussions until they've had sufficient time to reflect and process. Remind them that a good idea today will likely be an even better idea in a week or a month.

- **Reintegration:** Prompt clients to reflect on their original intentions. Now that they've reached the other side of the journey, how will they apply their insights? Thanks to the way that psilocybin mushrooms cleanse the lens of the mind and heart, the journey often reveals a clearer view of oneself and the world. Clients may notice that they are seeing more, feeling more, and experiencing a deeper connection to life's subtle details. Encourage them to use this heightened clarity to observe their surroundings with fresh eyes and open hearts. Remind them that this period of reintegration is also an opportunity to gently embody these insights—it's a chance to nurture the seeds of change planted during the journey. Slowing down, staying curious, and savoring their renewed sense of presence can help them anchor their experience in meaningful, lasting ways.

As clients navigate the waves of postjourney integration, it can be helpful to revisit principles from Stage Six: Closing Ceremony—Baseline Sobriety in chapter 6. This phase emphasized the transient nature of postjourney symptoms, offering reassurance that any discomfort is part of the natural recalibration process and will ease within a few days.

Reflection Questions

Once clients have adjusted and begun to stabilize, reflection becomes a valuable tool for deepening their integration process. Guided questions can help them uncover hidden insights, solidify lessons, and develop clarity around their experience. Consider offering the following prompts to support their journey of self-discovery:

- Did your intentions get addressed or resolved?
- What content emerged during your journey? Describe any memories, visuals, emotions, or recurring patterns you noticed.
- What aspects of the session felt positive? What didn't?
- What bodily sensations did you notice throughout your journey?
- Were any interpersonal relationship issues addressed?
- How has the journey changed you?
- Did the medicine help break down blockages or transform any stagnant material?

- What new possibilities have opened up as a result of your journey? Think about opportunities for personal growth, relationships, or creative endeavors.
- Is there a beautiful memory from the journey that stands out for you?
- What self-care practices can help you water the seeds of the intentions you planted prior to your journey?
- If you could write a letter to your prejourney self, what would it say?

Additionally, you may offer clients the opportunity to compose an integration statement. This can be a message to the medicine or a letter of commitment to the practices they believe will help maintain the journey's benefits.

These reflective practices help clients process their initial insights while laying the groundwork for deeper exploration. The next phase of integration builds on this foundation, with Gestalt therapy offering experiential techniques to sort through any unresolved material and enhance self-awareness.

Gestalt Experiential Integration

Gestalt therapy was developed in the mid-20th century by Fritz Perls as a departure from Sigmund Freud's psychoanalytic model. It has been the primary foundation of my own counseling practice and has influenced many other modern approaches, including Internal Family Systems (IFS), Somatic Experiencing (SE), Emotion-Focused Therapy (EFT), Process-Oriented Psychology, Experiential Therapy, and various other mindfulness-based therapies. It is rooted in present-moment awareness and emphasizes the integration of fragmented aspects of the self. Unlike purely cognitive methods, it is an experiential approach that engages the whole person in mind, body, and emotions.

The next phase of integration invites clients to explore the deeper emotional and psychological dimensions of their journey through experiential integration counseling, a process of embracing the entirety of one's journey and present state. By confronting individuals with their true selves, psychedelic mushrooms often compel an authenticity that can feel challenging yet liberating. This experience reflects Arnold Beisser's

"Paradoxical Theory of Change," which suggests that real transformation occurs when individuals fully accept themselves as they are, rather than striving to become something else.[1] By acknowledging and engaging with their authentic experiences—both comfortable and uncomfortable—clients create space for genuine growth and healing.

Psychedelic mushrooms, as both literal and metaphorical decomposers, enhance integration by breaking down emotional and mental barriers, thus revealing previously hidden aspects of the self. This quality makes them uniquely suited to integration work, as they help clients access disowned parts of themselves with greater clarity and courage.

Gestalt therapy is complementary to psychedelic integration counseling, as both are experiential activities that cultivate self-awareness, self-acceptance, and inner peace. They bridge fragmented and disowned parts of the self that have been cut off due to traumatic or challenging life experiences. By acknowledging and working with inner polarities and the multitude of parts within a person's psyche, psychedelic integration counseling that utilizes Gestalt therapy can help a person become more accepting of all their inner parts. Healing the relationship between inner parts allows them to coexist in a unified and balanced whole, ultimately creating more ease and freedom in the client's system.

The decomposing action of psychedelic mushrooms can help clients face unresolved emotions and unmet needs, which in turn makes them more receptive to Gestalt therapy techniques. Gestalt therapy then offers a structured framework for working through the insights revealed by the mushrooms, providing tools to process and integrate these revelations. Together, they form a powerful synergy that facilitates the exploration of buried material and supports the client's journey toward balance and wholeness.

Gestalt therapy interventions, including the empty chair exercise and dialogue with the self that you will read about below, can be instrumental in bridging the gap between a client's prejourney experience and postjourney life. Psychedelic mushrooms, by loosening ego defenses and dissolving emotional barriers, create an ideal environment for these techniques.

In the empty chair exercise, the client engages in a dialogue with an imagined or real other—whether it's another person or a part of themselves—by speaking to an empty chair, as if the other were seated there. In much the same way, the dialoguing-with-the-self exercise involves internal conversations between different parts of the client's psyche, with an aim toward fostering self-awareness and integration. The clarity and courage that the mushrooms provide often allow clients to approach these dialogues with greater openness and authenticity, facilitating breakthroughs that might otherwise remain inaccessible.

The role of the counselor or guide is to invite the client to explore what arises for them in the here and now as they reflect on their psychedelic journey. Facilitating a conversation between parts of the self can help the client identify what each part is seeking or needing from the other(s). Oftentimes, when each part is acknowledged, witnessed, and heard, the polarized parts will begin to work more harmoniously with each other. This reconciliation can sometimes create a third possibility or new perspective that the client was unable to previously see due to inner tension and/or confusion between the polarized parts.

When resolution between these parts occurs, the client can reframe their relationship to the parts of their story so they can experience them with more acceptance and compassion. By combining reflective practices like journaling with Gestalt's experiential methods, the client can integrate their experiences on a deeper level.

The transformative potential of psychedelic therapy combined with Gestalt therapy interventions is not a quick-fix process. Instead, it invites the client on a powerful journey of self-discovery that includes learning how to navigate the complexities of the human experience while weaving the insights provided by their psychedelic journey into everyday life.

While Gestalt therapy lays a foundation for exploring the emotional and psychological dimensions of integration, music offers another pathway to deepen this process. Much like psychedelic mushrooms dissolve blockages to reveal hidden aspects of the self, music serves as a catalyst to access emotions, memories, and insights. The soundscapes experienced during a journey don't just fade when the session ends—they become a portal back to these discoveries, offering a complementary tool to Gestalt's experiential methods.

Music for Psychedelic Integration

Relistening to music from a psychedelic journey can serve as a potent tool for integrating the experience. Much like Gestalt therapy's experiential techniques offer avenues for emotional and psychological exploration, music holds the unique ability to re-evoke emotions, thoughts, and visions from the journey, providing a portal for reconnecting with and making sense of those experiences in a nonpsychedelic state. By engaging with these soundscapes again, clients can tap into memories and insights that may have otherwise remained out of reach, allowing music to complement and deepen the integration process.

As guide or counselor, you can bring in music from the client's journey to open the integration counseling session. This can help clients drop into the space through breathwork or brief meditation, creating a calm and relaxing state conducive to exploring deep thoughts, memories, emotions, or body sensations.

Journey music can be a powerful tool for releasing stuck or incomplete emotions—those not fully processed during the journey itself. I often begin by asking the client if they recall a particular piece of music from the session, as this can provide valuable insight into unresolved emotional material. Although they may struggle to pinpoint pieces that correspond to specific memories from the experience, they usually have a general sense of when certain music was played during their journey, especially in relation either to the start of the journey, the booster dose and bathroom break, or toward the end of the journey when they returned to baseline sobriety. As the psychedelic guide, I meticulously track all playlists used during sessions. This practice allows me to revisit and identify the pieces and transitions that resonated with clients, so I can then reintroduce them in these integration sessions.

Much like Gestalt therapy emphasizes the importance of revisiting unresolved parts of the self, I've observed how relistening to these pieces of music can elicit strong emotional responses and bring hidden material into conscious awareness. Clients are frequently moved to tears or experience surges of excitement as the music transports them back to their journey. When this occurs, I encourage clients to focus on the emotions and

ASSEMBLING THE PARTS

memories stirred by the music. We can explore how that track resonates with their current emotional experience.

If the client cannot recall a specific piece, I select one from the journey playlist that aligns with their description of their mind-set or feels suited to facilitating emotional release. In choosing the music, I consider whether the emotions feel heavy, unresolved, or in need of a shift, opting for tracks with complex energy, unresolved chord structures, or a specific emotional resonance. As the client listens, I encourage them to fully engage with the feelings that arise, allowing the music to act as a soundtrack for emotional exploration and release.

I often recommend that clients listen back to their journey music regularly so they can continue to reconnect with the material that showed up during their experience. Intentional listening—fully immersing in the music while paying attention to its sounds, rhythms, and melodies—is especially effective. As clients listen, I suggest they take note of any thoughts, feelings, or memories that arise and explore whatever emerges with acceptance and curiosity. I also encourage creative follow-ups like painting, drawing, scribbling, or journaling to help reflect on the emotions evoked by the music and articulate their experience.

I also encourage clients to set an intention before listening to their journey music, such as intending to approach difficult emotions or memories with kindness and understanding. As the music plays, it can become the soundtrack for a self-guided meditation to experientially practice such skills within their creative imagination. Using the music during movement activities such as yoga, hiking, and biking can also help a client process and digest their experiences on a deeper level.

While the theoretical frameworks of Gestalt therapy and music for integration provide a road map for healing, their transformative potential truly comes alive in practice. In the next section, we'll step into the integration room to explore experiential vignettes that demonstrate these approaches in action. These stories reveal how music, alongside Gestalt techniques, supports clients in navigating emotional breakthroughs, reconciling fragmented parts of themselves, and weaving their psychedelic insights into everyday life. Each vignette offers a glimpse into the deeply personal and profound nature of this work, inspiring practical applications for guides and therapists alike.

Clinical Vignettes: Music, Gestalt, and Somatic Therapies in Action

Gestalt therapy and music create a supportive foundation for integration, offering pathways for clients to process emotions, reconnect with disowned parts of themselves, and anchor the insights gained from their psychedelic journeys. While these frameworks provide valuable tools, the true depth of integration is best understood through lived experience.

The stories in this section illuminate the subtle and profound ways music, somatic techniques, and Gestalt interventions can transform journey experiences into meaningful growth. Each vignette offers a glimpse into the art of holding space for healing, where theory and practice come together to gently support the client's unique process.

Every client's relationship with music is deeply personal, shaped by their needs and past experiences. Journey music becomes a dynamic tool for self-awareness and healing, encouraging past memories and emotions to surface in ways that feel accessible and safe. Rather than remaining buried in the subconscious, these experiences can be explored and integrated, fostering greater understanding and self-compassion.

The integration of focusing techniques, breathwork, and gentle physical exercises with journey music allows clients to connect with bodily sensations stirred by the soundscapes. This process creates a supportive environment where emotions can be safely revisited and expressed, helping to release patterns of avoidance and open pathways for healing. Over time, the client can develop healthier emotional responses, rooted in a sense of safety and inner balance.

Somatic modalities, such as Reichian therapy, which explore the connection between the body, emotions, and energy flow, provide another layer of support. These techniques can enhance body awareness and facilitate the release of tension, blocked emotions, and stored trauma. When a specific piece of music evokes feelings of sadness or grief, the counselor may guide the client through deep, steady breathing to gently engage with the accompanying sensations, such as a knot in the stomach or tightness in the throat. As the music plays, the counselor encourages the client to stay present with these sensations, fostering an embodied awareness that invites emotional release and relief.

Here is an example of a process that utilizes this type of therapeutic approach in an integration counseling session.

Therapist: Instead of describing your journey, take a moment to settle into your body and feel into what is currently emerging. Use your awareness to notice your breath and the weight of your feet on the ground. Allow yourself to be as fully present here as possible.

Client: (*Takes a deep breath and feels the tension in their shoulders.*)

Therapist: Good. Now, let's focus on any physical sensations. Is there tightness, warmth, or fluttering anywhere in your body?

Client: I feel lighter but my chest also feels constricted, like there's a knot still coming undone.

Therapist: That sensation might hold information. Imagine it as an energy block. Can you visualize its shape or color?

Client: It's dark, almost black. And it's pulsating.

Therapist: Let's explore its origin. What memories or emotions come to mind as you connect with this sensation?

Client: During the trip, I remember feeling overwhelmed during a family gathering last year. Lots of expectations, and I couldn't express myself.

Therapist: Take a moment to gently breathe into that area. Imagine the pulsations softening, releasing. Allow any emotions to surface.

Client: (*Takes slow breaths, feeling the knot loosen.*)

Therapist: Notice any images or symbols. Sometimes the body communicates through metaphors. What arises?

Client: I see a closed door. Behind it, there's light.

Therapist: I'm curious about the door. Does it represent protection? What could it mean? What could be on the other side of it?

Client: Maybe it's my authentic self, waiting to be acknowledged.

Therapist: Wonderful insight. As you breathe, imagine that door opening. Feel the warmth of the light. What emotions accompany this?

Client: Relief, joy. Like I'm stepping into my truth. (*Takes bigger breaths, shoulders relax, lips quiver, tears appear.*)

Therapist: OK great, try to stay with that sensation. Allow it to expand. And remember, there's no rush.

Remember, somatic processing is all about listening to the language of the body. The use of psychedelics can enhance this process by loosening ego defenses and releasing underlying subconscious material, leading to improved awareness. Trust what emerges, even if it feels mysterious or subtle. As each person's journey is unique, some clients may express themselves vividly, while others may find comfort in quiet gestures better expressed through an even less verbal but more artistic approach.

Here is an example of what that may sound like:

Therapist: I can totally understand how difficult it may be to put such a big experience into words. As you continue to explore what's happening now, I invite you to connect with your body. Notice any sensations, new openings, or any areas of tension or ease. You might feel the weight of

ASSEMBLING THE PARTS

your feet against the floor, the beating of your heart, the rhythm of your breath. Allow yourself to be as present here as possible.

Client: (*Takes a deep breath and settles back into the couch.*)

Therapist: Now, if you're interested, perhaps we can explore some nonverbal expressions. You have the option to draw, paint, or simply move your hands in the air. There's no pressure, no right or wrong way. Trust your instincts. If words arise, that's OK too.

Client: (*Picks up some pencils and starts sketching shapes on the paper.*)

Therapist: Let the lines flow uninterrupted. Imagine they carry messages from your deeper self and that your hand is the voice. What colors come to mind? What textures? Feel free to close your eyes if it helps.

Client: (*Adds some color to the shapes, blending blues and greens.*)

Therapist: As you create, notice any emotions or memories that surface. Sometimes the body speaks through art and can give words to the inexpressible. It's OK if it feels mysterious or abstract. Just let go and let it flow.

Client: (*Pauses, then continues drawing.*)

Therapist: And if silence feels right, that's welcomed too. We're holding space for whatever arises. Trust the process.

The choice between the artistic approach and the somatic Reichian approach in integration counseling depends on individual preferences, therapeutic goals, and what is emerging in the moment. The symbolism, colors, and shapes of an artistic approach encourage clients to bypass cognitive defenses and access deeper emotions, supporting emotional release and catharsis.

On the other hand, the Reichian approach focuses on the body and its energetic patterns. A client can use their refreshed awareness to explore bodily sensations, tension, and energy flow. As with psychedelics, this method further addresses stored trauma, promotes neuroplasticity, and connects emotions to specific bodily areas. Ultimately, some clients may prefer a blend of both approaches, integrating cognitive, emotional, and somatic dimensions. As guides, we honor each person's unique psychedelic journey and remain aware of sensitivities following such a powerfully life-changing experience.

Here is an example of what a session using a mixture of Gestalt, Reichian, and Somatic Experiencing might sound like as guide and client explore emerging material triggered by journey music.

> Therapist: As we begin today's session, I'd like you to take a few deep breaths and settle into the space. I'm going to play some calming music to help you ground yourself in the present moment. (*A few minutes transpire.*) How are you feeling now?
>
> Client: I feel a bit more relaxed.
>
> Therapist: That's good to hear. Now, I want to revisit a piece of music from your last psychedelic journey. You mentioned that it had a significant impact on you, so I checked the playlist and have it ready.
>
> Client: (*Shows emotional response.*)
>
> Therapist: I notice some emotion rising up. Can you tell me what you're feeling right now?
>
> Client: It's hard to explain... I feel a mix of sadness and relief.
>
> Therapist: That's OK. Let's try to stay with these feelings. Can you locate where in your body you're feeling these emotions? (*Invites the client to explore their emotional responses using either Reichian or Somatic Experiencing*

techniques.) As this song plays, I invite you to focus on your breathing. Taking deep, slow breaths. What do you feel in your body as you listen to the music?

Client: I feel a heaviness in my chest.

Therapist: OK, so focusing on that heaviness, without trying to change it, just observing it: What do you notice? What emotions come up?

Client: I feel sadness...

Therapist: Allowing yourself to feel that sadness, remember to breathe deeply. Let's continue to explore these feelings. I invite you to imagine that your sadness is sitting in the empty chair across from you. What would you like to say to it?

Client: (*Pauses.*) I would ask, "Why are you here? Why do you feel so heavy on my chest?"

Therapist: That's a powerful question. Let's take a moment and see if the sadness has a response. What does it want to say back to you?

Client: (*Closes eyes, breathes deeply.*) It says... "I'm here because you've been holding onto me for so long. You don't let yourself let go."

Therapist: That's really insightful. How does it feel to hear that?

Client: I feel torn. Part of me wants to push it away, but another part knows it's right.

Therapist: Stay with that tension for a moment. What do you notice in your body as you sit with these two parts—one that wants to push it away and one that understands its presence?

Client: My shoulders feel tight, but there's also this warmth in my chest ... like something is softening.

Therapist: That's important to notice. Let's thank the sadness for sharing its truth with you. When you're ready, you can let it know whether you're ready to let it go or if you need more time to sit with it.

Client: (*Pauses.*) I think I need more time. But it feels good to acknowledge it instead of avoiding it.

Therapist: Thank you for sharing that. Let's continue to explore these feelings. Remember, it's OK to feel these emotions. They are part of your journey toward healing and understanding. As we play this song, notice any sensations in your body. What do you feel?

Client: I feel a knot in my stomach.

Therapist: Focus on that knot. Don't try to change it, just observe it. What happens to the knot as the song continues?

Client: It's starting to loosen a bit ...

Therapist: That's great. Continue to observe the sensation. Let's see what else comes up as we continue to listen to the song ... Now, let's try to integrate these experiences. Can you connect the feelings and sensations you've just experienced with any memories you had during your psychedelic journey? What images come to mind? Can you describe them?

Client: I'm hiking in the woods at Yosemite ... I'm there with my family.

Therapist: Imagine you're there now. What do you see? What do you feel?

Client: I see Half Dome, it's huge and grey and beautiful ...

Therapist: Let's explore this memory further. Can you have a conversation with your family member who is there with you? What would you say?

Client: I'm so happy to be here sharing this moment with you. (*Makes connections between their current experiences and their psychedelic journey.*) This is reminding me of when I saw my family members during the journey. I felt so much love and gratitude for them and the experiences we shared when we were younger.

Therapist: That's beautiful. Let's take a moment to connect with that feeling of love and gratitude. Imagine you're holding it in your hands, like a glowing light. What color is it?

Client: (*Smiles.*) It's golden, like the sunlight on the trees.

Therapist: Hold that golden light and let it fill your chest. As it spreads through your body, notice what happens.

Client: It feels warm, like it's expanding. I can feel it in my arms and my legs.

Therapist: Let yourself be filled with that golden light. Now, as you hold this light, if you could share one thing with your family from this place of love and gratitude, what would it be?

Client: I would say, "Thank you for everything. Even the hard times, they've shaped me into who I am."

Therapist: That's a powerful message. Let's sit with this gratitude for a moment. As the music continues, see if any other feelings, images, or sensations arise.

Client: This is reminding me of when I saw my family members during the journey. I felt so much love and gratitude for them and the experiences we shared when we were younger. (*Becomes tearful.*)

Therapist: Focus on that joy you are feeling. Allow yourself to feel that joy and gratitude. Remember to breathe deeply. Let's continue to explore these feelings. As the song continues, do you notice anything else in your body?

Client: I feel an aliveness and tingling in my hands.

Therapist: Focus on that aliveness and tingling. Breathe deeply and just observe it. What happens to the tingling as the song continues?

Client: It's starting to expand, I feel airy ... ?

Therapist: That's great. Continue to observe the sensation as the music is the soundtrack for this experience. Let's see what else comes up as we continue to listen to the song.

The integration process is as unique as each client's journey. By blending somatic modalities with artistic or body-focused approaches, guides can help clients gently access and release emotions, supporting meaningful transformation. Through nonverbal expressions like drawing or exploring bodily sensations, clients can develop a greater sense of self-awareness, making it easier to integrate subconscious material into conscious understanding.

Incorporating music into the therapeutic process further nurtures emotional safety, fosters valuable insights, and deepens the client's connection to their inner world. Journey music serves as both a guide for exploration and a supportive tool for healing, offering clients the opportunity to revisit and weave the transformative aspects of their experience into daily life.

These experiential vignettes are intended to provide a window into the personal and profound nature of integration counseling. Each story showcases the interplay between a client's inner world, the therapeutic process, and the approaches used—whether music, somatic modalities, or Gestalt techniques—tailored to meet the client's unique needs. Yet integration is not confined to the session itself. True healing unfolds over time, through reflection and intentional practice, as the lessons and insights from the journey are gradually incorporated into everyday life.

In the final section, we'll consider the importance of follow-up and preparing for future journeys. Gathering client feedback, refining therapeutic approaches, and offering continued support help ensure lasting growth. By focusing on long-term integration, we create a bridge between the initial journey and the ongoing potential it holds for the client's life ahead.

Follow-up and Future Journeys

While I always strive to provide the best care, I also recognize that a single journey may not uncover everything a client hopes to explore or achieve. Recommending future experiences requires careful consideration, taking their unique preferences, needs, and safety into account. Without a deeper understanding, suggesting additional sessions too soon may inadvertently hinder their healing process. My priority is always to ensure their well-being, avoiding unnecessary complications in the pursuit of meaningful solutions.

Gathering client feedback throughout the treatment process—before, during, and after a session—is essential for tailoring the experience to their evolving needs. This ongoing dialogue creates space for individualized care, helping to adapt the therapeutic approach as the client's journey unfolds. As Scott D. Miller highlights in Feedback-Informed Treatment (FIT), continuous feedback is a vital tool for refining the therapeutic process and ensuring its effectiveness over time.

The integration of client feedback is central to this process, allowing me to fine-tune my approach and better support clients as they navigate their healing journeys. By actively listening to their experiences, I gain insight into what worked, what didn't, and how I can improve the therapeutic experience. This not only strengthens the connection between myself and my clients but also ensures the therapy evolves in alignment with their unique needs and goals.

To support this process, I have developed follow-up questions designed to gather meaningful feedback during either the final postjourney session or a 30-day follow-up call. These questions invite clients to reflect on their experience while offering insights that can guide future therapeutic work.

- **Client Satisfaction**: "Did you appreciate my approach and the way I conducted our sessions?"
- **Comfort Levels:** "Were you completely comfortable before, during, and after the journey?"
- **Counseling Effectiveness:** "Did my counseling approach help raise awareness or help you achieve your intentions and goals?"
- **Experience Enjoyment:** "Did you enjoy the setting, music, and journey space?"
- **Trust and Comfort:** "Was I a trustworthy and comfortable guide?"
- **Lasting Impact:** "Did our work together lead to lasting change in your life?"

Prioritizing client feedback not only helps me meet my clients' needs but also enhances my ability to improve my practice. By listening actively and reflecting on their experiences, I can refine my approach, fostering a therapeutic relationship that evolves along with the client's healing journey.[2]

11
PRACTITIONER SELF-CARE IN PSYCHEDELIC THERAPY

As guides and therapists, we hold a sacred role in the lives of those we support, especially in psychedelic therapy, where the work can be deeply transformative. But let's face it—this kind of work can take a toll on all of us. The emotional and mental demands are real, and without taking care of ourselves, we can quickly find ourselves overwhelmed, disconnected, or burnt out. So, what's the answer? We must take the time to check in with ourselves and develop the habits and boundaries that help us stay grounded and whole.

Our commitment to self-care is not just about our well-being; it is also an ethical responsibility. As highlighted in the ethics section, maintaining healthy boundaries and seeking support when needed are fundamental to ethical practice. By prioritizing our own self-care, we ensure that we are in the best possible state to provide safe, respectful, and effective support to our clients.

Checking In Before Sessions

Before diving into any session, we need to remember to pause and check in with ourselves. How are you feeling today? Take a moment to assess your emotional and physical state. Are there any stressors or concerns that might affect your ability to guide the session? What intentions would you like to set? Our ability to be present for our clients hinges on being emotionally ready ourselves. If we're carrying stress or emotional baggage into the session, it's going to be harder to truly attune to the journeyer's needs.

To give you an idea of how this looks in practice, here's what I do before each session.

When I wake on journey days, I can feel a variety of ways. Though I often feel invigorated and excited or calm and methodical, sometimes I wake up feeling unresolved about a personal conflict. Regardless of my emotional state, I dedicate 30 to 60 minutes to meditation—however long feels right in the moment. During my meditation, I focus on any emotions arising and work to clear them through deep, circular breathing and awareness. If I become aware of unresolved or distorted thoughts, I breathe into them while repeating affirmations like "All is well, all is safe." I envision the day ahead, from the client's arrival to their departure, seeing everything unfold smoothly. I visualize both myself and the client being grounded and capable of handling whatever emerges. Through repeated breathing and grounding, I offer encouragement to myself to trust and surrender, reminding myself that all will be well.

One additional practice I use is to reflect on the energy I want to bring into the session. Am I feeling open and grounded, or is there something I need to release before I begin? By asking myself these questions, I create a space of intentionality, which helps me remain fully present for my client.

Grounding Practices and Setting Boundaries

This work requires us to be deeply attuned to our clients, but it's crucial that we don't lose ourselves in their emotions. We can't pour from an empty cup, and if we're too enmeshed in the client's process, it can leave us drained or emotionally overwhelmed. Setting clear boundaries is key—boundaries around how much of their journey we take on and how we stay centered within our own experience. Knowing our role in the session and recognizing what we can and can't control is crucial. If we start feeling too involved, it's OK to pull back and ground.

Body awareness is also essential. We should always take a moment to check in with how our body feels. Is there any tension or discomfort? This simple practice helps us stay physically present.

Before, during, and after sessions, I practice mindful breathing and focus on my body in the present moment, allowing me to remain a grounding resource as the client journeys deep within or far outside themselves. I've learned to breathe into my root chakra and feel the ground beneath me. Each breath clears my mind and helps me reconnect with my body. I remind myself of my skills as a counselor, trusting my training and experience. When things become challenging, I try to remember the bigger spiritual picture: we can only do so much, and we trust that the medicine will guide the client in the way they need. We surrender to that process.

If I feel overwhelmed or unnecessarily concerned, I practice self-soothing techniques like affirmations, mindful breathing, and body scans, which help me remain present without overidentifying with the client's emotional state. These practices allow me to stay centered while offering the best possible support if the client asks for guidance.

Burnout and Compassion Fatigue: Building Resilience

Burnout and compassion fatigue can sneak up on us. In emotionally demanding fields like counseling and psychedelic therapy, it's easy to get lost in the needs of others and forget to take care of ourselves. While burnout is a predictable, cumulative process linked to stress, compassion fatigue is different. It comes up due to the emotional strain and preoccupation with clients' intense and transformative experiences. Therapists often internalize their clients' deep emotional pain and profound insights, leading to emotional saturation that impacts their well-being. This issue arises from our empathetic nature and the tendency to feel overly responsible for clients' therapeutic outcomes, resulting in the inevitable "cost of caring."

Five Phases of Compassion Fatigue

1. Zealot (Idealistic) Phase: Motivated by idealism, ready to serve, and full of energy, therapists in this phase, including ourselves, are often driven by our passion for helping others. However, this intense drive can lead to overextension, as we may set unrealistic expectations for ourselves or take on too much responsibility for our clients' well-being. This phase lays the groundwork for later emotional strain when those expectations prove unsustainable.

2. Irritability Phase: Over time, therapists may begin to feel emotionally taxed as the demands of the work outweigh their ability to recover. In

this phase, they may cut corners in their work or lose focus due to fatigue. Mocking peers or clients, while seemingly uncharacteristic, can arise as a defense mechanism against feelings of inadequacy or frustration. It can be easier to project negativity outward than to confront internal struggles, especially when a therapist feels they are falling short of their own high standards.

3. Withdrawal Phase: Feeling overwhelmed and depleted, therapists may begin to lose patience with clients and neglect their own self-care. Viewing themselves as victims can be a way to justify this withdrawal—shifting the blame to external factors rather than addressing their internal state. This phase often reflects a deep sense of hopelessness and disconnection.

4. Zombie Phase: In this phase, therapists may view others—including clients or peers—as incompetent or focus excessively on negativity. This reaction often stems from chronic emotional exhaustion, where the therapist has shut down emotionally as a way to cope with the overwhelming demands of the work. Losing zest for life reflects a broader disengagement from both personal and professional fulfillment.

5. Pathology and Victimization or Maturation and Renewal: If no action is taken, therapists can become stuck in a victim mind-set, perpetuating the cycle of depletion and disconnection. However, those who recognize the impact of compassion fatigue and commit to self-care and personal growth can initiate a process of renewal. This often involves reevaluating their boundaries, rediscovering their sense of purpose, and building resilience for the future.

Additional symptoms of compassion fatigue may include:

- Complacency: Avoiding difficult issues or failing to explore urgent concerns may reflect emotional fatigue and a subconscious effort to minimize additional stress. This can lead to faulty assumptions about clients or a reluctance to fully engage with their challenges.
- Impatience: Frustration with a client's progress or a desire for them to "get over it" often stems from feeling overburdened. Therapists may unconsciously want to accelerate a client's healing to relieve their own emotional load.

- Guilt: Feeling guilty for having a better life than a client or resentful of a client's inability to appreciate their circumstances reflects the emotional strain of maintaining empathy. This cognitive dissonance can arise when a therapist's capacity for compassion is stretched thin.

Symptoms of compassion fatigue are common among therapists and guides, manifesting as stress from the often intense emotional work we do. Though these symptoms can be disruptive, depressive, and irritating, being aware of them and their negative impact on ourselves and our clients can drive positive change, personal transformation, and newfound resilience. When we neglect self-care, we may find our capacity for compassion diminishing, leading to a gradual emotional, physical, and spiritual depletion. But with diligent self-care, we can maintain our ability to provide empathetic care while preserving our own well-being.

Recognizing the phases of compassion fatigue early on can help guide adjustments before burnout becomes irreversible. Signs of burnout include exhaustion, feeling drained even after taking time off, and disconnection. This can also include feeling detached from the work, feeling like nothing is making a difference, or experiencing cynicism—such as a "what's the point?" attitude that makes it hard to stay motivated.

There are ways we can all build resilience, strengthen our internal resources, and avoid burnout before it takes over. Are you taking regular time for rest and recovery between sessions? What practices or activities help you rejuvenate your energy after emotionally taxing sessions? Building resilience might involve setting a weekly time to review your emotional state and energy levels. Whether through journaling, meditation, or simply checking in with a peer, these practices help catch signs of burnout early. Additionally, learning to set clear work-life boundaries (such as designating specific days off) is essential for long-term sustainability.[1]

I always take as much time as possible to rest and recover between sessions. I recognize that burnout is happening when I feel stressed and my mind becomes scattered or excessively concerned about things I cannot control. I also notice it when I become overly sensitive to a client's struggles or when I start taking things too personally in my private life. I recognize burnout when my inner critic starts questioning my abilities, even though the more capable parts of me recognize the opposite truth and I know that the feedback I've received about my work has been positive.

To cope, I schedule personal time alone to meditate, hike, rock climb, take road trips, treat myself to lunch or ice cream, purchase or listen to music, or connect with close friends or colleagues. Most importantly, I connect with my wife—a fellow counselor and guide—who has an incredible ability to listen, empathize, and lighten the mood to counterbalance the heavy work I do daily.

Vicarious Traumatization and Somatic Countertransference

As guides in psychedelic therapy, we are often vulnerable to vicarious traumatization—the process by which we absorb the trauma of our clients, even when we're not directly involved in their traumatic events. Vicarious trauma can deeply affect us, manifesting as secondhand trauma that gradually takes hold and emerges as intrusive thoughts or physical tension. It can lead to PTSD-like symptoms, such as recurring intrusive thoughts and images or preoccupation with the client even during personal activities. In psychedelic therapy, where clients often undergo intense and transformative experiences, the impact of vicarious trauma can be even more pronounced, shaping our perception of the world, our beliefs, and our values.

Somatic countertransference refers to the physical responses we may have—such as tension or discomfort in our bodies—when witnessing a client's emotional pain during psychedelic sessions. Being mindful of these bodily reactions is key to preventing emotional overload. Recognizing these physical sensations can help you manage the emotional load and prevent it from affecting you in the long term. Paying attention to somatic countertransference—such as changes in body temperature, muscle tension, or breathing patterns—can help you notice when you're absorbing too much of the client's emotional state.

In psychedelic therapy, where emotional and energetic exchanges between guide and client are amplified, these effects can be even more pronounced. It's important to remain vigilant despite the intensity and recognize when the work starts to affect us physically or mentally.

When working with clients who have experienced trauma, do you notice any physical sensations or shifts in your own emotions? How do you manage these to ensure you're not taking on their emotional burden?

Strategies for managing vicarious traumatization and somatic countertransference include mindfulness and checking in with your body during the session to notice any tension, restlessness, or discomfort. A physical reset is also important; after emotionally intense sessions, take a few minutes to stretch, walk, bathe, shower, or do anything that helps you disconnect from the client's energy. Self-awareness is crucial too; know when to distance yourself emotionally from the client's process. It's important to maintain compassion without internalizing their pain.

When working with clients who have experienced significant trauma, I've noticed physical sensations like old injuries flaring up or a feeling of heavy weight on my back. I've also experienced headaches and discomfort shooting up my neck or behind my eyes. Sometimes, I become aware of strange thoughts that I know aren't my own. A few years ago, after working with a few challenging clients who requested to combine MDMA and psilocybin, I experienced overwhelmingly intrusive thoughts immediately following the sessions that I was sure weren't mine. The new experience was concerning and left me feeling confused. I knew I needed help, so I reached out to an experienced shamanic practitioner and psychedelic guide who helped me work through the process of understanding and clearing the vicarious trauma. Through recommended practices like tobacco work, energetic clearing techniques, and examining my decision to work with mixing natural and synthetic substances, I learned to reset and protect myself from such occurrences in the future.

It's essential to recognize when vicarious trauma might be affecting your work with other clients, and not just the ones from whom the trauma originated. Regular debriefing sessions with trusted colleagues or mentors, as well as journaling or using art and music, can help clear lingering emotional residues.[2]

Emotional Detox

Emotional detox is essential for our long-term well-being. Finding ways to release the emotional energy that may build up after a session is crucial to ensure we don't carry it with us. But how can we tell if we're building up an emotional energetic load? Common signs include feeling unusually irritable, fatigued, or emotionally drained after a session, experiencing difficulty concentrating, or noticing physical tension such as tight shoulders or an unsettled stomach. If left unaddressed, these signals can start to spill over into other areas of our lives, impacting our relationships and overall sense of work-life balance.

Engaging in activities outside of client work that help us to reconnect with ourselves and recharge is key to maintaining balance. Emotional detox strategies might include creative outlets (art, writing, music, singing), physical activity (hiking, biking, yoga, swimming), social connections (spending time with friends, family, or pets), or joining a peer-support group (such as the Psychedelic Guide Network). Any of these activities can help us process emotions and reconnect with ourselves and others.

To detox emotionally, I often discuss the sessions with my wife or other trusted colleagues. I also book sessions with mentors or therapists to explore concerns from challenging cases. I stay mindful of my mind and body, ensuring I don't carry the heaviness into my relationships. If I do, I engage in physical activities to help release that energy. Additionally, I use journaling and parts work for ongoing integration, reflecting on the session and my own emotional responses.

Incorporating regular mental health days where we completely disconnect from the demands of work can serve as a valuable emotional detox practice as well. These days give us space to recharge and reconnect with our personal lives.

Journey Planning: How Many Are Enough?

How many sessions do you find manageable in a week? What factors influence your decision to add another journey? How do you ensure you're not overextending yourself?

Some therapists or treatment centers believe guides can conduct numerous journeys per week, but the reality is that the emotional intensity of this work can be draining. In my experience, less is definitely more.

Over the years, I've experimented with multiple sessions at different times during the week but have learned that I do best facilitating one journey per week, with the option for an occasional additional session depending on my schedule and emotional state.

For example, I usually work with clients on Fridays, which allows both the client and me to enjoy the weekend off. If I add another journey, I'll schedule it for the following Tuesday and then follow up with the next journey on Saturday. This gives me at least three or four days of recovery time between sessions, ensuring I'm well rested and present for each client.

If I try to squeeze in too many journeys, either because I want to help everyone or because I'm overly concerned about my own financial needs and responsibilities, I know that I'm overextending myself. Booking sessions simply for financial reasons is never a good idea, as such desperation can lead to poor decision-making during the screening process. I also notice I'm overextended when I'm struggling to get good sleep, denying the fact that I'm pushing myself too far, or finding myself unable to stay grounded in subsequent sessions.

If I notice myself nearing a point of emotional depletion or overextension, I pause and evaluate whether I truly have the energy to give the client the full and ethical support they deserve. Recognizing when to say no or reschedule is just as important as scheduling in the first place. It's important to communicate openly with clients about the importance of rest, both for them and for ourselves.

Sustaining the Sacred Work

Self-care is not a luxury—it is a necessity in this work. The emotional and mental demands of psychedelic therapy are real, and without taking care of ourselves, it's easy to burn out or feel disconnected. The tools and practices we've covered here aren't just about protecting our own well-being—they're about ensuring we can continue showing up for our clients in the best possible way.

As guides and therapists, we aren't just doing a job—we're on the journey with our clients. We hold space for their transformation, and in doing so, we're also part of that process. If we want to continue helping others, we must first help ourselves. By checking in with ourselves before each session, setting boundaries, and building resilience, we can create the space to support others without losing ourselves in the process. It's about staying grounded and present, which means we're better equipped to guide our clients through their transformative experiences.

At the end of the day, you and I—all of us—are on this journey together. Taking care of ourselves isn't just for our own benefit—it's for the people we're here to help. The more skillfully we learn to balance our personal and professional lives, the more we can hold that sacred space for others. So, take a deep breath, honor your boundaries, and remember: by caring for yourself, you're contributing to a greater collective strength—one that allows all of us to show up fully for the work that matters most.

12
LIFE BEYOND THE JOURNEY—WHAT'S NEXT?

Whether you are a therapist, guide, DJ, client, journeyer, or recreational psychonaut, you came to this book seeking something—perhaps a spark of inspiration, clarity, or healing. For therapists and guides specifically, you may have been drawn to this material to deepen your understanding of how music can transform the therapeutic process or to gain insight into your own preexisting practices. Whatever brought you here, you've taken a big step toward growth, connection, and discovery. Along the way, I hope you've discovered an essential truth: the support you give and receive—before, during, and after a journey—is just as important, if not more so, than the journey itself.

When your clients began this process, something likely felt out of balance for them. They may have reached out for help to support their own journey or to gain insight into their path. Perhaps they trusted that the therapeutic power of psychedelics, paired with music, could provide clarity, healing, or transformation.

Now that your clients have completed their journey, they may wonder, "What do I do now?" It can be helpful to walk them through their entire process, which began with acknowledging a need for change. This led them to seek your guidance and support as they embarked on an inward journey. Acknowledging the courage it took for them to initiate this journey and enter into the unknown is powerful. Such unbridled strength is worthy of celebration.

Additionally, reflecting on any important revelations your clients experienced as a result of the journey, and how it did or didn't align with their initial intentions, can be supportive. From there, encourage them to consider what they have become aware of or what they are letting go of in light of the new possibilities that now exist beyond the journey.

In addition to these reflections, it's important to help your clients build a supportive network during the integration process. This could be like-minded friends, family, or a support community who understand and respect the powerful journey that has been undertaken. As a professional therapist or guide with training in psychedelic integration or transpersonal therapy, you can also provide ongoing support, though when searching for additional support for your clients, it's crucial to find other professionals who understand the unique nature of these journeys and can help the client process and apply insights with compassion and expertise. Look for individuals with specific training in psychedelic integration or transpersonal approaches, as they will be more equipped to support the nuances of the integration process and any emerging material. Reliable directories such as Psychedelic.Support, Third Wave, Psychedelic Passage, or The Power Path offer vetted therapists, guides, and shamans for ongoing care.

Encourage your clients to engage in self-care practices such as music, meditation, yoga, journaling, exercise, therapy, or spending time in nature to help ground and facilitate the integration process. For continued learning about psychedelic experiences and personal growth, books like *The Psychedelic Explorer's Guide: Safe, Therapeutic, and Sacred Journeys* by James Fadiman, *The Holotropic Mind: The Three Levels of Human Consciousness and How They Shape Our Lives* by Stanislav Grof, and *The Doors of Perception* by Aldous Huxley and documentaries like *Fantastic Fungi* and *How to Change Your Mind* are all highly recommended.

Websites and podcasts such as Psychedelics Today, *Adventures Through the Mind*, and *The Psychedelic Therapy Podcast* offer profound discussions around these substances. Online communities like the Multidisciplinary Association for Psychedelic Studies (MAPS), PsychedeLiA Integration, InnerSpace Integration, NEST Harm Reduction, Spirit Pharmacist, Psychedelic Passage, Psychedelics in Recovery, and Fireside Project provide valuable platforms for education, peer support groups, human connection, and a safe space for psychedelic self-expression.

LIFE BEYOND THE JOURNEY—WHAT'S NEXT?

As your clients reflect on life after the journey, their mind's eye cleansed and the lens of their heart opened, encourage them to reflect on questions such as:

- What has been decomposed and transformed?
- What dreams have surfaced in the wake of this transformation?
- What patterns have been resolved and what new ones have emerged?
- What energy do they carry now that wasn't there before?
- What burdens have they left behind?

With this refreshed sense of being, what can they see and feel that they couldn't before? How will they nurture the seeds of change that have taken root within them? Remind them that the medicine and the music are still with them. They can revisit the musical soundscapes from their journey as tools and companions to help process lingering material, spark new insights, and reconnect them to the moments that mattered most. They can let the music serve as a mirror for their inner world, whether during meditation, yoga, study, a walk in nature, or simply driving through beautiful places.

As they listen, they can allow the music to bring back memories of the person they were before the journey, the revelations that surfaced during the experience, and the growth they have experienced since. From this place of reflection, encourage them to create their own soundtracks—playlists that tell the story of their life through sound. Experiment with pairing these musical storybooks with their daily experiences. Continue falling in love with music and the infinite ways it can connect your clients to themselves, to others, and to the world. Celebrate music as medicine and let the amplifying effects of psychedelics remind them that all they've ever needed has always resided within them.

Just as seeds take time to grow and flourish, remind your clients that their journey is not a single event but an ongoing process of nurturing and tending to the inner garden they've cultivated. Each revelation, like a chapter in the Hero's Journey, marks a step in their personal evolution, leading them toward wholeness and transformation.

Whether you are integrating your own journey or helping someone else integrate theirs, these questions remain the same at their core: they invite us to reflect, to notice, and to honor the seeds of change that have taken root.

It is just as crucial to emphasize to your clients, however, that psychedelics are not a cure or a quick fix. Excessive use of psychedelics can result in unexpected outcomes such as unwanted disintegration instead of integration, a God complex, paranoia, psychosis, or the misguided belief that just one more psychedelic journey will provide the solution to problems that are often best addressed without the use of such substances. For those who experience psychosis or other forms of disintegration following a psychedelic experience, Marc Aixalà's book *Psychedelic Integration* offers valuable insights and guidance for navigating these challenges.

The essential work of integration between journeys is crucial to avoid any unexpected outcomes. Encourage your clients to be patient with their integration process and to take time tending to their inner garden. If, after some time, they feel the need to explore something deeper or keep coming up against old material, it may be a good time to revisit the process of safe psychedelic journeywork.

To the Guides, Witnesses, and DJs

To the guides reading this, I hope something within these pages has resonated with you and can be applied to your practice. Here are a few questions to reflect on:

- What have you learned about yourself as a guide, and how will you carry that forward?
- What insights did this material reveal about how you hold space for others?
- How has this information expanded your understanding of music as a therapeutic tool?
- What patterns or techniques can you refine or evolve in your practice?
- How can you continue to cultivate safety, trust, and growth in the spaces you create?

Adapt what works to your unique style and approach, and continue evolving your craft. The work we do is a profound honor—serving each soul who entrusts us to assist them on their journey is an extraordinary privilege.

Be grateful for the opportunity to help others navigate the mysteries of life and the psychedelic experience. Whether you find your strength in the guidance of a higher power, the universe, or simply the love and commitment you bring to your practice, honor the gift of this work. Together, we are part of something truly transformative for humanity.

As you incorporate music more deeply into your practice, let it continue to be a powerful tool for healing. Encourage your clients to collect, savor, and weave music into the fabric of their lives. Use music to complement their joys, challenges, and moments of awe. Help them dive deep into the sounds they love, allowing those vibrations to inspire a sense of home and well-being.

Celebrate the artists who give voice to the inexpressible and create soundtracks that accompany the most profound experiences. Use their work to fuel creativity, crafting soundscapes that tell the story of each client's journey. Keep discovering, keep creating, and above all, keep listening.

To those who use music in all settings, recognize the art of curating and blending sounds as a sacred act. This unique and beautiful form of therapy connects people to themselves and to each other. Continue experimenting, collecting, and presenting the incredible work of your favorite composers and musicians. Let their dedication inspire you to push boundaries and fearlessly create. There's magic in discovering the perfect track for a moment and sharing that joy. Keep chasing that magic, and honor the artists who make it all possible.

Stay in love with the therapeutic power of music. Keep digging, blending, and celebrating the sounds that remind us what it means to be alive.

Looking Ahead

As your clients reflect on their experience and begin to integrate its lessons, they may naturally wonder about what lies ahead. It's essential to guide them toward their next phase with intention and patience. As for the next journey, let the moment decide. Encourage your clients to use their refreshed awareness to stay connected to the present. Advise them to pay attention to the emerging material within—the emotions, memories, and longings that now have space to receive attention. Guide them to tend to their inner garden with care, watering the seeds of growth and addressing the needs of their ecosystem.

You might want to share the timeless wisdom of renowned researcher Myron Stolaroff with your clients as they consider future journeys:

Individuals vary greatly in their frequency of use of these materials. Some are satisfied with an overwhelming experience which they feel is good for a lifetime. Others wish to renew their acquaintance with these areas once or twice a year. Still others are interested in frequent explorations to continually push their knowledge forward. Regardless of the frequency, it is wise to make sure that the previous experience has been well integrated before embarking on the next one. Early in one's contact with these substances, where there is a wealth of new experience, this may take several months. As one becomes more experienced, the integration time grows shorter, and the interval between trials may be shortened.[1]

Allow the dust to settle and give the seeds of change time to grow before revisiting the process. Encourage them to address and change what they can with the new tools they've rediscovered or developed, and to stay attentive to emerging material as it arises within them.

The journey of self-awareness through self-discovery and healing is a lifelong process. Each step, each revelation, and each moment of clarity is part of the beautiful tapestry of life. Part of this tapestry are the supportive gifts of medicine, music, and therapy, which help us remember who we truly are. These unique tools, specifically in combination with one another, have the potential to provide immense healing and celebrate the human capacity for growth and transformation.

Thank you for taking this journey with me. May your path be filled with healing, inspiration, and self-discovery.

ACKNOWLEDGMENTS

First and foremost, I want to express my deep gratitude to all the journeyers and nonpsychedelic clients I've had the privilege of working with throughout my career. It's been an honor to assist them through life's various challenges and victories. Each journey is an opportunity to grow alongside my clients both personally and professionally. I would like to specifically acknowledge those whose presence in sessions played a crucial role in the development of this therapeutic guidebook and its associated music protocols. To all of you, I extend my eternal gratitude for allowing me the opportunity to guide you on your incredible journeys.

Most importantly, I wish to express my profound gratitude to my wife, Destiny. Her limitless love, patience, and guidance have been invaluable throughout this journey. Her extraordinary capacity to love, laugh, dance, hold space, and comprehend my expansive existence often leaves me speechless. I could not have asked for a better partner, companion, colleague, lover, and friend to stand at my side through it all. I also extend my heartfelt thanks to her parents, Jim and Rosie, for their warmth, love, and acceptance into their family.

My late father, Captain Richard, a brilliant man of sweetness and wit, instilled in me his love for the written word and continually inspired me to become the published author he aspired to be. My mother, Marjorie, merits special acknowledgment for her love and support, unwavering devotion to God, her nurturing nature as a registered nurse, and for imparting the importance of service, faith, and resilience in the face of life's challenges.

Thanks also to my brother, Michael, whose generous sharing of his innate musical talent and theoretical knowledge has significantly shaped the way I hear music and the career path I have taken. My sister, Danielle, who has been a guiding light both spiritually and practically since our paths crossed on the day she was born, has consistently aided me in better expressing myself through music, writing, and the therapeutic arts. The value of Danielle's crucial contribution to the refinement of my message and her assistance in telling my story to the world is immeasurable.

My heart brims with joy for my nieces and nephew—Carson, Cassidy, Farren, Soleil, and Cahlil. I hold them dear to my heart and derive immense joy from watching their extraordinary journeys unfold. I harbor the hope that the insights shared in this book may prove beneficial to them someday.

My Aunt Eileen, my mother's twin, deserves special recognition for the years of wisdom she imparted and the spiritual guidance she provided during my transition from a wildly fiery adolescent to a responsible, grounded young man. I am also grateful to my in-laws, Randall, Benny, Justin, Willma, and Doug, for the warm welcome into their family; they embraced me with love and acceptance from our first meeting.

I'd like to especially mention my mentors in Gestalt therapy: Dr. Allen Berger, Armin Baier, LCSW, and Roger Andes, whose wisdom, guidance, and professional support over the past 15 years have been instrumental in shaping my understanding of the human psyche and the potential for transformation through the practice of Reichian, classic, and relational Gestalt therapy. I am deeply grateful for the increased awareness I've gained as a result of my mentorship with them.

I am deeply grateful to Dr. Joseph Barsuglia and Dr. Jenna Abell, two pivotal figures in my journey. Their unwavering belief in my potential and early guidance gave me the confidence to develop the practice and protocols in this book. In a field that can often feel isolating, they provided essential support and camaraderie, helping me navigate uncharted territory, refine my approach, and trust my path. Their encouragement inspired me to teach others about my work with music and psychedelics and share my approach through writing. I consider them trusted allies who encouraged me to push beyond my limits into this transformative work.

ACKNOWLEDGMENTS

Many thanks to mentors, friends, colleagues, and fellow psychonauts in the Los Angeles psychedelic community who have shared their personal and professional expertise within the realm of psychedelic therapy. Their bold efforts to establish some of the first public psychedelic integration and harm-reduction support groups helped illuminate the transformative power of these experiences and inspired me to reengage with the world of psychedelics through a more intentional and therapeutic lens. I am especially grateful to Erica S, Shiri G, Skye W, Greg L, John S, Sel S, Ashley B, Bear G, Erica H, Tara R, Raph Q, Jay S, and many others for their support, guidance, and camaraderie as I navigated my return to this fascinating field of psychedelics.

I must also express gratitude to my chosen family, the extraordinary people I am privileged to call friends. Their companionship has significantly enriched my life experience. A special shout out to Sean DeGaray who generously sponsored my counseling education at a time when I needed it the most. His support has inevitably left a lasting impact on the thousands of clients I have assisted over the past 15 years.

I would also like to extend my deepest appreciation to Rob O, Chris C, Ben W, Diana D, Brian T, Alex K, Eli M, Phil Y, Carlo S, Joe C, Joe D, Brian S, Michael M, Eduardo and Manu L, Trevor W, Petey, Treavor W, Brad and Beatrice, Brian and Heather G, Amani F, Jill and Keith, Mesa M, Nicole F, Suni F, Ravel F, Erin D, Lauren S, Lucy & Hein H, Anne S, Andre E, Tressa and Hatem D, Sage G, Brad G, Charlie and Cat M, Jessica S, Alex G, Courtney W, Justin Scott D, Reagan D, Joel M and Linda, Cari L and Miia, James and Cynthia B, Jenna and Anthony S, Chris M and Oona D, Justin H and Taylor E, Parker A, DJ and Candace S, Byron M, Little DJ and Keely, Grant Q, Daryck T, Rhonda, The Sourcerer, CMH, and the entire Psychedelic Love Brigade family. Each of you has brought unique wisdom and presence into my life, and for that, I am eternally grateful.

In the realm of DJing, I owe a great deal to the vibrant, creative, and fearless community of national and international electronic music DJs and producers. Their knowledge and passion for electronic music inspired me to dive deep into the vast universe of psychedelic electronic music. I extend special thanks to such New York City and North American DJing

THE PSYCHEDELIC DJ

pioneers as Frankie Bones, Adam X, Jimmy Crash, Heather Heart, Reade Truth, Micro, Dave Trance, Jason Jinx, Mr. Kleen, Soul Slinger, Josh Wink, Danny Tenaglia, and the entire West Coast Moontribe family. I also want to acknowledge the invaluable contributions of event promoters and organizations like Dennis the Menace, Eddie Van Raven, Storm Rave, Scotto, NASA, The Shelter, Alan Sanctuary, Caffeine, Voodoo, Liquid Sky, Limelight, Disco 2000, Sound Factory, Twilo, Essence, Drop Bass Network, and Under One Sky, whose efforts helped shape the early '90s North American underground electronic culture. Their innovative techniques and unwavering dedication have been instrumental in the development of the DJ world and the community that surrounded it.

I've always harbored a dream to express my gratitude to at least a handful of the revolutionary artists who have shaped my musical tastes. Their relentless dedication to crafting such extraordinary pieces of music has forever altered the course of my life. For the music enthusiasts and vinyl aficionados reading this, I'd like to specifically acknowledge a few artists, in order of their appearance in my life: Mozart, Beethoven, the Beatles, Fleetwood Mac, the Doors, Run DMC, Beastie Boys, Eric B & Rakim, Epmd, Gangstarr, Special ED, Slick Rick, LL Cool J, Fatboys, Guns N' Roses, Def Leppard, A Tribe Called Quest, De La Soul, Digable Planets, Nice & Smooth, Digital Underground, Brand Nubian, NWA, Dr. Dre, Ice-T, Ice Cube, Snoop Dogg, Pink Floyd, Jimi Hendrix, Cream, Led Zeppelin, Bob Marley, Nine Inch Nails, Ministry, Utah Saints, Frankie Bones, Adam X, Joey Beltram, the Future Sound of London, Orbital, Moby, Vapourspace, Aphex Twin, The Orb, Plastikman, Richie Hawtin, Cari Lekebusch, Braincell, Fred, Joel Mull, Adam Beyer, Jesper Dahlbäck, Robert Leiner, Source Experience, The Advent, Luke Slater, Speedy J, R&S Records, Sven Väth, Harthouse Records, Resistance D, Union Jack, Art of Trance, Casper Pound, Rising High Records, Mixmaster Morris, Irresistible Force, Pete Namlook, Brian Eno, Tangerine Dream, Syzygy, James Bernard, Influx, Air Liquide, Jam & Spoon, Dubtribe Soundsystem, Higher Intelligence Agency, Spacetime Continuum, Rabbit in the Moon, DJ Three, Hardkiss Brothers, Freaky Chakra, Single Cell Orchestra, Soul Oddity, Simon Posford, Hallucinogen, Man With No Name, X-Dream,

ACKNOWLEDGMENTS

James Monro, Slinky Wizard, Total Eclipse, Transwave, Deedrah, Koxbox, Psychopod, Ian Ion, The Infinity Project, Celtic Cross, Shpongle, Raja Ram, Doof, Tristan, Electric Universe, Galaxy, Spectral, Eat Static, Vibrasphere, Cwithe, Metal Spark, Sibilant, Son Kite, Minilouge, Saafi Brothers, Flying Rhino Records, Blue Room Records, TIP Records, Tom Middleton, Jedi Knights, Global Communication, Oliver Lieb, LSG, Spicelab, Sasha & Digweed, Charlie May, Spooky, William Orbit, Underworld, Mr. C, Junkie XL, Red Jerry, Hooj Choons, Blackwatch, Voyager, John Graham, Andy Page, Lee Burridge, Luke Chable, James Holden, Chicane, Desert Dwellers, Liquid Bloom, Synkro, Burial, Jon Hopkins, Donato Dozzy, Lawrence, Tipper, Seba, Calyx, Teebee, Noisia, Tycho, Melorman, Purl, Yagya, Deepchord, Carbon Based Lifeforms, Detroit Escalator Co., Primal Code, awakened souls, marine eyes, Poemme, Helios, Halftribe, Tylepathy, Waveform Transmission, Sébastien Léger, Roy Rosenfeld, and Gelka, to name just a few. And the list goes on and on . . .

Last but certainly not least, I would like to close this book by expressing my deepest gratitude to the team of dedicated artists and professionals who helped bring this book to life.

A profound thank you to Danielle Polgar for her invaluable help in organizing my thoughts and notes, laying the foundation for the first draft of the manuscript. To Doug Reil, my publishing consultant, for his enthusiasm, guidance, developmental feedback, and generous professional referrals from the moment we met. To Noelle Armstrong, whose developmental editing raised important questions that sharpened the book's focus and expanded its potential. To Allison Felus, for her meticulous copyediting and essential coaching support, which carried me through the final, most chaotic stages of this project.

To Ruby Warrington, Donnel McLohon, and Chris Williams at Numinous for their expertise in transforming this manuscript into a tangible book. To my graphic designer and "human paintbrush," Myck Stewart, whose ability to translate my concepts into stunning visual storytelling—both for this project and my broader brand—has been nothing short of extraordinary. To Brad Burge, for believing in this project and offering his vast expertise in public relations and media management.

To my longtime friend and Chief of Staff, Trevor Wyse, whose support and creative consultation—throughout the process of writing this book and in life—have been invaluable.

To all mentioned here, I extend my heartfelt thanks for your invaluable contributions to my life and practice. Your inspiration, support, and friendships are an ongoing blessing, and I look forward to many more years of shared experiences and growth.

APPENDIX: AUDIO PROTOCOLS, QR CODE, RESOURCES, AND INSTRUCTIONS

If you've made it this far, thank you for taking the time to read this book. I hope you've found the information useful. Whether you're here to listen to the DJ mix while reading, to reference it for your own sessions, or to integrate these protocols into your personal or professional journeywork—welcome.

These DJ mixes are carefully curated to support psilocybin-assisted therapy, providing an auditory experience that enhances the depth and flow of psychedelic journeys. Whether you're exploring on your own, guiding clients, or using the audio for reference or educational purposes, this section ensures you have everything set up for an optimal listening experience.

Important Notice: Reference Use and Artist Support
These DJ mix protocols are for promotional and reference use only. By accessing them, you agree to support the featured artists by purchasing their music or donating directly to their work via their Bandcamp pages, personal websites, record labels, or other legal downloading sources. More information is available via the QR code.

For a deeper discussion on the importance of purchasing music versus streaming, refer to the "Sustainability: Purchasing Music Versus Streaming" section in chapter 9. Supporting artists financially is essential, especially when you are using their music in personal, client-based, or public psychedelic journeys. They've more than earned it!

THE PSYCHEDELIC DJ

Accessing the DJ Mixes and Resources

To access all related audio links and additional information about the artists, record labels, and other resources mentioned in this book, scan the QR code or visit https://integratedpsychedelics.com/book.

About the DJ Mixes

Each four-hour DJ mix has been curated live in a real session. The pacing reflects the common qualities of the first four stages of a psilocybin journey, following the mountain expedition metaphor outlined in chapter 7, "Stages of a Mushroom Journey."

Each mix includes a five-minute bathroom and booster dose window between 55 and 60 minutes, marked by underwater sounds—a natural cue to take that break or booster dose if needed. If more time is required, simply pause or rewind to the start of the water sounds before resuming the ascent. (Though, please note, this is the only planned break accounted for in the mix.) The priority is always comfort, flow, and alignment with the journeyer's rhythm—there's no need to rush or perfectly sync with the music. The goal is a seamless yet adaptable experience suited to the unique session's needs.

These mixes serve as guides, not rigid prescriptions—adjust them as necessary based on the journeyer and the session context.

APPENDIX

Session Timeline

This basic timeline is also available in the "Behind This Track" section on the SoundCloud app or in the "Show More" section on the desktop browser version. Each stage is also timestamped in the comments of the waveform file.

- Trailhead (0-10 mins): Consume medicine, start music, breathwork/meditation
- Stage 1 (10-55 mins): Hike (Onset)
- Basecamp (55-60 mins): Bathroom and optional booster break (play water sounds, pause, or continue as needed)
- Stage 2 (60-150 mins): The Climb (Ascent)
- Stage 3 (150-180 mins): The Summit (Peak)
- Stage 4 (180-240 mins): The Return (Descent)
- End of Mix: Music optional

Playback Setup

Smartphone Setup: SoundCloud App Playback

If streaming via the SoundCloud app, follow these steps for the best experience:

1. Download the SoundCloud app from your smartphone's app store.
2. Create an account and subscribe to a premium plan to remove ads, enable offline playback, and improve audio quality.
3. Open the QR code link or manually enter the URL to access the DJ mix.
4. Like or save the mix in your account for easy access.
5. Download the mix in the app for offline listening to avoid Wi-Fi or cell signal issues.
6. Close all other apps and activate Airplane Mode and Do Not Disturb to prevent interruptions.

Smartphone Setup: Playing the File Directly from Your Library

If you have downloaded the mix as an audio file, play it directly from your phone's library:

1. Transfer the file to your smartphone using iTunes (iPhone) or a file manager app (Android).

2. Import the file into your preferred music player (Apple Music, VLC, or any high-quality audio player).
3. Create a dedicated playlist to ensure uninterrupted playback.
4. Close unnecessary apps and enable Airplane Mode and Do Not Disturb to prevent notifications.

Laptop Setup

For playback via laptop:
1. Open the QR code link or visit SoundCloud directly.
2. Sign in and subscribe to remove ads.
3. Download the audio file (if available) for offline listening.
4. Add the file to iTunes, VLC, or another media player and create a dedicated playlist.
5. Close unnecessary apps and enable Do Not Disturb for uninterrupted playback.

Prelaunch: Sound Test and Connectivity

Check Device and Sound System
- Ensure your device is properly connected to the sound system.
- Test playback before starting the session.

Adjust Volume for an Optimal Experience
- Set the maximum volume based on the loudest part of the mix.
- The volume should be immersive—engaging but not overwhelming.
- For left/right stereo setups, an ideal range is 50 to 70 decibels (use a dB meter app to measure).
- Refer to chapter 8, "Psychedelic Audio Presentation—A Technical Guide to Journey Space Setup," for details.

Maintain Quick Access to Volume Control
- Keep volume controls easily accessible for real-time adjustments.
- The goal is to maintain an immersive yet supportive auditory space.

Additional Applications

Though designed for psilocybin-assisted therapy, these mixes can also be adapted for other four- to six-hour psychedelic sessions, including MDMA, MDA, and 2C-B.

Future protocols will be available via the QR code—stay connected for updates.

With your sound system set up and your DJ mix ready, you're now prepared to explore the role of music in psilocybin-assisted therapy and beyond. Whether you're listening, guiding, or facilitating, these protocols support a transformative, immersive, and educational sonic journey.

Enjoy the trip!

NOTES

Ethics and Training in Psychedelic Therapy
1. "Code of Ethics for Spiritual Guides," Spiritual Development, Council on Spiritual Practices, accessed February 28, 2025, https://csp.org/docs/code-of-ethics-for-spiritual-guides; "MAPS MDMA-Assisted Therapy Code of Ethics," *MAPS Bulletin*, Spring 2019: Vol 29, No. 1, https://maps.org/news/bulletin/maps-mdma-assisted-psychotherapy-code-of-ethics-spring-2019/; "5-MEO-DMT: A Recommended Model for Best Practices," Version 9.1, The Conclave, December 7, 2024, https://theconclave.info.

Chapter 1
1. David Huron, "Why is sad music pleasurable? A possible role for prolactin," *Musicae Scientiae* 15, no 2 (July 2011): 146–158, https://doi.org/10.1177/1029864911401171; Robert J. Zatorre and Valorie N. Salimpoor, "From perception to pleasure: Music and its neural substrates," *Proceedings of the National Academy of Sciences* 110, no. 2 (June 18, 2013): 10430–10437, https://www.pnas.org/doi/pdf/10.1073/pnas.1301228110.
2. "Why the Brain Seeks Out Sadness in Music," Integris Health, August 19, 2024, https://integrishealth.org/resources/on-your-health/2024/august/why-the-brain-seeks-out-sadness-in-music; David Nield, "Here's Why Listening to Sad Music Makes You Feel Better," ScienceAlert, June 16, 2016, https://www.sciencealert.com/new-research-reveals-the-pain-and-pleasure-of-listening-to-sad-music;

Simon McCarthy-Jones, "Why Sad Songs Make Us Feel Good," Neuroscience News, November 17, 2021, https://neurosciencenews.com/sad-song-psychology-19673/; Leigh Riby, "How music heals us, even when it's sad," Northumbria University Newcastle, https://www.northumbria.ac.uk/about-us/news-events/news/expert-comment-how-music-heals-us/.

Chapter 2

1. Giorgio Samorini, "The oldest archeological data evidencing the relationship of *Homo sapiens* with psychoactive plants: A worldwide overview," *Journal of Psychedelic Studies* 3, no. 2: 63–80, https://doi.org/10.1556/2054.2019.008.
2. "Magic mushrooms may have been used in Japan since Jomon times," *Heritage of Japan*, November 5, 2014, https://heritageofjapan.wordpress.com/2014/11/05/8816/.
3. "Psilocybin Mushrooms: Basic Info," Other Plants & Fungi, Info & Support, ICEERS, accessed February 28, 2025, https://www.iceers.org/psilocybin-mushrooms-basic-info/.
4. Osiris González Romero, "Ritual and Religious Uses of Psilocybe Mushrooms in Mesoamerica," Harvard Divinity School, News, October 9, 2024, https://cswr.hds.harvard.edu/news/2024/10/ritual-and-religious-uses-psilocybe-mushrooms-mesoamerica.
5. "Psilocybin Mushrooms," ICEERS.
6. Gastón Guzmán, "Species Diversity of the Genus Psilocybe (Basidiomycotina, Agaricales, Strophariaceae) in the World Mycobiota, with Special Attention to Hallucinogenic Properties," *International Journal of Medicinal Mushrooms* 7, no. 1 & 2: 305–332, http://dx.doi.org/10.1615/IntJMedMushr.v7.i12.280.
7. Justin Cooke, "Magic Mushroom Strain Guide (100+ Strains Explained)," Tripsitter, November 14, 2024, https://tripsitter.com/magic-mushrooms/strains/.
8. "Psilocybin Mushrooms," ICEERS.
9. Dominique Strauss, Soumya Ghosh, Zurika Murray, Marieka Gryzenhout, "An Overview on the Taxonomy, Phylogenetics, and

Ecology of the Psychedelic Genera *Psilocybe, Panaeolus, Pluteus* and *Gymnopilus,*" *Frontiers in Forests and Global Change* 5 (2022): https://doi.org/10.3389/ffgc.2022.813998.

10. *Britannica*, "Psilocybin Mushroom," last updated August 22, 2024, https://www.britannica.com/science/psilocybin-mushroom.

11. Strauss et al, "An Overview."

12. Huu H. Tran and Andrew L. Juergens, "Mushroom Toxicity," National Library of Medicine, StatPearls Publishing, last updated August 7, 2023, https://www.ncbi.nlm.nih.gov/books/NBK537111/.

13. Hernando de Alvarado Tezozómoc, *Crónica Mexicana* (Imprenta Y Litografia de Ireneo Paz, 1878), https://archive.org/details/cronicamexicana00alvaiala/page/n7/mode/2up.

14. Bernardino de Sahagún, *General History of the Things of New Spain: The Florentine Codex*. trans. and ed. Arthur J. O. Anderson and Charles E. Dibble, 12 vols (School of American Research and the University of Utah, 1950–1982), https://archive.org/details/generalhistoryof0000bern/page/n9/mode/2up.

15. Romero, "Ritual and Religious Uses."

16. Richard Evans Schultes, "Plantae Mexicanae II," *Botanical Museum Leaflets, Harvard University* 7, no 3 (February 21, 1939): 37–56, https://www.samorini.it/doc1/alt_aut/sz/schultes-identification-of-teonanacatl.pdf.

17. R. Gordon Wasson, "Seeking the Magic Mushroom," *LIFE* Magazine, May 13, 1957, https://archive.org/details/bub_gb_Jj8EAAAAMBAJ/page/n101/mode/2up.

18. "Psychedelic Research and Psilocybin Therapy Studies," Johns Hopkins Medicine, Psychiatry and Behavioral Sciences, accessed February 28, 2025, https://www.hopkinsmedicine.org/psychiatry/research/psychedelics-research.

19. "Psychedelic Research," Johns Hopkins.

20. Albert Garcia-Romeu, Roland R. Griffiths, and Matthew W. Johnson, "Psilocybin-Occasioned Mystical Experiences in the Treatment of Tobacco Addiction," *Current Drug Abuse Reviews* 7, no. 3 (2014): 157–164, http://dx.doi.org/10.2174/1874473708666150107121331;

Roland R. Griffiths et al, "Psilocybin produces substantial and sustained decreases in depression and anxiety in patients with life-threatening cancer: A randomized double-blind trial," *Journal of Psychopharmacology* 30, no. 12 (November 2016): 1181–1197, https://doi.org/10.1177/0269881116675513.

21. "Psychedelic Research," Johns Hopkins.
22. "Psychedelic and Dissociative Drugs as Medicines," National Institute on Drug Abuse, Research Topics, last modified January 2024, https://nida.nih.gov/research-topics/psychedelic-dissociative-drugs-medicines.
23. Álvaro Estrada, *María Sabina: Her Life and Chants* (Ross-Erikson, 1981); Andy Letcher, *Shroom: A Cultural History of the Magic Mushroom* (Harper Perennial, 2007).
24. Letcher, *Shroom*; Estrada, *María Sabina*.
25. Eric Blair-Joannou, "Drum (Teponaztli)," The Metropolitan Museum of Art, The Michael C. Rockefeller Wing, 2020, https://www.metmuseum.org/art/collection/search/312583; Arnd Adje Both, "Aztec Flower-Flutes: The Symbolic Organization of Sound in Late Postclassic Mesoamerica," https://www.mixcoacalli.com/wp-content/uploads/2007/07/both_2002.PDF.
26. María Sabina, *Mushroom Ceremony of the Mazatec Indians of Mexico*, recorded by V. P. and R. G. Wasson, July 21, 1956, Folkways Records FW08975, FR 8975, 1957, https://folkways.si.edu/maria-sabina/mushroom-ceremony-of-the-mazatec-indians-of-mexico/american-indian-sacred/music/album/smithsonian.
27. F. J. Carod-Artal, "Hallucinogenic Drugs in Pre-Columbian Mesoamerican Cultures," *Neurología* 30, no. 1 (2015): 42–49, https://doi.org/10.1016/j.nrl.2011.07.003.
28. Peter T. Furst, *Hallucinogens and Culture* (University of California Press, 1976).
29. Åke Hultkrantz, "The Drum in Shamanism: Some Reflections," *Scripta Instituti Donneriani Aboensis* 14 (January 1991), https://doi.org/10.30674/scripta.67194.
30. Heather Beltz, "The Power of Sound: Music and Magic in Pre-Christian

Irish Folklore," (master's thesis, Texas Tech University, 2017), https://ttu-ir.tdl.org/server/api/core/bitstreams/e1157f1f-8166-456e-825d-b4bcb7681f69/content; Letcher, *Shroom*.
31. Helen L. Bonny and Walter N. Pahnke, "The Use of Music in Psychedelic (LSD) Psychotherapy," *Journal of Music Therapy* 9, no. 2 (Summer 1972): 64–87, https://doi.org/10.1093/jmt/9.2.64; "Bill Richards: Psychedelic Therapy and the Perfect Psilocybin Playlist," Beatrice Society, accessed February 28, 2025, https://beatricesociety.com/bill-richards-psychedelic-therapy-and-the-perfect-psilocybin-playlist/.
32. Francesa Sciandra, "Music for Psychedelic Therapy: How to Create a Trip Playlist," Blog, May 9, 2024, https://francescasciandra.com/blog/music-for-psychedelic-therapy-how-to-create-a-trip-playlist.
33. Marc Shapiro, "Inside the Johns Hopkins Psilocybin Playlist," Johns Hopkins Medicine, News & Publications, October 30, 2020, https://www.hopkinsmedicine.org/news/articles/2020/10/inside-the-johns-hopkins-psilocybin-playlist.
34. Ryan O'Hare, "Magic mushroom compound performs as well as antidepressant in small study," Imperial College London, April 14, 2021, https://www.imperial.ac.uk/news/219413/magic-mushroom-compound-performs-well-antidepressant/.
35. Raluca Bilaşco Rusu, "The Role of Music in Psychedelic Therapy: A Review," December 2023, https://researchgate.net/publication/376893781_The_Role_of_Music_in_Psychedelic_Therapy.
36. Mendel Kaelen et al., "The hidden therapist: evidence for a central role of music in psychedelic therapy," *Psychopharmacology* 235, no. 2 (2018): 505–519, https://doi.org/10.1007/s00213-017-4820-5.

Chapter 3

1. "Rewind: Richie Hawtin—Decks, EFX & 909," Resident Advisor, Features, accessed February 28, 2025, https://ra.co/features/4422.
2. "Common Tempo Markings in Music," The Online Metronome, Blog, accessed February 28, 2025, https://theonlinemetronome.com/blogs/12/tempo-markings-defined.
3. L. Bernardi, C. Porto, and P. Sleight, "Cardiovascular, cerebrovascular,

and respiratory changes induced by different types of music in musicians and non-musicians: the importance of silence," *Heart* 92 (2006): 445–452, https://doi.org/10.1136/hrt.2005.064600; P. Gomez and B. Danuser, "Relationships between musical structure and psychophysiological measures of emotion," *Emotion* 7, no. 2 (2007): 377–387, https://doi.org/10.1037/1528-3542.7.2.377.

4. Joe Muggs, "How Richie Hawtin Transformed Electronic Music Again and Again and Again," *Mixmag*, July 3, 2019, https://mixmag.net/feature/richie-hawtin-mixmag-cover-feature-interview-2019; Declan McGlynn, "Richie Hawtin: Techno's Future-Focused Pioneer," *DJ Mag*, June 17, 2019, https://djmag.com/longreads/richie-hawtin-techno%E2%80%99s-future-focused-pioneer.

5. "Why Sasha & Digweed's 'Renaissance: The Mix Collection' is one of the best mix albums of all time," 909originals, October 14, 2020, https://909originals.com/2020/10/14/sasha-digweeds-renaissance/; Yakov Vorobyev and Eric Coomes, "DJ Sasha: How to Establish a Unique Sound," in *Beyond Beatmatching: Take Your DJ Career to the Next Level* (Mixed in Key, 2012), accessed online February 28, 2025, https://mixedinkey.com/book/find-and-play-unique-tracks/.

Chapter 4

1. Joachim Neumann et al, "Effects of Hallucinogenic Drugs on the Human Heart," *Frontiers in Pharmacology* 15 (2024), https://doi.org/10.3389/fphar.2024.1334218.

2. Agnieszka Wsół, "Cardiovascular safety of psychedelic medicine: current status and future directions," *Pharmacological Reports* 75 (2023): 1362–1380, https://doi.org/10.1007/s43440-023-00539-4.

3. Michael P. Bogenschutz et al, "Percentage of Heavy Drinking Days Following Psilocybin-Assisted Psychotherapy vs Placebo in the Treatment of Adult Patients with Alcohol Use Disorder," *JAMA Psychiatry* 79, no. 10 (2022): 953–962, https://doi.org/10.1001/jamapsychiatry.2022.2096.

4. Guy M. Goodwin et al, "Single-Dose Psilocybin for a Treatment-Resistant Episode of Major Depression," *The New England Journal*

of Medicine 387, no. 18 (November 3, 2022): 1637–1648, https://doi.org/10.1056/nejmoa2206443; Roland R. Griffiths et al, "Psilocybin produces substantial and sustained decreases in depression and anxiety in patients with life-threatening cancer: A randomized double-blind trial," *Journal of Psychopharmacology* 30, no. 12 (2016): 1181–1197, https://doi.org/10.1177/0269881116675513; Edward Jacobs, "A potential role for psilocybin in the treatment of obsessive-compulsive disorder," *Journal of Psychedelic Studies* 4, no. 2 (2020): 77–87, https://doi.org/10.1556/2054.2020.00128; S. Bhanot et al, "A systematic review to assess the use of psilocybin in the treatment of headaches," *European Psychiatry* 66, special issue S1 (March 2023): S617–S618, https://doi.org/10.1192/j.eurpsy.2023.1286.

5. The Oregon Psilocybin Evidence Review Writing Group, "Oregon Psilocybin Advisory Board Rapid Evidence Review and Recommendations," July 30, 2021, https://www.oregon.gov/oha/PH/PREVENTIONWELLNESS/Documents/Psilocybin%20evidence%20report%20to%20OHA%206-30-21_Submitted.pdf

6. R. R. Griffiths et al, "Psilocybin can occasion mystical-type experiences having substantial and sustained personal meaning and spiritual significance," *Psychopharmacology* 187 (2006): 268–283, https://doi.org/10.1007/s00213-006-0457-5.

7. Kathleen Davis, FNP, "Psilocybin (magic mushrooms): What it is, effects and risks," Medical News Today, October 31, 2023, https://www.medicalnewstoday.com/articles/308850.

8. "Shroom & Magic Truffles Dosage Calculator," Zamnesia, Shroom Shop, accessed February 28, 2025, https://zamnesia.com/us/magic-mushroom-dosage-calculator; "Mushroom Dosage Calculator," Mushly, accessed February 28, 2025, https://mushly.com/dosage-calculator.

9. Myron Stolaroff, "Using Psychedelics Wisely," GNOSIS 26 (Winter 1993), http://www.psychonautdocs.com/docs/stolaroff_using.htm.

Chapter 5

1. "Psychedelic Research," Johns Hopkins; Rachel Yehuda and Amy Lehrner, "Psychedelic Therapy—A New Paradigm of Care for Mental

Health," *JAMA* 330, no. 9 (2023): 813–814, http://dx.doi.org/10.1001/jama.2023.12900; Gregory S. Barber and Scott T. Aaronson, "The Emerging Field of Psychedelic Psychotherapy," *Current Psychiatry Reports* 24 (2022): 583–590, https://doi.org/10.1007/s11920-022-01363-y.
2. Spirit Pharmacist, https://spiritpharmacist.com.

Chapter 6

1. Stacey L. L. Couch, "Calling the Directions and The Medicine Wheel," Wild Gratitude, September 22, 2013, https://www.wildgratitude.com/medicine-wheel/.
2. Sandra Ingerman, "A Ceremony to Greet the Cardinal Directions," Sounds True, Blog, January 3, 2019, https://resources.soundstrue.com/blog/a-ceremony-to-greet-the-cardinal-directions/; "The Ancient Roots of Psychedelics in Religious Ceremonies," Sacred Sacraments, Blog, November 24, 2023, https://www.sacredsacraments.org/post/the-ancient-roots-of-psychedelics-in-religious-ceremonies; "Liturgy of the Ancient Celtic Church," The Ancient Celtic Church—Alt-Keltische Kirche, Faith & Spirituality, accessed February 28, 2025, https://www.alt-keltische-kirche.de/en-gb/our-liturgy.
3. Matthew M. Nour et al, "Ego-Dissolution and Psychedelics: Validation of the Ego-Dissolution Inventory (EDI)," *Frontiers in Human Neuroscience* 10 (2016), https://doi.org/10.3389/fnhum.2016.00269; Frederick S. Barrett et al, "Psilocybin acutely alters the functional connectivity of the claustrum with brain networks that support perception, memory, and attention," *NeuroImage* 218 (September 2020), https://doi.org/10.1016/j.neuroimage.2020.116980.
4. Sara Gael, MA, "Understanding and Working with Difficult Psychedelic Experiences," Global Drug Survey, 2017, https://www.globaldrugsurvey.com/past-findings/gds2017-launch/understanding-and-%20working-with-difficult-psychedelic-experiences/.

Chapter 9

1. Tom Newman, "How much music streaming services pay per stream in 2025," RouteNote Blog, February 18, 2025, https://routenote.com/

blog/how-much-music-streaming-services-pay/; Oksana, "How Much Streaming Services Pay Artists in 2024," LALAL.AI, Blog, April 9, 2024, https://www.lalal.ai/blog/how-much-streaming-services-pay-artists-in-2024/.
2. Harry Jackson, "Streaming Royalties & Pay Outs for Every Platform," Whipped Cream Sounds, Best Music Distribution, Streaming Services, February 2, 2023, https://www.whippedcreamsounds.com/streaming-royalties-pay-outs-for-every-platform/.
3. Mikayla Howard, "Tuned Out: Exploring Music Streaming Services' Unfair Compensation Practices," The Ohio State University, Moritz College of Law, OSTLJ Blog, https://moritzlaw.osu.edu/sites/default/files/2024-02/Howard%20Blog%201.pdf.
4. "How do I get paid on Bandcamp, and how often?" Bandcamp Help Center, Artists & Labels, Getting Paid, accessed March 5, 2025, https://get.bandcamp.help/hc/en-us/articles/23020694353047-How-do-I-get-paid-on-Bandcamp-and-how-often.

Chapter 10

1. Arnold Beisser, MD, "The Paradoxical Theory of Change," 1970, https://ngfo.no/wp-content/uploads/2017/06/THE-PARADOXICAL-THEORY-OF-CHANGE-beisser.pdf.
2. International Center for Clinical Excellence, https://centerforclinicalexcellence.com/; Scott D. Miller, PhD, https://www.scottdmiller.com/.

Chapter 11

1. Sulabha (Su) Abhyankar, "Gift of Empathy: Burn Out, Vicarious Traumatization and Compassion Fatigue in Clinicians," conference handout, the Evolution of Addiction Treatment Conference, Los Angeles, CA, February 5, 2017.
2. Abhyankar, "Gift of Empathy."

Chapter 12

1. Stolaroff, "Using Psychedelics Wisely."

INDEX OF ARTISTS AND REMIXERS

This index celebrates the artists, composers, and remixers featured throughout this book. By acknowledging their contributions, it serves as both a tribute and a guide for readers eager to explore, appreciate, and support their work.

#

36, 124; & awakened souls, 120, 124. *See also* awakened souls.

A

about : forest, 123
Above & Beyond, 45
Alaska x Synkro, 124
Alucidnation, 123, 129
Amandra x Mattheis, 45
Anna, 129
Another Fine Day, 129
Arcade Fire, 17, 54, 72
Archivist, 122
Arkaean, 124
Art of Trance, 45
ASC, 123
Autumn of Communion, 54
awakened souls, 120, 122, 124

B

Babicz, Robert, 45
Bach, Johann Sebastian, 33
Barwick, Julianna, 123
Beethoven, Ludwig van, 33
Benisch, Peter, 45, 124
Bernard, James, 44, 122, 123
Black Swan & Endless Melancholy, 43, 123
Bluetech, 124, 148
BT, 120
Buchert, Jens, 123
Budd, Harold, 54

C

Carbon Based Lifeforms, 125
Chicane, 125
Chillage, Mick, 124
City of Dawn. *See* zakè & City of Dawn

D

Dahl, Öona; & Giddyhead, 120
Damm, 120
Deepchild, 125
Desert Dwellers, 120, 148
Dettmann, Marcel, 45, 124
Digweed, John. *See* Sasha & Digweed
Disneynature Soundscapes, 121
Divasonic. *See* Liquid Bloom, Telepathy & Divasonic
Doctrina Natura, 45
Dozzy, Donato, 45, 127
Dreamfish, 121, 127
Durand, Federico, 129

INDEX OF ARTISTS AND REMIXERS

E

Eamo, 124
Eat Static, 45
Einaudi, Ludovico, 54
Endless Melancholy, 122, 129. *See also* Black Swan & Endless Melancholy
Eternell, 126

F

For the Good of All, 72
Four Tet, 45
Frahm, Nils, 45
From Overseas, 120
Future Sound of London, The, 7, 69, 122

G

GAS, 126
Gelka, 132
Gerrard, Lisa, 17
Giddyhead, 120. *See also* Dahl, Öona & Giddyhead
Goldman, Jonathan, 116
Goldmund, 129
Grandbrothers, 123
Grateful Dead, 33
Greenwood, Jonny, 17, 123

H

Halftribe, 120, 132
Haquin, 129
Harrison, Ed, 124
Hashizume, Cherif, 46
Hawtin, Richie, 6, 39, 57. *See also* Plastikman
Helios, 120, 125, 129
Henrik B, 121
Hiatus, 54, 123

Hopkins, Jon, 46, 70, 118, 122, 123, 126, 130, 148
How to Disappear Completely, 121
Hutchings, Sophie, 123
Hypnowave, Kryss, 124

I
Illuvia, 124
Influx, 124
Inquiri, 71, 126
Irisarri, Rafael Anton, 45
Ishq, 46, 96, 118, 134
Iyakah, 72

J
Jóhannsson, Jóhann, 17, 54, 72, 129
Junkie XL, 44

K
Kenniff, Hollie, 123, 132

L
Lapsed Pacifist, 126
Last, David, 124
Lav, 44, 123; & Purl, 71
Lekebusch, Cari, 6
LF58, 127
Ligovskoï, 126. *See also* Mora, Valentino, and Ligovskoï
Liquid Bloom, 45, 71, 124, 148; & TRIBONE, 127; Tylepathy & Divasonic, 129
Lusine ICL, 129

M
M83, 125
Malibu, 124
Marconi Union, 120

Margraf, Jonas, 124
marine eyes & zakè, 126. *See also* zakè
Mattheis. *See* Amandra x Mattheis
May, Charlie, 45, 72
Mayhall, Brian, 123
Melorman, 123, 124
Metcalf, Byron & Steve Roach, 45, 124
Moby, 7, 96
Mora, Valentino, and Ligovskoï, 126
Morker, Evigt, 124
Mozart, Wolfgang Amadeus, 33
Music for Sleep, 96, 120

N
Neel, 120
Newman, Thomas, 17
Nobel, Mathilde, 45, 124
Nonstatic, Martin, 124

O
Ólafsson, Vikingur, 54
Orbital, 129

P
Pink Floyd, 6, 33
Plastikman, 6, 56. *See also* Hawtin, Richie
Poemme, 120, 124, 126
Primal Code, 124, 127
Pulse Emitter, 120, 127
Purl, 70, 123, 126; & Deflektion, 96, 134. *See also* Lav & Purl

R
Rize, Alex, 123
Roach, Steve. *See* Metcalf, Byron & Steve Roach

Robertson, Matt, 125
Roth, Martin, 123
RxGibbs, 72, 132

S

Sacred Seeds, 44, 123
Salt of the Sound, 122, 129; & Anita Tatlow, 120
Saphileaum, 45, 71, 122
Sasha, 45; & Digweed, 59
Seven Fields of Aphelion, The, 122
Shaman's Dream, 71, 127
Sheehan, Rhian, 129
Slap, Robert, 116
Slow Dancing Society, 122
Slow Meadow, 129
Speedy J, 124
Spinger, 45, 124
State Azure, 129
Synkro, 123, 124, 125; & Indigo, 123. *See also* Alaska x Synkro
Syzygy, 123

T

Tatlow, Anita. *See* Salt of the Sound & Anita Tatlow
Tipper, 70
Totally Enormous Extinct Dinosaurs, 72
Treeboga, 124
Trentemøller, 123
TRIBONE. *See* Liquid Bloom & TRIBONE
Tycho, 45, 123, 148
Tylepathy, 71, 127; *See also* Liquid Bloom, Tylepathy & Divasonic

U

Unique Matter, The, 123

V
Vibrasphere, 45

W
Wagner, Richard, 123
Warmth, 120
Waveform Transmission, 127
Woods, Michael, 45

Y
Yagya, 70

Z
zakè, 120; & City of Dawn, 54, 96, 126
Zimmer, Hans, 17

ABOUT THE AUTHOR

Matt Xavier's remarkable career spans more than three decades at the intersection of music, healing, and expanded states of consciousness. As a full-time psychedelic guide, DJ, and mental health counselor, he has dedicated his life to blending artistry with compassionate care, helping clients navigate transformative journeys.

In the early 1990s, Matt gained prominence as "Matthew Magic," a pioneering force in New York City's underground electronic music scene. As cofounder of Tsunami Productions, he helped introduce psychedelic Goa trance to the North American East Coast. He later founded the influential techno label Railyard Recordings and held DJ residencies in both New York and Los Angeles, performing at renowned festivals and clubs around the world.

Alongside his music career, Matt has spent fifteen years working in clinical mental health as a certified Gestalt therapist and addiction counselor. He has provided evidence-based care to individuals with co-occurring disorders at leading treatment centers across Los Angeles. Educated at Loyola Marymount University and credentialed in California, Matt's approach combines deep empathy with grounded clinical expertise.

In 2019, Matt merged his lifelong passion for sound with formal training in psychedelic-assisted therapy, launching Integrated Psychedelics—a private practice offering harm-reduction therapy, integration counseling, and immersive, music-centered psychedelic journeys. Through his innovative work in what he describes as Therapeutic DJing and Psychedelic Soundtracking, Matt teaches others how to harness the powerful synergy

THE PSYCHEDELIC DJ

between music and psilocybin-assisted therapy to support emotional release, healing, and deep personal transformation.

With a rare blend of artistic instinct and clinical mastery, Matt empowers both facilitators and journeyers to unlock the therapeutic potential of intentional sound design. His work bridges the intuitive art of Therapeutic Music Curation with humanistic, trauma-informed counseling and ancient ceremonial practices, creating a transformative space where healing, insight, and self-discovery flourish through the combined forces of psychedelics, therapy, and music.

www.ingramcontent.com/pod-product-compliance
Lightning Source LLC
Chambersburg PA
CBHW020457030426
42337CB00011B/135